6/29/04
$ 15.00
B+T
☆S

# Withdrawn

D0555463

*Lisbon*

# Cities of the Imagination

*Cities* of the Imagination

# Lisbon

## A cultural and literary companion

## Paul Buck

Interlink Books
An imprint of Interlink Publishing Group, Inc.
New York • Northampton

First published 2002 by
**INTERLINK BOOKS**
An imprint of Interlink Publishing Group, Inc.
99 Seventh Avenue • Brooklyn, New York 11215 and
46 Crosby Street • Northampton, Massachusetts 01060

**Library of Congress Cataloging-in-Publication Data**

Buck, Paul, 1946–
    Lisbon: a cultural and literary companion / Paul Buck.
        p. cm. — (Cities of the imagination)
Includes index.
    ISBN 1-56656-395-X
1. Lisbon (Portugal)—Description and travel.    2. Lisbon (Portugal)—In Literature.
3. Lisbon (Portugal)—History—Miscellanea.    4. Lisbon (Portugal)—Social life and
customs.  5. Popular culture—Portugal—Lisbon.  I. Title.  II. Series.
DP756  .B83  2001
946.9'425—dc21                                                        2001000106

Reproduction of *The Policeman's Daughter* (p. 200) by kind permission of Paula Rego
Photographs by Paul Buck
Cover Design: Baseline Arts
Cover images: Paul Buck; Action Plus; Sue Cunningham Photographic;
© Almada Negreiros/SPA, Lisbon, 2002

To request our complete full-color catalog, please call
**1-800-238-LINK**
visit our website at: **www.interlinkbooks.com**
or write to us at: Interlink Publishing, 46 Crosby Street
Northampton, Massachusetts 01060
e-mail: info@interlinkbooks.com

# Contents

# Foreword

Lisbon, as viewed by Paul Buck, was revealed to my eyes during those distant years of 1967, 1974-5 and 1998 as the eye of Europe on the horizon: the search across oceans and exploits of caravels. Today it is reviewed, street by street, on the screen of my inner eye.

As too is the epic of "The Three Marias," touched upon in the author's journey, presenting me with the condensation of the Lisbon dream. In 1972 their book, *New Portuguese Letters,* was published: a resurrection of those *Letters of a Portuguese Nun* that Rilke translated into German for his own pleasure. Maria Isabel Barreno, Maria Teresa Horta and Maria Velho da Costa released it in the penultimate year of the Salazarist regime. They were charged immediately with an outrage against public decency and abuse of freedom of expression. The book was seized. History gives the impression that the "captains' movement," the MFA (Armed Forces Movement), unfolded on April 24, 1974 mainly to gain liberty for the Three Marias. And the new Portuguese nun.

Today we believe the *Letters of a Portuguese Nun,* dating from the seventeenth century, were written by a man disguised as a woman who had taken the veil, and that they attest to the French fascination with Portugal, that world beyond the great Spanish and Austrian empire which encircled the kingdom of Classical France at the time. When the Braganças rose against the annexation carried out a century earlier by Philip II, they received the support of Louis XIV—himself half-Spanish through his mother and, perhaps, half-Italian through Cardinal Mazarin. It need not be improbable that the latter was the originator of the "miracle" of the birth of the "Sun King" after the thirty barren years of his father's marriage. As far as I am concerned, it would please me if the most celebrated of the French kings was a Spanish Italian—an illustrious "immigrant"—for Portuguese emigration invented the unity of the world.

As Paul Buck clearly underlines, the New Letters of the "nun" are a form of the relationship between woman and man. They could even take as their subtitle the beautiful phrase that Lou Salomé coined in 1901: "the man as woman," *Der Mensch als Weib*—where *Mensch* (as distinct from *Mann*) designates as much the woman as the man, a word which has no equivalent in either the English or French language.

Thus I am able to understand Paul Buck's description of Lisbon as that of a "woman-city" (*femme-cité*). He has perceived it as a "micro-country," a word borrowed from the title of the beautiful Portuguese poems by Carlos de Oliviera that I discovered earlier when the Russell Foundation entrusted me with an inquest into the mysterious events of the "second *coup d'état*" in 1975—the one that resulted in finally imprisoning the liberator of Lisbon, Otelo de Carvalho; and the one on which we opened a debate of historic research at Westminster that was both passionate and extensive.

Later, we wanted to create a mode of opera or sacred music that was not an Oratorio, but a *Relatorio*, the name of the official Report written on the role of Otelo de Carvalho in the Portuguese revolutions of the 1970s. That Portuguese magic I can hear today in the revolts in East Timor, and in the emergence of the Nobel Peace Prizewinner, José Ramos Horta, in that antipodal part of the world. Also with José Saramago, another Nobel winner in the Portuguese language, whom I met at the Union of Writers during the uncertain weeks of January 1976 following the military events in Lisbon of November 25, 1975. And whom I met once again at the centenary celebrations for Jorge Luis Borges, in Buenos Aires, where he described in magnificent fashion the inverted labyrinths of Borges and Pessoa.

This micro-country in the labyrinths of Lisbon is drawn to my eyes through two great painters, at two edges of time: Nuno Gonçalves, the Master of the *retábulo* (retable) of the São Vicente on the one side; and Maria Helena Vieira da Silva on the other side of the diptych. With her I also recall that Velázquez was a *da Silva*. And that *Las Meninas* could have been a game of Portuguese mirrors. The historian of Spanish art, Francès, has subtly reconstructed, with *three* mirrors in place of one, the interior space of this incomparable painting signed by Velázquez. This book in your hands is a micro-country mirrored to the nth degree. Its author offers Lisbon to our desire.

*Jean-Pierre Faye*

# Preface

A book like this owes to those it references, owes to a library and the spirit of collecting. Over the years a library can become a cumbersome and unwieldy burden, can take over a house, indeed become the house. Yet, at times like this, a library can become invaluable and need no justification. As a result, the only other library required for assistance to any degree was the Canning House Library in London, which rose to the challenge.

My resources are listed at the back. All translations not noted in the bibliography are my own.

Those who have helped, friends and people met along the way, are: Stephen Barber, David Barton, Eduardo de Gregorio, Hanna de Heus, Jean-Pierre Devresse, Wolf Gaudlitz, António Guerreiro, Martin and Sarah James, Frances Lee, Cameron Lindo, Elina Lozinsky, Paul Mayersberg, Darius Misiuna, Jacques Parsi, Sara Plácido, Paula Rego, Danièle Rivière, Ruth Rosengarten, Patrick Rousseau, Anthony Rudolf, Paulo Scavullo, Barbara Spielman, Ian Taylor, Catherine Timmers, Joaquim Vacondeus, and Sarah Wilson. I offer them all my heartfelt thanks. Also thanks to my editor, James Ferguson.

Two others from Portugal, whom I met in the course of writing this book, both having shown immeasurable friendship and patience in the face of my questions, are Jorge Mantas and Fernando Guerreiro. For them a special thanks.

Likewise, to Jean-Pierre Faye for his positive response away from home in the depths of the German countryside.

In Paris, for her support and encouragement over many years, as well as for seeking references unobtainable here, and also introducing fresh research, I offer my deepest thanks to my friend Mireille Andrès.

My final thanks and love goes to Catherine, my wife, to whom this book is dedicated. She has been my partner on this trip, both in the physical sense of our stays in Lisbon as well as through its research and readings, for she has accompanied me step by step, and step for step.

*Paul Buck*

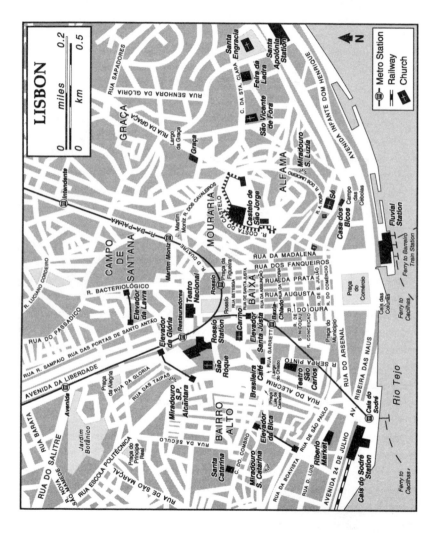

# PART ONE

# *ARRIVALS*

*"The afternoon passed and darkness fell. Lisbon is a tranquil city with a
wide river of legendary fame."*
José Saramago, *The Year of the Death of Ricardo Reis*

## 1. Introduction

The picture of Lisbon that forms in most of our minds revolves
around a handful of images seen in travelogues and movies. Select
monuments and locations like the Torre de Belém (Belém Tower), the
Mosteiro dos Jerónimos (Jeronimos Monastery), or the pinched
streetways of the old Alfama quarter. Dried salted cod and grilled
sardines. Or clanking trams wheezing up and down hills. Hills. Many
hills. Seven, they say. Panoramic views across the city. And the river,
the Rio Tejo (Tagus). That wide river that yawns in the sun and invites
our eyes to dream with it, dream of voyages that started or ended on
this stretch of water. Or else dreams that money can't buy, dreams that
will remain forever dreams.

All this is here. And more. The quota that makes for a heavy dose
of romance and nostalgia. As if we haven't enough of such enticements
in the cities from where we come. And those who venture to this
western city on the edge of Europe are mainly from other points in
Europe, notably Germany, Holland, France, Italy and Britain. With an
added sprinkling from the US and Japan. These are the tourists.

Those in abundance from Africa and South America, from the former colonies, are here to stay, here to make a new life, hopefully to help shape the new Lisbon.

Why do foreigners, travelers, come to Lisbon? Why *did* they come? Because it was the farthest point in Europe, a launching pad to the world, whether for exploration or escape. Others used it later as the pivotal point when traveling from America to North Africa. These eras are at an end. Air travel has opened up numerous other routes, and the use and excuse for visiting Lisbon has had to become other. Today romantic notions ride high on the list, clinging to vestiges of the old has become the draw. The idea is to see the city itself, not to pass through.

Lisbon is a city that has a number of notable architectural monuments and places of historical interest, but not so many that one is trapped by them. It is a beautiful city, for it is built on a series of hills and valleys whose steepness give rise to a multitude of viewing points, such that the city can become almost narcissistic, encouraging one to keep re-viewing it, akin to stepping inside a house choked by mirrors, continually catching the reflections, sucked into the space of admiration.

The houses appear to cling to near cliff-like sides, an array of white and gray walls, mixed with color-washes of mellow shades of yellow, green and pink, all topped by pinkish-red roof tiles. The impression is almost Mediterranean, despite the proximity of the Atlantic and its cruel tendencies, delivering mists and chill rains at unwelcome times. Lisbon is just inland and sheltered enough to be significantly dominated by palm trees.

Seven hills, like Rome, Constantinople, Liège, Sheffield… Seven indeed. Nearer twenty-two. Another myth dispelled.

And a river wide enough to be more than a river, wide enough to be a setting, a sea with a discernible far shore, a frame to work with, to give perspective to the water vessels.

A city whose frontage is all water, a dock that stretches as fast as the imagination. Dreams to compare with our childhood ones of running away with the circus. Or, conversely, dreams that welcome the exotic ashore with "mythical kings and iguanas" (Dory Previn). A city where the map reveals a route that is quick and manageable, yet underfoot offers a challenging climb, or an unsteady stagger downward.

This is a city that has become a work-in-progress, a poem, a novel being rewritten for another generation. A city striving to remove its decay, yet keen to retain its fragile air of mystery, excitement and tumultuous enjoyment. A city actively modernizing and rejuvenating, making some residents nervous for its future, while others celebrate and chase with the foot balanced above the accelerator. While consternation is caused by the amount of old property transformed into an accumulation of boutiques, bars, restaurants and discos, there is pleasure at the wealth of houses being renovated rather than demolished to erect new and excessively expensive apartments. Suggestions are rife to visit before modernity sets hard. Other suggestions are voiced to watch modernity become the savior of the city. It depends on your view. And views there are a-plenty, practically and metaphorically.

The idea of *saudade*, that special feeling of nostalgia for the past as the future can never offer better, that feeling that is regarded as part of the Portuguese soul, might be sustained by some, while others wish to sweep it away and rid themselves of that clammy restraining hand of tradition. They want to be European, and they want more, they want to be numbered as players in the world without the necessity to venture abroad to achieve their aims.

My own attachment to Lisbon started a good few years ago, shortly after the dramatic political changes in 1974, when I read *Portugal: The Revolution in the Labyrinth*, the book edited by Jean-Pierre Faye for the Bertrand Russell Peace Foundation. Cinematic interests brought the next illumination, with Alain Tanner, Wim Wenders, Raúl Ruiz, Eduardo de Gregorio and others all heading for the capital and its environs with their casts and cameras to shoot film. The music of *fado* was the following seduction, hotly pursued by an awareness of some of the city's literature through the many hands of Fernando Pessoa, José Saramago and others. Visiting only enhanced the allure.

Lisbon as a place of departure for other points in the world was always a given, an historical fact. Little interest was expressed in its being a city in which to halt. I hooked onto Pessoa and his resolution to remain firmly seated in his native city. Lisbon was not only there to be enjoyed for itself, it also came with a sense of romance, my wife's own earlier attachment to the city, before our meeting, pulled the threads tighter on our intimacy.

Lisbon is not a large city. In fact, it is the smallest of the western capitals. It invites the idea of a brief trip, a long weekend, nothing more extensive. It is not packed with unmissable monuments. Witness the visitors checking in and out the hotels "before they've had time to wash their dirty underwear," as one local delicately observed. They shift around the city as speedily as their coaches can take them. Or march hungrily through the Alfama as if in the maze at Hampton Court. How do I get out? Yet Lisbon is not like other cities. Lisbon has a relaxed pace. Lisbon demands that you can only reap its rewards if you fall in with that pace. There is nothing wrong with sitting on a *miradouro* (belvedere) in the sun for the whole afternoon, gazing across the rooftops, watching the boats ease along the Tagus. The locals enjoy it; it is not the decadence of the visitor to be seen to take things easy. Nor is there anything wrong with ambling through the narrow alleyways of the Alfama one day and then returning the next for more. You'll probably be hard pushed to repeat your steps a second time, something new will surprise you. Besides aching limbs—if you can manage a succession of days on steep inclines and sweeps of steps that make the flight before the Sacré Coeur in Paris barely more than a practice slope. That is one of the pleasures of Lisbon. One has to adopt a more relaxed view, to stay longer, to breathe the city, not to assert one's own home pace on its life, but rather to fall in step with this tranquil place and the laid-back manner of its residents. There is always time to stand at a bar for *uma bica*, the exquisite demitasse of strong espresso coffee. To capture that aroma and atmosphere is at the heart of the writing of this book.

Once you have understood that notion then you can take in the other parts of the city, the everyday life of the modern city, visit the new shopping complexes that are mounting the city, compare them to your own capital, your own cities. Perhaps you will discover the same brands, the same names, the same stores, even the same store-fitting designs in each center. The homogeneous blend that is Europe. Once we were assured that the grand hotels were the same the world over.

Businessmen never knew in which city they woke each morning as each Sheraton hotel room looked much the same. It was intentional. That was the game of being international. And then there was McDonalds. Now the same multinational chainstores proliferate throughout Europe. With the added bonus, in Lisbon's case, that the fashion chain of Zara from neighboring Spain seems to have a bigger grip than in other cities. Almost every street in the main areas seems to have another branch. And in the night the big pantechnicons slide into place to refill the stock, ready to be emptied the following day given the number of youngsters walking around clutching their Zara-logoed shopping bags. The old rivalries and the dynastic marriage alliances between the two countries that went drastically wrong is perhaps a thing of the past, forgotten, dead and buried... or perhaps just less noticeable. One can still be sharply reminded of the ructions when a cutting remark slices the air during a conversation, or silence and indifference greets you as a result of a Spanish reference. But who is to blame them when the European Union omitted the border between the two countries on a poster in 1998, giving the impression that Portugal was part of its neighbor? If you can't manage to speak Portuguese, it's best to speak French, English, German or other languages than Spanish.

My approach to the city is as a visitor, a traveler, not as a resident. Needless to say there are as many commentators on a city as there are viewpoints. In Lisbon's case this takes on an added and appropriate meaning, for it is a city of *miradouros*, both the recognized and the unexpected. Every person in the city could make a composite picture from their own choice of these viewpoints.

We don't expect every artist to paint the same portrait of a given subject. Each will present their own impression, the notion of "capturing a likeness" often shown the door, verisimilitude directed at photography, even though today we recognize that there as many artists with the camera as those with brushes, each able to use light to create a different portrait. And that's without combating the latest digital technology, image manipulation making it virtually impossible to know what is "true" any longer. Thus, to paint the portrait of a city, whether with brush or various cameras, will produce an even greater range of views. Similarly for a writer. My view of Lisbon is selective, my preferred angles.

One of Lisbon's filmmakers, Paulo Rocha, spoke critically of the Swiss filmmaker Alain Tanner (along with Wim Wenders) who has twice filmed here, the first time for *In the White City* (1983), and more recently for *Requiem* (1998): "These are people who are uncomfortable in their own land, and set out to dream elsewhere. They don't really see Lisbon, which is more varied than their decorative vision. They only speak about Pessoa, who has become a multinational, and who only affects fifty years of Lisbon's history. The city is more dynamic, more desperate, richer in hypotheses than the ones these filmmakers present." Tanner parried the "decorative" attack and agreed: "I'd perhaps say the same if I was a *Lisboeta*. The intention of *In the White City* wasn't to explore Lisbon society. My character knew nothing of the city's culture...Some Portuguese have reproached me for making tourism, showing places they no longer want to see. They've had enough of people speaking to them of Pessoa, *saudade*, the nostalgia of the Portuguese. They want to be Americans." My view is that if a city has a richness, it can sustain more films, books and paintings than are ever likely to be produced, even if all are not to my taste.

I have chosen to draw from a selection of visitors as well as the Portuguese, for I note that in the twentieth century many Portuguese writers and artists left their country either for political reasons, or because they wished to be part of a foreign cultural world, often found in Paris. Some never returned to live, yet their work is shaped by their native country and its capital, Lisbon. Others decided to return having supped at the foreign feast, bringing back their bounty to display to their fellow compatriots. And not only the creative people, but the ordinary citizens too, many venturing abroad as their only means to earn a living, sending money home. The Portuguese are not alone in this approach to survival. However, it is interesting that the majority of those who traveled within Europe made Paris their destination. The largest community of Portuguese abroad today is still in Paris. This is reflected in the amount of Portuguese literature translated into French as opposed to the paucity translated into

English. As a consequence, French writers have shown more interest in Portuguese culture than has the English-speaking world. One result is that the visitor to Lisbon will find more old people able to converse in French than in English, although the younger ones, as everywhere, are entranced by the English language, or perhaps have accepted it with reluctance if they wish to venture forth from their homeland, or need it as an aid to understand more of the world's output of television and popular culture.

I outline these ideas because the approach of this book takes its lead from the Portuguese. José Saramago, their 1998 Nobel Prize-winning novelist, is a prime example of this inventiveness in literature. In his earlier book, *Manual of Painting & Calligraphy: A Novel*, Saramago presents us with the world of a portrait painter in Lisbon. "'I have decided to write an account of my travels until another commission turns up,'" he tells his lover. She has read the text he has given her. She is perplexed. "'I don't understand why you've called this article (...) a first exercise in biography. How can a travel book be considered biography?' 'I'm not sure that it can, I really don't know, but I couldn't find anything more interesting to write about.' 'Either it's a travel book or a genuine autobiography.'" He tells her of his belief that we reveal something of ourselves in all that we do. He reiterates his contention that the travel book is just as good as an autobiography. "'The problem is knowing how to read it.' 'But anyone who reads a travel book knows what he is reading and it never occurs to him to look for anything else.' 'Perhaps people ought to be warned. If they don't need to be told that a picture has two dimensions rather than three, then they should not have to be warned that everything is biography, or to be more precise, autobiography.'" One of the attributes that has made Saramago a writer of our time is that he has consistently re-evaluated the forms of writing itself. This has helped the younger generations in Lisbon to have the courage to pursue brave adventures in their work.

My position does not lead me into the shanty towns, except by default, with a film like *Ossos* (1997) by the young Portuguese filmmaker, Pedro Costa. In this memorable, if extremely bleak film, set in one such area, Costa has given us a picture of Lisbon that most outsiders would prefer not to see. Travelers venture to other lands to find what is missing in their own. We prefer to see the good sides if at all possible, for we know the bad in our own cultures only too well.

Fortunately I am here as a writer, not specifically to capture the city with the camera. Lisbon today is partly closed for renovation and rejuvenation. To photograph with any intention of capturing many of the famous sights is not feasible. Tarpaulins and scaffolding are dominant features. For good reasons, in many cases. It certainly takes the shine off some romantic notions. The city will probably be in this state for some while as everyone is pushing forward at the same time, pushing until the grants from the European control center in Brussels cease to flow.

## Literary Snapshots

Thomas Mann, writing his last novel, *Confessions of Felix Krull, Confidence Man*, in the 1950s, though set in 1895, is quite intent on underlining that Lisbon is not just a stopping point en route to elsewhere, Buenos Aires in this case. His main character meets a resident of Lisbon journeying home on the train from Paris. Professor Kuckuck, Paleontologist and Director of the Museum of National History in Lisbon, "an as yet insufficiently known institution of which I am the founder," discourages him from being too hasty on his embarkation for an educational year in Argentina, laying it on for his fellow traveler and for us, the reader:

> However long your journey may be, you ought not to neglect its beginning simply because it is a beginning. You are entering a very interesting country of great antiquity, one to which every eager voyager owes a debt of gratitude, since in earlier centuries it opened up so many travel routes. Lisbon, which I hope you will have time enough to see properly, was once the richest city in the world, thanks to the voyages of discovery. Too bad you did not turn up there five hundred years ago—at that time you would have seen gold by the bushel. History has brought about a sorry diminution in those fine foreign possessions. But, as you will see, the country and people are still charming. I mention the people because a good part of all longing to travel consists in a yearning for people one has never seen, a lust for the new—to look into strange eyes, strange faces, to rejoice in unknown human types and manners.

Before insisting on places to visit, he prepares us for the people themselves in great detail:

*Thus you will find, in the country you are approaching, a racial mixture that is highly entertaining because of its variety and confusion. The original inhabitants were mixed—Iberians, as of course you know, with a Celtic element. But in the course of two thousand years Venetians, Carthaginians, Romans, Vandals, Suevians, West Goths, and especially the Arabs, the Moors, have co-operated to produce the type that awaits you— not to forget a sizeable admixture of Negro blood from the many dark-skinned slaves that were brought in at the time when Portugal owned the whole African coast. You must not be surprised at a certain quality of the hair, a certain lip, a certain melancholy animal look in the eye that appear from time to time. But the Moorish-Berber racial element, as you will find, is clearly predominant—from the long period of Arab domination. The net result is a not exactly heroic but decidedly amiable type: dark-haired, somewhat yellowish in complexion and of delicate build, with handsome, intelligent brown eyes.*

A few years later, Mann's German compatriot Erich Maria Remarque took us back to more recent history in his novel *The Night in Lisbon* (1962), reminding us that it was a destination for those fleeing across Europe: "We live like the Jews on their way out of Egypt. Behind us the German Army and the Gestapo, on both sides the sea of French and Spanish police, and ahead of us the Promised Land of Portugal with the Port of Lisbon, the gateway to the still more Promised Land of America."

Lord Byron some years earlier in July 1809 was only briefly there, though wrote good and bad of the place, famously: "I am very happy here, because I loves oranges, and talks bad Latin to the monks, who understand it, as it is like their own, and I goes into society (with my pocket pistols) and I swims in the Tagus all across at once, and I rides on an ass or a mule and swears Portuguese, and I have got a diarrhoea, and bites from the mosquitoes. But what of that? Comfort must not be expected by folks that go a-pleasuring." Not that he kept that spirit for long, as we will see.

Rose Macaulay, who wrote a marvelous work in the 1940s about Byron and other travelers to Portugal, had been used to bicycling around London, "but in Lisbon bicycling would be fine exercise for a trick cyclist. Indeed to this day a pedal cyclist in Lisbon is a rare bird."

She was undoubtedly right, but more than half a century later, by chance one Sunday morning, we came across a group of cyclists in the Praça do Comércio about to undergo a race. This, however, was more a fun race, because there were families on less than state-of-the-art bikes among the pack of determined-looking cyclists lined up at the front, all geared up and ready for the gun. One can only hazard that though they were obviously adept at cycling hills, this ride (or race) was destined to go along the river front to avoid overly steep climbs.

A rare bird in her ability to describe her circumstances and write her experiences was Simone de Beauvoir. Her first visit to Lisbon occurred in 1945. It was a trip with more than one intention. Her sister Hélène, an artist, had married Lionel de Roulet, an ex-student and disciple of Jean-Paul Sartre. Prior to the war, Lionel's mother had met a Portuguese man and remarried, moving to Portugal, requesting her son to join them to help alleviate his health problems. Hélène raised money and joined them later, becoming stranded for the duration of the war, in the process consenting to marry Lionel. He worked at the French Institute in Lisbon, and was editor of a Franco-Portuguese review called *Affinidades*.

His invitation to Simone was a way to bring her to visit her sister whom she had not seen in five years. She related this in *Force of Circumstance* (1963), the third volume of her autobiography. "He invited me, on behalf of the Institute, to go to Portugal and give some lectures on the Occupation." Albert Camus made Beauvoir an official correspondent for *Combat*, which helped speed up obtaining the required papers, and she set off via Madrid for Lisbon. Her biographer Deidre Bair summed it up: "When she arrived in Portugal as a social commentator, she was struck for the first time by the contrast between rich and poor, excess and poverty, and her articles reflected this dichotomy in absolutes, without shading or nuance. The prose is simplistic, but the outrage and emotion are genuine."

Happy to see her sister, she thought Lisbon "was like Marseilles, like Athens, like Naples and like Barcelona: a burning city, whipped by the smell of the sea; the past suddenly became alive again in the novelty of its hills and promontories, its soft colors, its white sails." To show how she transformed with little more than a slight shift this experience in her subsequent novel, *The Mandarins* (1954), she replaced herself with Henri, a thinly veiled Sartre, accompanied by his young lover (again working in facts from her personal irritations of the time). No sooner had they arrived than Henri, too, commented as the taxi plummeted down steep streets and sped around the city:

> *A southern city, a fresh, hot city with its ancient clanking streetcars, and on the horizon the promise of salty winds and the sea beating against high walls. Yes, he recognized it, and yet it astonished him more than ever had Marseilles, Athens, Naples, Barcelona. Because now everything new, everything unknown, was a thing to be marvelled at. It was beautiful, that capital, with its quiet heart, its unruly hills, its houses with pastel-coloured icing, its huge white ships.*

Overcome by the "opulence of the stores," Beauvoir entered that world. Her sister was determined to renew her wardrobe. "Never in my life had I surrendered to such a debauch; my lecture tour was very well paid, and in one afternoon I assembled a complete wardrobe: three pairs of shoes, a bag, stockings, lingerie, sweaters, dresses, skirts, blouses, a white wool jacket, a fur coat." Dressed to the nines, she attended the cocktail party at the French Institute. "There I met some of Lionel's Portuguese friends, all opposed to the regime; they told me resentfully about Valéry, who had not wanted to see anything in Portugal except the blue sky and the pomegranate trees in bloom. And all that nonsense about the mystery and the melancholy of the Portuguese soul! Out of seven million Portuguese, there are seventy thousand who have enough to eat; the Portuguese are sad because they're hungry." And again she related those facts in almost identical terms and situations through Henri in *The Mandarins*.

She was given tours around Lisbon and Sintra and, despite petrol rations, taken on a long tour through the Algarve in a borrowed car. She described the pleasures of the land, but she also noted the plight of the peasants, despite their colorful clothes "dazzling in the sunlight." "I no longer allowed myself to be deceived; there was a word whose weight I was beginning to appreciate: hunger." And though she related stories in her autobiography of the poverty she saw as she went north and south, countering it with the simple need to bask in her joy of being alive in the sun and away from post-war Paris, in the novel version she highlighted the experience in a visit to the Alfama:

> *Barefooted women—everyone here went barefooted—were squatting before their doors frying sardines over charcoal fires, and the stench of stale fish mingled in the air with the smell of hot oil. In cellar apartments opening on to the street, not a bed, not a piece of furniture, not a picture; nothing but straw mats, children covered with rashes, and from time to time a goat. Outside, no happy voices, no laughter; only sombre dead eyes. Was misery more hopeless here than in the other cities? Or instead of becoming hardened to misfortune, does one grow more sensitive to it? The blue of the sky seemed cruel above the unhealthy shadows.*

The positive outcome of Beauvoir's lectures were her meetings "with the Portuguese anti-Fascists; most of the ones I met were ex-teachers, ex-ministers of state, men of middle age or older...they provided me with a host of documents on the population's standard of living, on the economic organization of the country, on the budget, the unions, the incidence of illiteracy, and also on the police, the prisons and political repression." A young doctor took her into working-class homes and gave her details of health conditions, although "one had only to walk through Lisbon and keep one's eyes open to be aware of such things. The people were deliberately kept in a state of filth and ignorance: Fátima was being launched." They wanted the attention of the French, to awaken public opinion in France.

On her return to Paris, Beauvoir began her series of articles on Portugal for *Combat*, using the pseudonym, Daniel Secrétan, "in order not to compromise my brother-in-law." But as Camus was away in North Africa at the time, Pascal Pia, his replacement, halted the series, and she continued the articles in another paper, *Volontés*. Later came her long novel, *The Mandarins*, in which she used the fictional form to explore the limits of commitment by intellectuals, incorporating her Lisbon experiences as part of her discourse.

For the French film director, François Truffaut, Lisbon just happened to be the city where Pierre (Jean Desailly) in *La Peau Douce* (Soft Skin, 1964) was taken on a flying visit to give a lecture on *Balzac and Money*, joining the ranks of businessmen, lecturers, artists and performers who pass through all major cities as a result of their work. There he started an affair, "adultery as existential act," as critic James Monaco defined it, not with a resident, not in the outside world of the city itself, but within the hotel and with a real itinerant worker, the air hostess, Nicole (Françoise Dorléac). As with the modern businessmen, the specific city is not important, just a location when going about one's job, the hotel or venue being the focal points rather than the particular delights of the city's attractions or culture.

In 1997, the British novelist Julie Myerson visited the city:

*We were blown away by its unassuming beauty, but surprised too by its shambolic poverty. It felt like a city stuck in the Fifties. In 1997 we found hatters and glove shops and cobblers and mothball-smelling joints selling swathes of nylon and polyester. On every street corner you could buy feathery heads of grass dyed every imaginable shade of orange, green and purple. Elderly women struggled up the steep, narrow streets with baskets, while above their heads huge bras and mammoth knickers flapped on lines in the dusty, stolid breeze. There were thin grubby children and even thinner, mangier cats, and piles of rotting rubbish flung out on every pavement.*

She had expected things to be a bit different: "something a little more chic, more comfortable. We were unnerved. Maybe it's just that we avoided the tourist drag, but we kept wandering into scenes that made us feel impossibly rich and clean and well-shod, like voyeurs, like tourists."

This, she determined, was a result of not seeing the signs advertising the forthcoming Expo. Her next visit revealed a different city, one that had been cleaned and "groovied up," even "the grubby *Torre de Belém* that's flaunted on everything from ashtrays to key-rings has been cleaned to a creamy Disneyland white." But not all was so bad: "What I really love about Lisbon is its messy jitteriness, its sense of flux. You never know quite where you are with it. Unlike, for instance, Paris or Rome, you feel that no-one has quite summed it up—and because of that, you can make it your very own."

A few snapshots by travelers give a mood to what lies in store. Perhaps it's no wonder that there appears to have been some reluctance on the part of the Argentinian Jorge Luis Borges to acknowledge his Portuguese origins. Emir Rodríguez Monegal, an authority on the author, informs us that: "his surname is undoubtedly Portuguese: Borges means a citizen of the *burgos* or cities, a bourgeois." But it was not until an interview late in his life in 1970 that he talked about a trip to Lisbon and his ancestors. "When I visited Lisbon many years ago, I tried to do some research on my origins. I looked into the phone book and got the scare of my life: all the people there were my relatives, because those who were not Borges were Ramalho or Acevedo! I didn't know I had such a family and just in Lisbon!"

The novelist Almeida Faria told the British poet, Paul Hyland, for his venture up the Tagus in *Backwards out of the Big World* (1997), that "the greatness of Portugal, if that exists, is in its cultural life, in literature." Over an evening meal with a group of writers and artists, one told us that there was weakness in the arts throughout Portuguese history. "Naturally, there are some who are good, but few real greats in any of the arts. There have been long periods when little has emerged. Of course the Salazar period didn't help last century." He was then hard pushed to mention a contemporary classical composer of merit. I mentioned one, not a resident of Lisbon or indeed Portugal, and he nodded reluctantly. "At least Lisbon has its literature, its poetry," he added.

And for most that means Pessoa, although others can become exasperated at the thought that Lisbon is Pessoa, as if a cross to bear. "There's more to the city than Pessoa," they say. And there is. Culture is not only the arts; it's the people, their customs, their food, their daily life and how it all ties together. And yet there is something noteworthy, something outstanding, that can be placed up front for all to see as they go about their daily business in Lisbon, and that lies beneath their feet in the Metro. There one can follow with wonder and admiration the bountiful display of artists' commissions that have made it a public art complex. "At least that's one public exhibit to be proud of. At least we've something," another at the table added, nominating her favorite of the station displays. "Why do you go to the Museu de Arte Antiga (Museum of Ancient Art) if not to look at the Bosch there?... nothing else, certainly not the Portuguese art." True, the Bosch triptych is not Portuguese art, but it is housed in Lisbon and it's not here by chance.

Whatever the opinions, this is Pessoa's city. He made it his own in many ways, as we will discover. He left his stamp in a multitude of forms, even if the print wasn't truly read until after his death. In his major prose work, *The Book of Disquietude* (1934), which he attributed to his semi-heteronym Bernardo Soares, he wrote: "I love the Tagus because of the big city along its shore. I delight in the sky because I see it from the fourth floor on a downtown street. Nothing nature or the country can give me compares with the jagged majesty of the tranquil, moonlit city as seen from Graça or São Pedro de Alcântara. There are no flowers for me like the variegated coloring of Lisbon on a sunny day." His work is irredeemably connected to the city. His work is the city. He is the city. It was a way for Pessoa to tackle the problem of being that lay at the heart of his writings.

The suggestion is that there is a pliability to the city, for each to make of it their own. The poet, Virgílio de Lemos, who originates from Mozambique, said that Lisbon is a city that demands we reinvent it: "It sees itself as an unfinished, incomplete city, open to metamorphoses." A city that "opens itself to the delirious imagination of its lovers."

José Cardoso Pires, one of the most important of Portuguese contemporary writers, warned us, however, in *Lisboa—Livro de Bordo*, (Lisbon—Book of the Edge, 1997), shortly before his death, not to fall into the trap: "There are scholars in transit who practice the Stations of the Cross with the monuments in order to be at peace with their cultural conscience." We note your warning. Let us be selective, not only in seeking among the expected attractions, but seeking out some other stations. Let us not make it a penitence, but a pleasure. This is a city where pleasure can be had even after your final breath, if you are buried in the Cemitério dos Prazeres (Pleasures Cemetery).

The final word here to João de Melo, who hails from the Azores: "Sometimes I dream that Lisbon doesn't exist and will only be a legend that one can recount, not to those who live here, but to those who come here visiting."

# 2. A Brief History of Lisbon

Legend suggests that Lisbon identifies Ulysses as its founding father, strangely adding that it was even here that the sea nymph Calypso fell in love with him, turning herself into a snake whose coils formed the seven hills. Perhaps that myth has more to do with a similarity to the place's later name, Olissipo, for historians are more inclined to date its origins at 1200 BC, when the Phoenicians came along.

John Dos Passos, the American novelist of Portuguese descent, wrote: "The Rio Tejo had another course and the coastline was gracefully curved. There must have been a reason why, over three millenia ago, the Phoenicians called the entire coast formation 'Gentle Bay' (Ubis Ubbo). Much later called 'Olisippo' or 'Olissipum' by the Romans, in Caesar's time the city was called 'Felicitas Iulia,' a shorter form of 'Urbs municipium civium Romanorum Felicitas Iulia cognominatum,' more or less 'Roman Capital of Happy Julia.'"

The Romans had arrived in 205 BC, fortifying the city and introducing road-building, the growing of grapes, wheat and olives, as well as bequeathing the basis of the Portuguese language. At the decline of their Empire, a succession of barbarians followed, until the Visigoths, of German origin, settled in the sixth century.

In AD 711 the Moors landed at Gibraltar, worked their way through Spain and entered the city in 714. They improved the fortifications of the castle, walls that still remain in places, and built houses on the southern slope down to the river. This district was called al-Hamma (Alfama), which means "hot springs" or "public baths." The Alfama today remains virtually intact, having later survived the Great Earthquake. The city at that time was called Luxbona, Lixbuna, Ulixbone, and Olissibona, variations of Lisboa. While Lisboa appears to derive from Roman titles, others contend that the name in fact derives from *água boa* (good water).

When the Moors ventured northwards they were halted by Alfonso VI, who was creating a Catholic kingdom. The succeeding king, Afonso Henriques, determined to extend his rule towards the south and pushed the Moors back as far as Lisbon. Unable to penetrate the fortifications, he sought the assistance of a band of Crusaders (Flemish, Norman, German and English) en route to the Holy Lands. Offering them riches if they sacked the city, the Siege of Lisbon in 1147 became a bloody affair. Afonso Henriques established himself as the first monarch of Portugal, although it was a further hundred years before the rest of the country south of Lisbon was wrestled from the Moors.

In 1150 Lisbon's Sé Catedral was built, although it was not until 1260 that Lisbon took over the mantle of capital from Coimbra. The city was expanded: one area, the Mouraria being built on the north side of the castle walls, where the Moors were allowed to live; the other area, today called the Baixa, in the valley bottom, where once flowed a Tagus tributary, before it silted.

Dom Dinis, known as the "poet king" and the "farmer king," encouraged literature and learning, and established the first university in Lisbon in 1288, although it later moved to Coimbra. During his rule he strengthened the country's frontiers and signed a treaty with Spain in 1297 to formalize the demarcations.

**Era of Exploration**
Through the early 1300s, a succession of earthquakes and bouts of the Black Death did their job in keeping the city and population in check. After further strife with Spain, a new alliance with England was sealed in the 1386 Treaty of Windsor, calling for true and eternal friendship. Within a year Dom João I had married Philippa of Lancaster, the daughter of John of Gaunt. Their third surviving son, the Duke of Viseu, Master of the Order of Christ, was to change the map of the world. He was known as Prince Henry the Navigator. He developed a school of navigation in the Algarve, where he gathered astronomers, cartographers and other scientists to aid the skills of the mariners associated with it. Over the next forty years he set up expeditions that pushed back the horizon, exploring the islands of Madeira, the Azores, and sailing down the west coast of Africa.

In a sense it was fortuitous that Spain had Portugal blocked off, for there was only the sea to venture across at this edge of Europe. In 1487 Bartolomeu Dias rounded the southern tip of Africa, the Cape of Good Hope, without seeing land. Christopher Columbus who had served in earlier expeditions along the African coast in connection with Henry the Navigator's school, asked the Portuguese crown to finance his plan to go west and find a route to the Indies. When rejected, he turned to Spain, and under its banner sailed off in 1492 to "discover" America. Now that Spain was a player in discovering—and colonizing—the world, she negotiated with Portugal to divide it for further explorations. The Treaty of Tordesillas of 1494 allocated all lands west to Spain and all the lands east of 360 leagues west of the Cape Verde Islands to Portugal. Such an arrangement included Brazil in the Portuguese allocation, later giving the impression that the Portuguese already knew of its existence.

In 1497 Vasco da Gama opened the sea route to India, starting and returning to Belém, going around the Cape of Good Hope. He found what Columbus had been seeking in the wrong direction, the sea route to the spices of the East, ending the Venetian monopoly on eastern trade and attracting European merchants to Lisbon. Further discoveries that followed included the accidental arrival in Brazil by Pedro Alvares Cabral in 1500, after setting off to follow in Vasco da Gama's traces, and the first circumnavigation of the globe accomplished under a Spanish flag, though the captain, Fernão de Magalhães (Magellan) was Portuguese.

The monarchy benefited from overseas exploration, making it the richest in Europe. With the building of the Paços da Ribeira (Ribeiro Palace) in the Terreiro do Paço, the focus moved away from the castle. During the sixteenth and seventeenth century the city expanded onto the surrounding hills. In 1496 Dom Manuel was forced to expel many Jews who had flooded in from Spain a few years earlier, a condition set by Spain to fulfill a marriage alliance. He hoped to alleviate the situation by compelling the Jews to become New Christians, only succeeding in driving their practice underground.

Dom João III established the Inquisition in 1531, victimizing the converted Jews, killing many of them in public executions, the infamous *auto-da-fés*. These inquisitions continued until the social reforms instigated by the Marquês de Pombal in the eighteenth century.

In 1570 when the economy began to collapse, its wealth wasted in attempts to sustain its foreign acquisitions, Portugal became vulnerable to Spain. After the death of Dom Sebastião in 1578, the cardinal-king Henriques ruled without an heir, leaving the way open for Philip II of Spain to take over as Filipe I of Portugal. From 1581 the Spanish ruled for sixty years.

Subsequent Spanish foreign policy was to be a disaster for Portugal. Provocation was set up when Spain used Portugal against its allies, the British and Dutch. By refusing the Dutch entry to the Tagus to go about their business as carriers and distributors, Spain ensured that they would bypass Lisbon and sail around the Cape themselves, venturing directly to the source for their merchandise. In the process they found the colonies unprotected and took control of the territories, as did the British. It was not long before the Portuguese empire was considerably reduced, for the Dutch then turned to Angola, followed by Brazil. Eventually the Portuguese tired of Spanish abuse. When an opportunity arose, a group of conspirators took over the palace in Lisbon, threw out the Duchess of Mantau, its Spanish caretaker, and crowned the Duke of Bragança as Dom João IV. He promptly signed treaties with the Dutch and the British to salvage what he could. December 1, 1640 is a date still celebrated as Portugal's Restoration Day, the day when Spanish rule was finally overthrown.

Intent on strengthening the alliance with the British, Dom Afonso's sister, Catherine of Bragança, was married to King Charles II, bringing with her a massive dowry that included two million *cruzados* ($500,000 then), the right to trade with the Portuguese colonies, the cession of Tangier, which was soon abandoned, and, as an afterthought, Bombay. Catherine also brought to England the ritual of afternoon tea, a device to keep an eye on her ladies-in-waiting, who were within orbit of her philandering husband, although he still managed to produce a number of children from his various mistresses.

**The Great Earthquake**
The eighteenth century saw further prosperity with gold and diamonds flowing from Brazil, although Dom João V did his best to counterbalance that and bankrupt the country by building his palace-convent at Mafra as a rival extravagance to Philip II's Escorial in Spain. When the monarch died there was not even enough money left to pay for his funeral. Dom José I, next to the throne, left power to the Marquês de Pombal. Although a tyrant, he happened to be the right person at the right place and time, for the shake up arrived with the

Great Earthquake of 1755, at 9:30AM on November 1, All Saints' Day, when most of the population was at Mass.

Three major shocks with a minute in between struck Lisbon, the second bringing down the walls and roofs of houses, shops, churches and palaces with a deafening roar. It took fifteen minutes for the fog-like cloud of dust to settle. As it did, fires could be seen spreading, most originating from toppled candles in the churches. As those who survived tried to scramble from the devastation, many made their way to the waterfront, to what they thought would be relative safety. Within an hour the tidal waves arrived, three in succession. Although the waves, which had started out at sea, had been tempered at the river bar, they were still between fifteen and twenty feet high as they flung themselves at the city, hurling people and debris as flotsam.

Observers on the hilltops said that the city swayed like corn in the wind before crumbling, with the fire completing the destruction and leveling buildings that might otherwise have stood. It took a week to extinguish the smoldering ruins. Figures vary, but estimations suggest that 40,000 perished as a result of the earthquake and its repercussions.

Other countries felt the disturbance, the tremors running up through Portugal, Spain and into the Bordeaux region of France, with reports also coming from Switzerland, northern Italy, Brittany and the Scilly Islands. The disturbed sea-waves reached England and Ireland by 2PM and the West Indies by 6PM. Nearly thirty shocks were felt the following week, with further alarms over the next few months. Although Lisbon had experienced earthquakes before, this was its first major destruction.

Dom José, who was at his palace at Belém at the time, wanted to decamp to Brazil, but Pombal insisted that he stay with the Court and remain under canvas in the palace garden to maintain morale. Many others followed his example and camped out in the open, even if their homes were still intact.

On hearing of the catastrophe, the French philosopher and writer, Voltaire, penned a 200-line poem, *Poem on the Disaster of Lisbon* (1756), and within ten days delivered it to his publisher. While sympathetic to the plight of the people, he was also concerned with commenting on the philosophical viewpoints of the day, the era of optimism. The particular target was the German philosopher Leibnitz and his affirmation that God was good, and thus created the best of all possible worlds, a view expressed by the English writer Pope in his *Essay on Man* as "whatever is, is right." Voltaire remarked that exponents of that philosophy would be hard put to explain the disaster as being part of the best of all possible worlds. In the preface he hits at such thinking: "The heirs of the dead would now come into their fortunes, masons would grow rich in rebuilding the city, beasts would grow fat on corpses buried in the ruins; such is the natural effect of natural causes. So don't worry about your own particular evil; you are contributing to the general good." The beliefs of Leibnitz and his ilk, he observed, were an insult to those in suffering.

Voltaire took it further with his most popular philosophical novel, *Candide* (1758), his satire on the optimistic creed. Shipwrecked within sight of Lisbon, Dr. Pangloss and his student Candide are washed ashore. "Scarce had they set foot in the city…when they perceived the earth to tremble under their feet, and saw the sea swell in the harbor, and dash to pieces the ships that were at anchor." It continues as fine fiction, but, like some of the engravings of the time, was scarcely a true report of the devastation that had occurred.

Pombal set about rebuilding the city, not only physically, but also re-establishing tax systems, setting up export companies and other manufacturing companies, abolishing slavery, as well as the Jesuit order that had dominated education and religious life. Though there were undoubted benefits, he was cruel. He had no regrets. "The prisons and the cells were the only means I found to tame this blind and ignorant nation," he remarked.

## Invasion and Dictatorship

With Napoleon's rise in France came the demand that Portugal declare war on Britain, her ally. To do so would be to commit economic suicide, for Britain would be sure to take over Portugal's overseas possessions. As Portugal hesitated, Napoleon invaded in the shape of General Junot's army, the Portuguese royal family fleeing to Brazil by boat just before the army's arrival in Lisbon in 1807. After three invasions by the French in successive years, they were forced to give up, the Duke of Wellington, as he was to become, driving them back to Toulouse.

Portugal was at one of its lowest points, being virtually a colony of Brazil, and a protectorate of Britain. Finally, in 1821, Dom João VI returned from Brazil, and the following year Brazil declared its independence. The rule of the monarchy was by now on unsteady ground, for the impetus was towards republicanism. When Dom Carlos attempted to rule dictatorially, he was assassinated, along with one of his sons. In 1910 the other son, Dom Manuel II, was overthrown by a republican revolution and went into exile in Britain. Turmoil reigned for a number of years, and in 1926 General Carmona became president and suspended the constitution.

In 1928 Dr. António de Oliveira Salazar, an economics professor at Coimbra University, became finance minister and his success at balancing the budget brought him control of the country, becoming prime minister in 1932. Salazar stayed in power until 1968, when he toppled himself, falling from his deckchair and suffering a stroke from which he never recovered, although it took him two years to die, all those around his bed maintaining the illusion that he still held power.

Salazar's regime, the *Estado Novo* (New State) was a repressive one, bearing many facets of a Fascist regime. The price paid for forty years of dictatorship was the retardation of Portugal, with censorship and the exclusion of outside influences to prevent "contamination," as well as the coterie of third-raters around the dictator that allowed mediocrity to blossom. "I consider more urgent the creation of élites than the necessity of teaching people how to read," was a typical Salazar remark. It sometimes seems that only football, *fado* and the promotion of the Fátima vision, encouraging the pilgrimage industry to flourish, were allowed for the populace.

In 1968 there were 100,000 Portuguese troops fighting in the colonial wars in Africa. Many conscripts should have been at university. The international student unrest was in their blood. Finally, dissent among the armed forces generated the necessary step. On April 25, 1974, Major Otelo Saraiva de Carvalho led a bloodless revolution, termed the "red carnation" revolution, after people stuffed the flowers down the barrels of the triumphant soldiers' weapons. The government was overthrown. Political instability followed with a curtailing of the colonial wars and independence for Angola, Mozambique and the other colonies, drawing to Portugal three-quarters of a million Portuguese citizens called *retornados*, which in turn placed an enormous strain on the shambles of an economy.

**European Nation**
Various political combinations have taken place since then, giving forms of democracy to the country. It seems that what many had thought was in substance a people's revolution in 1974 was in fact a middle-class movement, more intent on reform than revolution. With intentions of developing closer ties with Europe, Portugal took the next step and joined the European Union in 1986, the subsequent surge of funding allowing Lisbon to start rebuilding and investing in its future with a vengeance. Not for two hundred years has such renewal been seen.

In 1992 Portugal held the presidency of the European Union, building a new center at Belém for the purpose. In 1994, as European City of Culture, Lisbon began to show new confidence. And with Expo 98, a new cityscape was generated and further hope for the future. Other international events are looming; the European football championships are on the horizon and a bid for the Olympics is in progress.

All this ambition is not without its problems. Unemployment, housing shortages, and poverty are being tackled, but are far from eradicated. Spanish business appears to have its hands on a sizeable amount of Portugal's economy, tied in more closely than many might wish.

These few facts might be helpful, as you push forward: a brevity that excludes much, but as Saramago wrote, in relation to his book, *The History of the Siege of Lisbon*: "The truth is that history could have been written in many different ways."

# 3. Rio Tejo

The main entrance to Lisbon has always been the river, the Rio Tejo (Tagus). Arrival by boat as key to the door. Lisbon's history is narrated in terms of its relationship to the sea. These days the choice is wider, the preference for other means: motorways, bridges, railway stations and airport. Not that crossing the river is a forgotten approach. Anything but. For those who live south of Lisbon and who do not wish to get entangled in the traffic on the bridges, daily travel to work is best accomplished by ferry, a regular service, one that continues throughout the night.

Departure can be effected directly opposite at Cacilhas, or from its neighboring towns of Barreiro, Montijo and others, necessary too if connecting to trains heading south to the Algarve or other beaches. Arrival in Lisbon is either at Cais do Sodré or Terreiro do Paço. Arrival at the hub of the city. If you wish to bring your car, it's Cais do Sodré.

The ferry is not the only traffic on the river. It might well have to wend its way past an ocean liner, cruise ship, naval boats, tankers, freighters and tugs, as well as lighter craft working on the river. All are either coming in to dock and unload, or heading for the Lisnave yards opposite for repair work, or perhaps departing for a Mediterranean cruise, or somewhere further afield, perhaps the ports of the old Portuguese territories from Rio de Janeiro to Maputo. There is still plenty of activity, though you might not see the old *fragatas*, the traditional boats with their large sepia triangular sails that ferried goods from one bank to the other. German director Wolf Gaudlitz's film, *Taxi Lisboa* (1997) admirably captures this sense of wending and weaving of the cross-cutting river traffic with angles that suggest imminent collisions.

### First Impressions

A few celebrated figures have arrived by boat, engraving their names in different ways on the memories of the city. Lord Byron's brief passage and writings, immortalized in a few quotes, and part of his poem *Childe Harold's Pilgrimage* (1812), did more to discourage travelers of the nineteenth century than others we are led to believe. His visit to

Lisbon was little more than an accident, a casual decision. "The Malta vessel not sailing for some weeks," he wrote, "we have determined to go by sea by way of Lisbon." There are a number of important points to be borne in mind with regard to Byron. This was his first trip abroad, and his first port of call, thus no yardstick for comparison was on offer. Byron was twenty-one, out of university at Cambridge by one year. The Lisbon packet that took him and his fellow university friend, John Hobhouse, set sail from Falmouth in Cornwall on the July 2, 1809. They were accompanied by three or four servants, although only one continued beyond Gibraltar. It took four and a half days to reach Lisbon. "Only four-and-a-half days—good sailing," as the Byron scholar Allan Massie noted. Byron was fortunate that it wasn't longer. He wrote to his friend Francis Hodgson back in England, not entirely seriously: "I have been sea-sick, and sick of the sea." It was barely fifty years since Lisbon had been destroyed by the Great Earthquake of 1755, yet the city had been rebuilt quite remarkably. Byron's view to his mother in a letter written later from Gibraltar was nonetheless dismissive. "It has often been described without being worthy of description for, except for the view from the Tagus which is beautiful, and some fine churches and convents, Lisbon contains little but filthy streets and more filthy inhabitants."

Byron's attitude towards the Portuguese is revealed in the First Canto of his long poem:

*What beauties doth Lisboa first unfold!*
*Her image floating on that noble tide,*
*Which poets vainly pave with sands of gold,*
*But now whereon a thousand keels did ride*
*Of mighty strength, since Albion was allied,*
*And to the Lusians did her aid afford:*
*A nation swoln with ignorance and pride,*
*Who lick yet loathe the hand that waves the sword*
*To save them from the wrath of Gaul's unsparing Lord.*

This "malevolent, contemptuous sneer" as Rose Macaulay called it, has never endeared Byron to the Portuguese, as one can imagine. Many scholars are still bewildered as to why he should have been so sharp. There seems to be little evidence to account for it, though some try to relate it to an incident that occurred at the theater when Byron was struck by an angry husband as a result of the poet's advances towards his wife. It might have upset the romantic, but it was scarcely a disaster or anything out of the usual, one supposes. Nor was it so bad that he should seek revenge in such a low fashion. When it was suggested that he should modify some of his attacks, he noted: "As I have found the Portuguese, so I have written of them." His watchful friend and mentor Mr. Dallas remarked that: "Resentment, anger, hatred held full sway over him, and his gratification at that time was in overcharging his pen with gall that flowed in every direction." Whatever it was that fired him, Byron's attack on the Portuguese seems to have cleared the rage from his system, for he made angels of the Spanish in the next step of his travels.

As a specific counter to Byron's "sneer," Dorothy Quillinan, Wordsworth's daughter, determined to "assist in removing prejudices which make Portugal an avoided land." Her stay in Portugal in 1845 was recorded in a journal. Yet the power of the pens of others more famous appears to have held sway.

Another of those was Henry Fielding, who was likewise not given to much praise, although his situation was somewhat understandable. The great novelist left Britain in ill health, jaundice, dropsy and asthma being his main troubles. He sought warmer climes as a last resort to his ailments, unable to stomach the bad English summer. He determined to go to Lisbon because it would be the easiest by boat, rather than to Aix-en-Provence, which would necessitate a lengthy and uncomfortable overland journey. But the boat trip was not as simple as perhaps anticipated; all manner of upsets and irritations beleaguered the voyage. This is documented fully in *The Journal of a Voyage to Lisbon* (1755), though little exists of the visit itself, probably because it was short-lived, terminated within a couple of months when he died. Today he is buried in the English Cemetery, across the Jardim da Estrela from the Basílica.

The year was 1754, just prior to the Great Earthquake. As their boat, *The Queen of Portugal*, awaited procedures for disembarkation, Fielding noted his impression of Lisbon from the deck: "Lisbon, before which we now lay at anchor, is said to be built on the same number of hills with old

Rome; but these do not all appear to the water; on the contrary, one sees from thence one vast high hill and rock, with buildings arising above one another, and that in so steep and almost perpendicular a manner, that they all seem to have but one foundation." He continued, written after the fact: "As the houses, convents, churches, etc., are large, and all built with white stone, they look very beautiful at a distance; but as you approach nearer, and find them to want every kind of ornament, all idea of beauty vanishes at once." The interminable procedures and the dishonesty of the officials could not have helped this infirm man, for the book ends barely has Fielding stepped, or been carried, ashore, with the description: "the nastiest city in the world"– a judgment which did not lighten later according to the scant information that has come down to us.

In order to begin to bring back some color to this sea-borne approach to the city, we need to note the angle that José Saramago gave to the arrival of his character, albeit in fictional form, at the start of *The Year of the Death of Ricardo Reis* (1984). However, we will move one step at a time. Lisbon was not blessed with sun that day in 1936, rather suffering another day of inclement weather and rain. Reis was arriving home from Brazil on the *Highland Brigade*, set to cast anchor at the Alcântara quay. The steamer was sailing up the Tagus, the children pressed at its windows. "Behind windowpanes ingrained with salt the children peer out at the gray city, which lies flat above the hills as if built entirely of one-story houses. Yonder, perhaps, you catch a glimpse of a high dome, some thrusting gable, an outline suggesting a castle ruin, unless this is simply an illusion, a chimera, a mirage created by the shifting curtain of the waters that descend from the leaden sky." They asked the name of the port. "Lisboa, Lisbon, Lisbonne, Lissabon, there are four different ways of saying it, leaving aside the variants and mistaken forms."

### Departure Point

Lisbon was the place from which Vasco da Gama set off to discover the sea route to India, departing from the beach at Restelo (now called Belém). This major expedition, as others, was not all plain sailing, as a few potted lines in history outlines can suggest. Looking at the small print, the details of the expeditions, one reads of the terrible hardships endured, the numbers who did not survive the trip, scurvy being one of the reducing agents: "All our people again suffered from their gums, which grew over their teeth, so that they could not eat. Their legs also swelled, and other parts of the body, and these swellings spread until the sufferer died." Of the fleet of four (two *naus*, a smaller *caravel* and a large store ship) that set sail with 170 aboard, it was one *nau* and the *caravel* that returned triumphant with 55 aboard.

Not only a place from which to set off by way of adventure and exploration, Lisbon was also a place to flee from itself. When Napoleon threatened the Portuguese with invasion in 1807 unless they turned on their allies, the British, it was from here that Dom João VI (as he was to become) and his entourage of something in excess of 8,000 departed for a fourteen-year sojourn in Brazil. They were escorted by Sir Sidney Smith's squadron, leaving the people of Lisbon stranded, and baying for their blood, as their removal was accompanied by a vast store of treasures and around half the currency in circulation. Some months later, when General Junot's army was being escorted by British transport ships back to France after its defeat at Vimeiro, it was the turn of the Lisbon people to curse the British and French, for the terms of the agreement (the Convention of Sintra), which had excluded the Portuguese from involvement, allowed the defeated to withdraw with their personal property, which in the event meant most of their spoils.

### Escape Point

"The beautiful way to arrive at Lisbon is by flying boat," the British poet Sacheverell Sitwell wrote in the 1950s. "Coming by any of the other airlines you touch down at Portela Airport, and miss the sensation of gliding up the Tagus parallel to the city." He compared this pleasure to arriving in Rome. "The approach by flying boat only compares in completeness and rounded fullness of feeling to that moment when the aeroplane makes a half-circle around the dome of St. Peter's, and in another few moments you have arrived in Rome."

This means of arrival was on offer for a limited period. The era of the seaplane or flying boat was short-lived, superseded by the larger and more reliable jets. Yet for a time they were useful as a connection with North Africa or Madeira, and also to set off across the Atlantic.

Anaïs Nin wrote in her diaries of her experience in 1939. Forced to flee Paris, she headed home to America via Lisbon, there to climb aboard a hydroplane, as she called the flying boat:

*Portugal. I cannot smile at the sun. I cannot smile at the white buildings, the women in black, at the wild flowers and the singing in cafés. I am in mourning for France. The hydroplane is poised on the water. The refugees cheer. Escape! A woman takes me to the ladies' room to search me, to see that I am not carrying a revolver, a camera, or gold. To get inside the hydroplane we walk on its wing and enter through an opening in its belly. The metal is the same color as the sea. It seems too heavy to fly. As it courses along the water with one engine starting, then another, gathering speed but bumping against the waves, I feel as if in a nightmare when one cannot fly upward even though menaced by great dangers.*

Various American writers destined for North Africa came through Lisbon. Jane and Paul Bowles, who formed a group with others such as Truman Capote and Tennessee Williams came this way, along with Libby Holman, the original torch singer, who was a close friend and intimate of Jane Bowles. In 1958 the Bowles stopped for a while in Lisbon and Funchal in Madeira, forced from Tangier by political pressures and Jane's deteriorating health, before continuing across the Atlantic. "I do rather like Portugal," Paul Bowles wrote in a letter, "if only because the people are pleasant. I'm fed up with being surrounded by hostility, which is the rule rather than the exception in the countries where I've been living: Morocco and Ceylon."

To return to the ships and the scene of wartime Europe. Erich Maria Remarque was no stranger to books that dealt with war. His novel *All Quiet on the Western Front* (1929) has remained a classic, albeit as a result of Lewis Milestone's landmark film. Remarque had himself fled Nazi Germany for Switzerland and later America. *The Night in Lisbon*, which concerns us, revolves around the flight of Jews and anti-Fascists from Germany, told through the story of one man as he recounts his plight as a condition for handing over his tickets and passports to another who wants to board the freedom boat at Lisbon. He reminds us just what a monumental role Lisbon was playing in history:

*The ship was being made ready for a voyage — like the ark in the days of the flood. It was an ark. Every ship that left Europe in those months of the year 1942 was an ark. Mount Arata was America, and the flood waters were rising higher by the day. Long ago they had engulfed Germany and Austria, now they stood deep in Poland and Prague; Amsterdam, Brussels, Copenhagen, Oslo, and Paris had gone under, the cities of Italy stank of seepage, and Spain, too, was no longer safe. The coast of Portugal had become the last hope of the fugitives to whom justice, freedom, and tolerance meant more than home and livelihood. This was the gate to America. If you couldn't reach it, you were lost, condemned to bleed away in a jungle of consulates, police stations, and government offices, where visas were refused and work and residence permits unobtainable, a jungle of internment camps, bureaucratic red tape, loneliness, homesickness, and withering universal indifference. As usual in times of war, fear, and affliction, the individual human being had ceased to exist; only one thing counted: a valid passport.*

### Terra Firma

The person who travels through this book, who makes his impression on various Lisbon districts is Pessoa. There can be no apologies for featuring him so readily. One way or another, he has something to offer at regular steps on our course. In *The Book of Disquietude*, he said of the Tagus: "When one's feelings are overwrought, the Tagus is a nameless Atlantic, and Cacilhas another continent, even another universe." In other words, he did not actually cross it regularly. "Very often it occurred to me to cross the river, a ten-minute trip between Terreiro do Paço and Cacilhas. And almost always I have been intimidated by all those people, by myself and by my idea. Once or twice I have crossed over, always feeling oppressed, only putting a foot on terra firma once I was back."

This reads well alongside an unpublished guide to Lisbon that was found among his papers. Although it was generally written in a no-nonsense style, in English, Pessoa chose to open the text with a poetic ring. "For the traveller who comes in from the sea, Lisbon, even from afar, rises like a fair vision in a dream, clear-cut against a bright blue sky which the sun gladdens with its gold. And the domes, the monuments, the old castle jut up above the mass of houses, like far-off heralds of this delightful seat, of this blessed region."

Pessoa may travel through this book with us, touching down at various points, but traveling on land, let alone sea, was anathema to him.

It was not that travel had not featured earlier in his life. As a child of seven, he had been taken by his mother to Durban in South Africa, returning alone at seventeen to pursue his studies. It was not Durban he wrote about. All that South Africa offered was an education that provided him with his love for English literature. It was Lisbon he thought about. It was Lisbon he returned to. It was Lisbon that was his city and his focus.

In a poem, *Lisbon Revisited*, titled in English, he wrote:

*Once more I see you again,*
*City of my childhood dreadfully lost...*
*Sad, cheerful city, once more I dream here...*
*I? But am I the same who lived here, and came back here,*
*And returned back here, and back,*
*And returned afresh back here?*

There was just no place for travel with Pessoa, as he explained: "What is travel and what use is it? All sunsets are sunsets; there is no need to go and see one in Constantinople. The feeling of freedom engendered by travel? I can feel that by going from Lisbon to Benfica, and I feel it more intensely than someone who travels from Lisbon to China, since, if the feeling of freedom does not exist in me, it does not exist for me anywhere at all."

## Sea of Straw

Seen from the ferry as one approaches, Lisbon reveals its hills, whether the official seven hills of Castelo, Graça, Monte, Penha de França, São Pedro de Alcântara, Santa Catarina, and Estrela, or the variations on that number. They seem to fluctuate in number, like the population of the city, which is variously quoted as three-quarters of a million to one million, depending on the extent of suburbs included, I suspect. Rodney Gallop, a British traveler, recalled his favorite view of Lisbon in the 1960s: "One pale, clear winter's dawn, when a low mist lay over the milky water and there floated above it, earthbound no longer, the three hills of St George, Bairro Alto and Estrela, opalescent and ethereal as a mirage. Through the mist the dark sails of anchored barges could be dimly discerned, hung out to dry in the windless calm. Lisbon that morning had the dreamlike quality of a Turner."

In her diary, the writer Maria Gabriela Llansol noted: "Viewed at length, Lisbon is unlike anywhere else; it is itself, without ostentation; the Tagus already is dead many times over and the town has no strength to cling to it; rivers sweep along with them the form of the towns they pass through." This is a view I had not observed in other river-bearing towns or cities, although standing before the Tagus it might well seem true, as it is so wide, its physical presence so grand as to be overwhelming. But then again, it is so wide that one almost thinks of it more as an ebbing and flowing sea than as a river that flows past.

Lisbon is a city of poets and poetry, and though we use the phrase "poetic city" with some regularity, besides Pessoa not many other poets seem to be quoted. As with elsewhere, not all write directly about a landmark, or landscape; more seek to convey the feelings evoked by the city. However, one of Lisbon's major contemporary poets, Sophia de Mello Breyner, wrote, in *Navigations* (1983):

*I say "Lisbon"*
*When I arrive from the south and cross the river*
*And the city opens up as if born from its name*
*It opens and rises in its nocturnal vastness*
*In its long shimmering of blue and of river*
*In its rugged body of hills –*
*I see it better because I say it*
*Everything is more clearly where it is*
*Everything shows more clearly what it lacks*
*Because I say*
*Lisbon with its name of being and nonbeing*
*With its meanders of astonishment insomnia and shacks*
*And its secret theatre sparkle*
*Its madlike smile of intrigue and complicity*
*While the wide sea stretches westward*
*Lisbon swaying like a sailing ship*
*Lisbon cruelly built next to its own absence*
*I say the city's name*
*I say it to see*

Yet there is more poetry. There is the poetry of painting, photography, music, film... most of which offer us direct imagery of the city, not just its soul or the soul of the people expressed by its writers. The young Lisbon filmmaker Pedro Nunes has been making films around the various transportation systems in the city. Recently he made one on the ferries, *Cacilheiros* (1998), which had been in preparation for two years, awaiting the right time, the right light. He told Elizabeth Nash: "I wanted to film in late October. It's the most important moment in the year to catch the magic of the city. The sun is low in the sky, and has a silky softness that reflects on the water and makes the colors of the riverside jump out with incredible intensity." Of course, when all was finally set to film, it rained, and rained, delaying filming for days.

What Nunes sought to capture, like many filmmakers who cast their cameras at the Tagus, is the near dusk reflection of the sun on the rippling water, an effect termed *mar de palha* (sea of straw), a golden straw-like reflection, as if the straw has been spread out to dry. The effect occurs here because the Tagus, which has journeyed from the mountains of Spain, and then across Portugal, is six miles from the mouth of the river and has widened, forming an inland sea, one that is more often rippling than choppy, giving breadth for eyes to play across the expanse from its northern bank, from Lisbon itself, when the sun is low in the sky in the west. This sight is not just for tourists, but for residents too. While we stand in our turn, we watch the waiting children salvage flat stones from the road-works and skim them across the water, inadvertently playing into the hands of the effect, as they too are drawn in and become part of this long tradition.

Nunes added from on board the ferry: "This is the moment I like best. There's a sudden stillness, it's as though everything stops. You're on a floating lookout, suspended, and your head fills with thoughts of absence, voyages, farewells. It's a disconcerting feeling."

*Taxi Lisboa* is another of the films that seeks to portray a love for the river as well as for the city itself. Although Augusto Machedo, the old driver, chugging up to a hundred and still holding a valid license, steers his equally old taxi, a grand Oldsmobile, across the Ponte 25 de Abril in the morning en route to work in the city, he leaves for home via the ferry on this occasion. Or at least he appears to. And as the ferry in all its orange splendor slips across the water, Machedo works his jack to change a tire, bemoaning the rubbish in the streets that punctures his tires and takes the wind out of his sails. As he spins away, and we smile at the pleasure we have had from Gaudlitz's film, comparable to watching that other city compendium, Fellini's *Roma*, I see the novelist Lídia Jorge, in playful mood, suggesting that if she was a particular type of bad poet, she "could speak of the shadow of the ferries gliding on the water like souls."

## Cacilhas

Having placed our soles on terra firma at the Terreiro do Paço, there is no earthly reason why we cannot go back, follow Machedo off into the night. It is very popular to spend the evening in Cacilhas eating seafood in one of the restaurants in the vicinity of the ferry dock, admiring Lisbon by night, across the water. *Arroz de marisco* is one of the specialties to eat, which I have seen variously interpreted as seafood stew, seafood risotto, and seafood paella. I guess it's whether you sit as an Englishman, Italian, or Spaniard, not necessarily in that order, that you take your pick.

You can always bypass the restaurants and walk along the narrow quay, the Cais do Ginjal, in the direction of the bridge. What appears as a long row of derelict warehouses is in fact a number of derelict warehouses and homes interspersed with other houses that are still habitable, or have been resuscitated. Eventually, after ten minutes, rounding the bend, you are greeted by a small bay with a couple of converted warehouses made into restaurants, from where you can eat and gaze once more across at the city. But beware of ghosts along the quay. Alain Tanner opened his film version of Antonio Tabucchi's novel *Requiem* along this quay. It enabled him to parade the panoramic view of the city, to make an opening statement of the urban landscape. Ironic that the figure he should be waiting for, "the bloke," was in fact Pessoa, whom, as we know, claimed to have barely set foot outside Lisbon, not even on the other side of the Tagus. Having arrived twelve hours too early for his meeting, our hero sets off to explore, taking the ferry across to the city. Later, almost twelve hours later to be precise, on his return, he meets up with his mysterious ghost, and together they talk as they walk off to have a meal, back along the quay, cloaked by atmospheric lighting. It is almost as if Orson Welles had moved from Vienna. And like the Third Man, Pessoa is gone, vanished. The critic, Pierre Hourcade, who knew Pessoa at the end of his life, remarked: "Never, when I bade him goodbye, did I dare to turn back and look at him; I was afraid I would see him vanish, dissolved in air."

This quay, opposite the city, is a peaceful spot to roam and ruminate. Bernard Comment, the Swiss-born novelist, who scripted *Requiem* for Tanner, favors this stretch, and one of the two restaurants, Ponto Final, around the corner, his preference *arroz de tamboril* (monkfish risotto, stew…). Perhaps it was Tanner himself who introduced him to this spot, as he had ventured here years before when seeking a location for *In the White City*, creating a quiet and isolated spot for the romance of his couple Paul and Rosa, with the bridge as backdrop.

There is no getting away from it, whether by day or night, whether sitting or standing, whether on the ferry or at the quay: to view what is termed the "white city" across that stretch of water is an unforgettable image. Preferably by day if the white city analogy is to be maintained. A place of inspiration for any artist, or would-be artist, notoriously faced each day by the white page, the white canvas, or the white screen.

# PART TWO

# *THE CENTER*

*"By day Lisbon has a naïve theatrical quality that enchants and captivates,*
*but by night it is a fairy-tale city, descending over lighted terraces to the*
*sea, like a woman in festive garments going down to meet her dark lover."*
Erich Maria Remarque, *The Night in Lisbon*

## 1. Baixa

Entry to the city over the years has been opened up greatly, not only by
flying in through the back door (the airport), or coming down the sides,
over the bridges, or even through the Windows with the internet. Yet we
have elected to arrive, at least for the purposes of this book, by the oldest
route, and step up to the front door from our boat, albeit the ferry
service. Coming across from Cacilhas without a car, the best way to see
the city rather than a surfeit of other rear ends, we choose to land beside
the Terreiro do Paço (Terrace of the Palace) as it is still known, though
officially it is called Praça do Comércio (Commerce Square).

A word of warning before we step ashore. We can afford time to wait
for the gangplank to be firmly secured, unlike the locals who swarm
from the ferry before the boat even appears to have settled in place.
There is a tendency in Lisbon for the residents, and even for official
documents, to call a place, or a street, by its former name rather than its
official name, even if the new name has been in operation for years.
Perhaps one exception would be the Ponte 25 de Abril, which, though

opened in 1966 as the Ponte Salazar, was changed in 1974 to commemorate the bloodless revolution. That change is fixed. (Except for the temporary graffiti re-instating the old dictator on the bridge support—but how permanent is chalk?) All others vary, from former names to nicknames. You can look in vain on the map, find yourself lost from a local's instructions, or a reference in a book. And then there are the names that even with the latest map, and your confidence high that you've found the spot, are different from the sign on the wall. The street sign looks worn enough to have been attached there for years, yet you wonder whether you have the new name, the old one, or the wrong one.

The others have gone. We step ashore. We have arrived in Lisbon, "the most beautiful city in the world"—an endorsement from Cervantes that I read somewhere in passing and have never been able to put my finger on since.

## Terreiro do Paço

We are at the Terreiro do Paço, named with reference to the Paços da Ribeira (Ribeiro Palace or Palace of the River Bank) that stood there before the earthquake of 1755. And still they call it by its former name! This vast square, about 300 yards square, one of the finest in Europe, and "perfectly square" as Pessoa wrote, is the "reception room to the city," as countless others have pointed out. It really is that grand, and can always be spotted from afar. In fact, to get a good perspective it is best seen from afar, from the other side of the river or from the ferry as one approaches.

Thomas Mann noted: "The Praça do Comércio, a dignified and rather quiet square, is open on one side to the harbour, where the River Tagus makes a deep bend; the other three sides are lined with arcades, covered walks from which one enters the Customs House, the main Post Office, various ministries, and the bank for which I was bound." Its appearance, three sides of tall arcades topped with pink-washed façades, has been variously described as "classical," "simple and graceful," or "one that lacks imagination." The style is called Pombaline, after the city-planner, the Marquês de Pombal, who was given the task of lifting Lisbon back on its feet after the devastation caused by the earthquake and its subsequent flood and fires. Lisbon might well be a city of modest people, but Pombal wanted to present an extravagant touch in the rebuilding, to commemorate the king's generosity and make a mark right on the doorstep, "a regal climax" as another observed. Thus, in the center of this square he elected to place a large bronze of the monarch, Dom José I, his patron, seated on a horse. It more than dominates the space. In the tradition of trying to turn things their way, to unseat the rider one could say, the British call this Black Horse Square, although this has neatly back-fired because the horse is more green these days, as a result of the salt in the air from the river, and has been for quite some years.

The statue was made by Joaquim Machado de Castro, and stands 46 feet high. The plumed helmet is the main feature of the head, reputably because the king was too ill to have his likeness made. It took five years to create and was cast in a single piece from "eighty-four thousand pounds of bronze in eight minutes." The king's horse is seen to trample serpents and the pedestal is flanked by Triumph leading a horse, and Fame guiding an elephant, a reference to the nation's conquests in the East. More than a thousand people were required to place the statue, taking over three and a half days, the whole affair carried out with great ceremony.

At the front of the pedestal there is a bronze bas-relief medallion depicting Pombal, but when he was later displaced, after his dictatorial era, the craftsman who had made the medallion was ordered to remove and destroy it. Contrary to orders, instead of melting the metal, he

bricked it into a wall of the Arsenal, revealing the secret to his nephew on his deathbed. Sixty years after removal it was retrieved and reinstalled.

In the sixteenth century, in the days before the earthquake, when the Ribeira Palace stood firm, this area saw scenes of bullfighting, royalty standing on their balcony to watch. Until recently, a different form of battle was taking place at the tail end of the twentieth century, with the area little more than a lot where cars sparred for a place to park. Now they have been pushed aside to other spaces, some underground, and the square has been reclaimed as an expanse for people to wander around, perch on the foot of the statue, and to contemplate, lean or graffiti the large sculptural objects that are scattered across the north side, unbalancing the space so that it does not become just a symmetrical square with a very large statue in the middle.

In the northwest corner, where the Rua do Arsenal begins, and almost directly before the Post Office, Dom Carlos and his elder son, the prince Luíz Filipe were assassinated on the February 1, 1908. As a result, the successor to the throne, the younger son, Manuel, went into exile two years later in 1910, Portugal being proclaimed a Republic. It was no surprise to learn that, in 1974, one of the objectives of the troops who moved into the city to aid the replacement of the dictatorship with democracy was to occupy this square, to take control of "the symbol of power."

In the center of the northern arcade is the Arco Triunfal, a magnificent arch that offers a sculptural flourish into the Rua Augusta and the Baixa grid. It is dated 1873, though it was designed by Verissimo José da Costa and begun in 1755. The years to completion are reflected in the nineteenth-century influence on the uppermost part. "The allegoric group which crowns the arch, sculptured by Calmels, personifies Glory crowning Genius and Valour; and the recumbent figures, which represent the rivers Tagus and Douro, as well as the statues of Nun'Alvares, Viriato, Pombal and Vasco da Gama, are due to the sculptor Victor Bastos," Pessoa wrote in his book, *Lisbon: What the Tourist Should See.* Though the text was written in 1925, it was not published, and the manuscript was not found until many years after his death when scholars were sorting through the famous trunk containing all his papers to start archiving and publishing more of his work. Written in English, it amounts to a car drive around the city, with notes and details on the various landmarks. There is little room for poetic elaboration. Poetry was not his intention with the project. From time to time I will draw on it mainly as a contrast to other guides.

Not included by Pessoa, who was keen to cover all matters to do with reading, was reference to the outstanding library of music manuscripts and music books in the palace, accumulated primarily through the patronage of Dom João IV before the earthquake in 1755 when fire reduced all to ashes. It appears that some copies that were made and taken elsewhere earlier have recently come to light. Along with the destruction of the library, there was also the destruction of a great many paintings, although no inventory is known. Sitwell speculated: "and who knows what lost paintings of Spanish provenance, pictures by Hieronymus Bosch left in Lisbon by Philip II, paintings, it is possible, done by Jan Van Eyck during his visit to Portugal, or portraits by Velázquez taken there during Spanish rule."

Today the project for the square is to make it more of a cultural spot, to open up the arcades to more cafés than the famous Martinho da Arcada, and to reduce the traffic further by sinking it into a tunnel above the new Metro station.

A favorite place to sit, or stand, has always been on the fourth wall, the front of the city stage before the river. Here one does not necessarily perform oneself, but watches the great river float by. One could stand at the top of the Venetian-style steps that lead up from the Tagus, formerly used by the royal barges for access to the palace, which is probably why the square has also earned comparison to Venice's Piazza San Marco. Although the palace went, the steps remained. But all is not as before. There is work in progress, part of the rejuvenation program, and even the two columns, the famous Cais das Colunas have been removed, with promises that they will be returned, though not all residents are certain. It would not be the first occasion in the current renovation scheme that a monument or statue has been removed or relocated while work was carried out, never to return.

There are times while walking around the city that words like reconstruction, rejuvenation, and regeneration should perhaps give way to a word like *deconstruction*. At what point does a city that is being dismantled and rebuilt come apart enough to offer thoughts of being in the process of deconstruction? Perhaps the very idea that one can get exasperated at times and think of it as deconstruction means that point has been reached.

So while it is not possible for the foreseeable future to see the features of the two columns in their rightful place, at the beginning of the 1990s, the Dutch writer Cees Nooteboom could write in his novel *The Following Story*: "I was drawn to that strange structure on the Praça do Comércio, where two columns rise from the gently rippling water like a gateway to the ocean and the world beyond. The dictator's name is carved in the marble, but he has gone now, taking his anachronistic empire with him, leaving the water to pursue its slow erosion of those columns." Or, as the British writer Oswell Blakeston wrote: "the Cais das Colunas, so called from the two famous columns on the steps of the quay which feature on posters and are known to all tourists and are lapped daily by the silk-sewn wavelets of the Tagus, the estuary with its ferries and sailing craft that glide out of another age and yet are here on the smooth waters." Glancing at the jetty where the ferries tie up, a stone's throw away, is not quite the same thing. But that is all there is at this time.

The terrain was re-trodden by the Italian novelist Antonio Tabucchi a few years ago with his exquisite hallucination, *Requiem* (1991). The book takes place "on a Sunday in July in a hot, deserted Lisbon." Tabucchi's character, to whom he refers as "I," has arranged to meet a "bloke," he says in the first lines, at twelve o'clock. A bloke? "I can't call him a 'bloke,' he's a great poet, perhaps the greatest poet of the twentieth century, he died years ago, I should treat him with respect or, at least, with deference." He is referring, of course, to Pessoa. Tabucchi is an authority on Pessoa, also translating him into Italian. He wants to write about an imaginary meeting with his subject, to dream, to mingle the living and the dead on equal terms. The framework stems from the confusion over twelve o'clock. Which twelve? Midday or midnight? "And it was then that I remembered: He said twelve o'clock, but perhaps he meant twelve o'clock at night, because that's when ghosts appear, at midnight." We are party to the strategy to meet with someone who is a dream, arranged in an earlier dream, or more appropriately, a daydream. Here, as everywhere, Tabucchi plays on facts that the Pessoa expert knows, not that it is crucial to any enjoyment of the book. For example, Pessoa was known to be late for appointments. Or early. Not punctual, anyway. So the twelve o'clock confusion is a valid device for the narrative. Pierre Hourcade confirms that sense of time-keeping: "He was there, without warning, late or early—never to time—always unexpected, even when I had long arranged the meeting. And in the short moments of his presence, he seemed to live double, triple, as if to concentrate the time, and to recoup the non-existent time that had gone before."

With twelve hours to kill, or dream away, Tabucchi sets off in search of adventures and answers to questions that have been nagging at him. At one point he is back at the square, seated on the pedestal beneath the statue of Dom José. "It really was a magnificent night, the moon was full, the air was warm and soft, there was something sensual, magical about it." The square was deserted. "A ferryboat bound for Cacilhas sounded its siren before leaving, its lights were the only lights you could see on the Tagus, everything else was utterly still, as if caught in a spell." A Seller of Stories accosts our author, and offers to sell him a story, although why he should accept becomes a debatable point as his whole day has become a series of stories, whiling away the hours until his appointment. In the event, he agrees, although first he asks for advice on where he should take his guest, as he is meeting him at the Cais de Alcântara and wants to eat nearby:

> There is one, said the Seller of Stories, right opposite the quay, it used to be a station or something, but now it's a kind of social club, it's a restaurant, a bar, a disco and who knows what else, it's very trendy, I think it's what's called post-modern. Post-modern? I said, post-modern in what sense? I'm not sure I could explain, said the Seller of Stories, I mean that it's been done up in lots of different styles, for example, the restaurant is full of mirrors and the food they serve is sort of unclassifiable, I mean, it's a place that broke with tradition by embracing tradition, you could describe it as a compilation of several different styles, that's what I would call post-modern. It sounds like the ideal place for my guest, I said.

Again we learn more about Pessoa. In fact, this book conveys insights into the Portuguese character, the Lisbon character, at every turn. It is as much a guidebook to Lisbon as any other named guidebook.

## Café Martinho da Arcada

All this attention to Pessoa, and yet none of our quoted writers has deigned to venture into one of the two most famous haunts referred to when talking about Pessoa, the Café Martinho da Arcada, in the north corner of the square. This famous café-restaurant was founded in 1782 and was not only the haunt of Pessoa's generation, but of writers, artists, and intellectuals from decades before.

The nineteenth-century Portuguese novelist of note, often compared to Flaubert, was José Maria Eça de Queirós. Though he mostly lived abroad, working in the consular service, he wrote social novels, attempting to expose the vices and foibles of the dominant classes in Portugal, particularly the bourgeoisie and clergy. One of the qualities usually highlighted about his work is that he produced a wealth of detail without affecting the narrative, even if his social stance often gave his characters a certain lack of warmth or individuality. In the novel, *To the Capital* (1925), the young, aspiring writer, Artur Corvelo, sets off for Lisbon from his provincial town, clutching his inheritance, in search of fame and all that goes with it. His desire is to enter fashionable circles, social and intellectual. Before he departs, his friend warns about the continual need to be dipping into one's pocket: "'You are in a café with the girls, a visit is arranged to the Dafundo with nice girls... it is essential to scrape up at least three or four milreis, for a cab, a drop of Colares, etc...' 'But that's not it,' said Artur impatiently. 'I am not going to Lisbon for debauchery. It is to study, to work.'" No sooner has he arrived than he is outside the fashionable Martinho:

> *He thought it splendid, with the gathering of top hats between the gilded mirrors, beneath a cloud of tobacco smoke, in the endless buzz of conversations. He didn't dare to go in. At the entrance, a group was chatting, and Artur watched them from a distance, attentively, thinking that they must be poets and politicians. His head was suddenly filled with an exciting stream of intellectual feelings; he was in a hurry to get into that life—to become involved, to enjoy discussions on Art and the Ideal, "to belong also to Lisbon."*

Later, stretched out on his bed, he was "murmuring voluptuously: 'I'm in Lisbon, I'm in Lisbon.'"

How different by the end of the book, when failure has made its mark, and he is again in the area. "He had only to go over the parapet, to jump, and he would be free… There would be a moment of agony, convulsive suffocating, gulps of water swallowed—and peace…"

Pessoa was a regular at the Martinho not only to meet people, but to read and write at a table. A famous stylized portrait of him, painted in 1954 by José de Almada Negreiros, shows him there seated alone, bespectacled, wearing his hat, smoking, paper and pen on the table before him along with a coffee and a copy of *Orpheu 2*, the issue of the magazine he was responsible for. Another photograph of him with friends taken in 1921 in the Martinho is also regularly reproduced, as are two others, one from 1931, in discussion, a text in hand, and another, alone, in the final months of his life in 1935, the image less sharp, as if his disappearance is imminent. This café is one of only a few places Pessoa frequented still in existence. Today it is not the place it once was, although it still has a trace of charm, and *uma bica* and *pastéis de nata* (custard tart) never go amiss if one is passing, and one remains at the counter rather than venture into the more expensive restaurant that seems to cater mainly to businessmen. There are no literary connections any longer, "unless it's to have the illusion, between its walls," as French writer Gérard-Georges Lemaire suggests, "of communicating with a world which no longer exists except in and through his books."

**The Grid**

Initially, when the Marquês de Pombal set about rebuilding the lower part of the town, called the Baixa, he stipulated that it be constructed in a grid fashion, and that it be made more functional with straightforward architecture, the roads and pavements at least 40 feet wide, and, naturally, that it be earthquake proof. It was noted that the façades were "broken only by regular lines of plain stone-framed windows, reminiscent of Adam's London, where Pombal had been the Portuguese envoy for some years, but there is a subtle difference in the proportions, and the eaves of the tiled roofs turn up in an amusing Chinese manner." Manuel da Maia, assisted by the Englishman Elias Sebastian Pope, and Eugénio dos Santos de Carvalho, were mainly responsible for the rebuilding, until succeeded in 1760 by Charles Mardell, who later signed himself as Carlos Mardel.

The grid of fifteen streets that rose behind the Terreiro do Paço stretched back to the next square, the Praça Dom Pedro IV, commonly known as the Rossio, which remained in place, off-center in the formal structure, with its neighboring square, Praça da Figueira. The three main streets that link the squares are Rua do Ouro, Rua Augusta, and Rua da Prata. From the beginning each street was assigned a specific function, reflected in its name. Thus Rua dos Sapateiros (Cobblers' Street), Rua da Prata (Silversmiths' Street), Rua do Ouro (Goldsmiths' Street), Rua do Comércio (Commercial Street), Rua dos Correeiros (Saddlers' Street), Rua dos Douradores (Gilders' Street) and Rua dos Fanqueiros (Cutlers' Street). Many of these streets still retain their crafts, though not necessarily in great numbers. And if you think there will be no saddlers, then walk along Rua dos Correeiros and be greeted by one in all its splendor of leather and gleaming metals. One of the most intriguing sights is the huddle of haberdashery and button stores on Rua da Conceição, with their dilapidated Art Nouveau fronts, completely incongruous to the flash décor of those around the corner in Rua Augusta.

Today, the central street, Rua Augusta, and some of the cross streets have been closed to cars, making them pedestrian walks, where street performers and beggars abound. I nearly wrote easier for window-shopping, but most are cobbled underfoot and not the easiest streets to walk on.

The Baixa by day is a business area as well as a shopping center, but at night, apart from a few restaurants, it is reduced to a ghost town, stragglers passing through from one side of town to the other being its only signs of life. A few hotels and some inhabitants are also visible, but generally there is little life. But that does not mean that it is peaceful, far from it, for though most cities find the rats scurrying at night, here workmen can be heard clearing rubble out of the buildings being refurbished, stores are refilled with stock, and the garbage is carted off. At different stages of the night there is always some disturbance.

"On these streets, until the night falls, I have a sensation of life like the life they have. By day they're full of meaningless activity; by night they're full of a meaningless lack of it. By day I am nothing, and by night I am I. There's no difference between me and the streets next to the Customhouse, save their being streets and I a soul, which perhaps is irrelevant when we consider the essence of things." So wrote Pessoa. The main areas for his literary life are to be found here and the Bairro Alto.

Pessoa himself worked in this area as did his semi-heteronym Bernardo Soares, the central character of *The Book of Disquietude*. There are countless references in his work and it would be possible (and I think it has been done) to create a full map of the places populated by Pessoa in his life and writings. Suffice to pick up on a handful as we proceed.

While the functions of the streets have been shuffled, the silver and gold mixed, the shoes tiptoed into other streets, the cafés and *pastelarias* (pastry shops) sprinkled like icing sugar and cinnamon on a *pastéis de nata*, they still cluster together where they can, whether fabric stores in Rua dos Fanqueiros, or the haberdasheries one after another in Rua da Conceição. Or in Rua do Ouro three stationary shops in quick succession. Although Olivier Rolin, the French writer, states that he goes into Papelaria da Moda to stock up during each of his visits to Lisbon, I see nothing there, or in the others, that one cannot buy in London, New York, and undoubtedly other major cities of the world, whether cheap notebooks or expensive recycled or handmade *cahiers*. Perhaps it is a habit, a preference that he has adopted. He writes that if he is not writing on Lisbon itself, which he has done in many articles and chapters in his novels, then he is writing on Lisbon, because he is using paper purchased in Lisbon.

The Rua do Ouro (now Rua Aurea officially on the maps) was regarded by Pessoa as a street with luxury. "Many of the shops, especially towards the upper end of the artery, will be found to be as luxurious as their Parisian equivalents." Untypically, this street also bears the rudest *pastelaria* I've encountered, but perhaps those who work there are unappreciative or tired of *fado*, for next door is the record shop Discoteca Amália, specialists in *fado*, named after the celebrated Amália Rodrigues, the music playing loudly, *blaring* in relative terms in Lisbon, into the street.

Saramago's Ricardo Reis puts a different perspective on the street. It's New Year's Eve, and he's out for a walk:

> All the way down the Rua do Ouro the ground is strewn with litter. From windows people are still chucking out rags, empty boxes, cans, leftovers, fish bones wrapped in newspapers, it all scatters on the pavement. A chamberpot full of live embers bursts into sparks in every direction, and pedestrians seek protection under balconies, pressing themselves against the buildings and shouting up at the windows. But their protests are not

*taken seriously, the custom is widely observed, so let each man protect himself as best he can, for this is a night for celebrating and for whatever amusements one can devise. All the junk, things no longer in use and not worth selling, is thrown out, having been stored for the occasion, these are amulets to ensure prosperity throughout the New Year. At least now there will be some empty space to receive any good that may come our way, so let us hope that we are not forgotten.*

Some still keep to the custom today, although not necessarily to part with the quantity that our increasingly materialistic society would threaten those below with, but more as a symbolic gesture. The poet Adília Lopes says she used to toss out dolls and such like.

## Rua Augusta

Behind the triumphal arch is the paved walkway of the Rua Augusta, these days given over to shopping, eateries, including the fast food joints, and a space for street performers. Temporary stages are erected for showcases, whether music or fashion displays. The Ecuadorians make their regular appearances, these days their pan pipes and accessories miked up to overcome and take full advantage of the noisy bustle. By comparison, later in the day when the shops are closed and the crowds have thinned, when tourists are out strolling, an African sets up his pitch: a series of cardboard boxes with lengths of salvaged string running from each, his speakers and amplifiers; a piece of driftwood strung and slung across his chest, not honed in the shape of a guitar, and a mike stand suitably constructed. This wood, card and string ensemble makes no attempt at style, or rather, the style is to give just the most basic resemblance. And then when ready, no sooner, he slowly starts mumbling into his mike, gradually starts to issue sounds, humming, little more, no attempt at a fitful arrangement of the music, no Eddie Murphy clone, just the occasional words, or humming, the rest of the music undoubtedly continuing in his head, in his body. He sways. Some think he is mad: where is the full show? In fact, it is the ultimate performance, a rare sight. Here is an art that would leave many so-called "performance artists" for dead.

While having a *sesta* (siesta) in our hotel I could hear singing, *fado* singing, or a lone female voice, a series of sad songs, unaccompanied.

I thought perhaps it was a distant radio, music coming from nearby, from another hotel room, or living quarters on the opposite roofs. It went on for ages. I dozed in and out the notes, balancing on the top stave. When I stood, stretched, opened the window, I could place the voice in the street below, round the corner. I went down into the Rua Augusta and there sitting up against a shopfront was a blind woman, a box before her, singing her plaintive songs, barely a pause from one to the other. She had been singing for an hour or more uninterrupted. Three years later, I find her there again, moved along slightly, as a Zara store had commandeered her space. The beggars in Lisbon still seem to be the old and/or infirm. Some find other ways to retain their dignity, selling matches, or lottery tickets.

Passing up and down the Rua Augusta, it becomes noticeable that there are many shoe shops. It is not that the surrounding streets of this area, or other areas, don't have their share, but that as a pedestrian space it becomes more noticeable. Portugal is famous for its leather goods, including its shoes. The markets attest to that. And yet why do such delicate shoes abound? Perhaps the residents are more adept at using the transport system to go up and down the hills rather than walk. Fortunately transport is not expensive. But even walking anywhere that is flat, such as here in the Baixa, where the pavements are cobbled, made up of mosaic stones, is a test to any footwear. No one who walks the streets could survive in fashionable shoes, on a ground that is treacherous for high heels. And yet the displays on offer invite that masochism.

Beneath this lower area there exists another wealth, dating back to the first century, with the Romans. It appears to be a subterranean series of tunnels, a labyrinth of galleries, bridges and rooms. Until the early eighteenth century, the people of Lisbon had been using what they thought was a well, now situated at the junction of Rua da Prata and Rua da Conceição, but then the water was found to be pestilent. Lisbon had more epidemics through lack of clean drinking water than many other cities. After the earthquake, when the whole lower town was being rebuilt, they discovered the underground remains, lifted by the land disturbance, and then duly forgot about them again until recent times. The true extent of the area is not really known, nor whether it was part of a public forum, or a spa as many have thought.

Perhaps the drinking water problem was resolved and it was forgotten about. For between 1729 and 1748, to the north of the city, the authorities built an aqueduct, Aqueduto das Aguas Livres (the aqueduct of free-flowing water) that survived the earthquake and still stands. It is a feat of which Lisbon has remained proud, not only as an architectural splendor, for it had the tallest stone arches in the world when built, but because it provided the citizens with clean drinking water. It comprises twenty-one round and fourteen great pointed arches, the central one being 200 feet high and nearly 94 feet wide, the aqueduct stretching across the Alcântara valley. This is the visible part of the water line; other parts are concealed or underground. It runs for over twelve miles from its source at the springs in Belas and ends just short of the Largo do Rato. The aqueduct was closed in 1844 (until recent times) when what we would now call a serial killer, one Diogo Alves, murdered people by hurling them head first from the arches.

**Rua dos Douradores**

The saddest and most dreary of streets in the Baixa grid has to be the Rua dos Douradores. It is such an unremarkable street that it seems no surprise that it housed not only one of the offices in which Pessoa worked, but was the setting for his semi-heteronym, Bernardo Soares, who lived and worked in this street, whose social world extended to the three or four people in his office, and whose territory was restricted to the streets of the Baixa, rarely further:

*How refreshing for the soul to see a hush fall, beneath a high, still sun, over these carts with straw, these crates to be bundled and these unhurried pedestrians—all from a transplanted village! I myself, alone in the office and looking at them through the window, am transported: I'm in a quiet little town in the country, I'm stagnating in an unknown hamlet, and because I feel other I'm happy. I know if I raise my eyes, I'll be confronted by the sordid row of buildings opposite, the grimy windows of all the downtown offices, the pointless windows of the upper floors where people still live, and the eternal laundry hanging in the sun between the gables at the top, among flower-pots and plants. I know this, but the golden light shining on everything is so soft, and the calm air surrounding me so*

*gratuitous, that even what I see is no reason to renounce my make-believe*
*village, my rural small town where commerce is tranquil.*

Another office located in this street, and suitably so, is to be found in a tale by Eça de Queirós called *The Yellow Sofa* (1902). Set for the most part in his office, or in his home in the Estrela, it tells of Godofredo da Conceição Alves who returns home early one day to find his closest friend and colleague on the sofa embracing his wife. After the eruption, the story follows the events, explanations and compromises made by Godofredo as wife, colleague and friends calm the boat and smooth the cloth, maintaining the hypocritical stagnancy of bourgeois life.

### Rua da Madalena

On the eastern edge of the Baixa, running parallel to the grid but traversing the bottom of the hill to the cathedral and beyond is the Rua da Madalena. It, too, comprises businesses that cluster together, this time orthopedic shops, and is a feature of José Cardoso Pires' acclaimed novel *Ballad of Dogs' Beach*, which appeared in the 1980s. This is one instance of a considerable body of writing since 1974 that has used the period of the Salazar dictatorship and its aftermath. This novel is based on a true story that occurred during the regime, with Inspector Elias Santana unraveling the mystery of an unidentified body. The Inspector knows the area well, for he lives close at hand, in the shadows of the Sé Catedral with a view over the Tagus from his third-floor flat in the Travessa da Sé. Standing in the Largo dos Caldas, he takes in:

*(…) the barber's with the flyblown mirror and solitary chair, the sound*
*of cabinet-makers, unseen in rear workshops, the big house with the*
*barred windows, where you saw a small light wandering at night; and*
*the pigeons preening along its roof you saw on any sunny morning. It was*
*across the square that there was plenty to look at and ample food for*
*thought, in the orthopaedic shops on the slope of Rua da Madalena.*

*At each shop-door of that steep street, as if under the starter's flag in*
*some impromptu rally, stood an invalid chair. From above, these shining*
*conveyances might have been poised to roll downhill and, gaining speed*
*and height, soar crazily and vanish over the roofs of Lisbon. At day's end*
*they would be taken, like pets, indoors, but the showroom lights burned*
*on in shrine-windows stocked with ex-vetos and permanently illumi-*

*nated for the benefit of the stroller, who could admire dramatic corsetry
designed, one would think, for a torture-chamber, metal collars, and an
exhibition of prostheses and trusses. In one window Professor Hasaloff,
framed in what resembled a velvet reliquary, delivered his revivalist
message on the subject of dead portions of the body.*
These shops barely seemed to have changed, some still bearing the
antiquated display signs and advertising boards.

In *The Relic* (1887), Eça de Queirós sends his main character,
Teodorico Raposo, into the arms of a young woman, Adélia, in the Rua
da Madalena, near Largo dos Caldas, where he has spent a few hours
ravishing her before returning to the piety of his aunt's home and
guidance. Finally, in his efforts to please his auntie, and to pave the way
to inherit and become wealthy, he sets himself the task of a daily coverage
of such an array of churches that by the time he arrives at the bed of his
lover he is exhausted, and fit only to be derided by her. In time,
uninspired by his lack of stamina, she rejects him and takes another lover.
Upon discovery of his rejection, distraught beyond belief, Teodorico
takes to wandering nearby, around the Baixa: "But every window open to
the evening breeze, every starched muslin curtain reminded me of
Adélia's cosy boudoir. A pair of stockings in a shop window was enough
to fill me with nostalgic longing and I would see again the perfection of
her legs; any luminous object I saw would remind me of her eyes and
even the strawberry ice cream I ate in the Café Martinho brought to my
lips the taste of her exquisitely sweet kisses."

Eventually he makes one last vain effort to visit her, beseeching his
rival to allow him to enter, calling to the window above. "And from
within, from amongst the curtains round the bed, where I imagined her
lying all rumpled and beautiful, came my Adélia's angry voice: 'Empty
the bucket of dirty water over him!'"

## Beginnings of Cinema
Tales of sordidness, or sexual explicitness, are not spread across the streets
of Lisbon, as yet. Lisbon might be catching up fast with the rest of so-
called civilization, but lurid sexual posturings are not entirely everywhere
for all to see. Amusingly, or sadly, depending on the way one looks at it,
the oldest cinema in Lisbon is to be found in the Baixa, on the opposite

side of the district from the Madalena, at the top of the Rua dos Sapateiros. It is called Animatógrafo do Rossio and lies just through the archway from the Rossio. The cinema's entrance is one of the finest Art Deco examples to be seen, with its virgins bearing shining electric lamps in tiles on both sides of the richly ornamented entrance. Films have been shown here since 1907. And indeed they still are, but of the more salacious kind, for the cinema is now a cheap porno movie house. João César Monteiro, one of Lisbon's most independent and oddest film-makers, decided to include this cinema in his film *Recordações da Casa Amarela* (Recollections of the Yellow House, 1989) with his lead character, himself, walking past the beautiful façade, accompanied by the sound from the cinema, a dirgy music overlaid with a strong sexual dialogue pulsating from the film within onto the street without and thus further onto Monteiro's film and into the cinema in which we are sitting.

Perhaps a more conducive parting shot should be made from the bottom of the Rua da Madalena, where Wim Wenders placed his camera in the *Lisbon Story* (1994), welcoming us to the city when his main character arrives. He has persuaded a truck driver in the countryside to drive him into Lisbon (in exchange for his abandoned car, and more importantly, its radio with cassette recorder—and Dolby stereo). The driver, having little knowledge of the city, drives back and forth in jumpcut footage, across the Rua da Conceição, back and forth, near and far, across the grid of junctions from early dawn until full of day, finally stopping in the road and forcing the Tram 28 to grind to a halt and its driver to climb down and provide directions. Though I'm not so sure they are convincing ones, if one works out where they are supposed to be bound.

# 2. Mercado da Ribeira

Lisbon smells of fish. At least that's the idea one has until one is there. Portugal is a sea-bound country; fish and seafood are the staple diet. But that doesn't mean there's an all-pervading smell of fish in the city. Or indeed that the smell of fish is unpleasant, which is the implication. What people probably mean is that one particular fish experience, dried salted cod, is the culprit. It's true, it smells strongly. But it's not everywhere, and it can only be bought in certain outlets. The best place to inhale that smell is to walk along Rua do Arsenal, from the Praça do Comércio, east towards the Cais do Sodré, the station where trains run along the coast to Estoril and Cascais, and the ferries cross to Cacilhas. Before you arrive at the clutch of shops, holding out together, that sell the dried salted cod, the smell hits you hard. Thirty seconds later, you have passed, and the air is sweet again.

Fish is one of the pleasures of Lisbon. In front of the station at Cais do Sodré is the daily market, the Mercado da Ribeira (Ribeira Market), where everything, fish, meat, fruit, vegetables and flowers are traded. This domed building is a hive of activity from early morning to well into the afternoon. The morning is best, the time when the fish are sold. For fish are still the focus, their display an array that stretches from the most common and cheapest, sardines and mackerel, through hake, sea bass, sea bream, turbot, sole, skate, swordfish, whiting, all the way to two others of prominence, the *peixe espada* (scabbard fish), which is around three feet long and eel-like, and the *tamboril* (monkfish), which wears the ugliest look this side of a horror movie.

The fish seem to attract prime attention because of the tradition that accompanies them in the shape of the *varinas* (fishwives), who once carried their trays on their heads. It is still possible perhaps to glimpse them in the market, or along the quay on the other side of the station, but traditions fade or adapt. The last person I saw balancing with an upright poise was an old lady in black, a full plastic bin liner square on her head, walking through the Praça da Figueira, an earlier market area.

You are more likely to see people in the countryside or along the coast bearing trays or baskets on their heads than in the city. The *varinas* who bore the baskets and filled the streets with their piercing cries were described almost a century ago by the British writer, Aubrey Bell, with "their flat baskets, saucer-shaped black hats and large gold earrings, their kerchiefs of black or, more often, of bright gold, yellow, orange or green, flowing down to the waist, their stiffly folding skirts of dull green, mauve or blue," making them, for him, "the most curious sight and sound of the city." Fifty years later, Oswell Blakeston described their piercing cries: "We were woken in the morning by the cries of the fish-women, forced through mouth and nose like a steam organ. At times it was a shrill unwavering note fortissimo; but there were different cries for different fish. Whiting had a downward glissando."

The cries can still be heard from time to time, though more often in the streets of the Alfama, in the open fishmarket that we will come to later, for most of the women selling fish in the Ribeira go about their work, gutting and selling, talking and laughing, as any other seller. Or perhaps I arrive too late each time, and need to come in at dawn to catch the vocal activity and any other traditional features.

The real briskness of trade is seen with the vegetables and fruit. The trucks bringing the produce arrive first thing and by six selling is under way. The people of Lisbon have a particular relationship with lettuces. *Lisboetas* call themselves *alfacinhas* (little heads of lettuce), and one who is born in Lisbon is an *alfacinha de gema* (little head of lettuce with yolk). The smell that lingers in the air all day, even after the bulk has been sold, belongs to coriander. Upstairs around the perimeter is the flower market, much of whose contents is whisked away to the cemeteries, which one doesn't believe until one visits them.

Old traditions die to be replaced by others. A new one is being built as the nightlife that has moved out to the clubs on the docks stretches the twenty-four hour clock. Some tired clubbers making their way home at dawn choose to stop off at the market for an early morning drink while they await the train schedules to wake and get underway at the Cais do Sodré. The market traders are already used to the garish sights, a regular carnival display, and skimpy at times. Katarina Wind in her story, *All Wrapped Up* (1999):

> *I was so tired, yet still up. My cells were jumping, even if I was down on my platforms. One day I'll regain equilibrium. Too itchy to stand with my*

*drink, I needed to walk… barely manoevering out the way of those blurred*
*before my toes. My boa dangled down my back, dragged its mouth along*
*the floor. Red. My Lisboa. The joke was stale. I need a fag. I offered to swap*
*for a scabbard on the slab last week, but I couldn't stomach its eyes.*

And then she staggers off in search of her train, more body paint than
clothes, her feet stomping six inches from the ground.

The real perversity is that cod, the basis of the national dish, *bacalhau,*
is not fished around the Portuguese coast. Centuries ago, probably at the
end of the fourteenth, before America was discovered, the fishermen
began to catch cod off the coast of Newfoundland. The fleet was away for
long periods. To preserve the fish they salted it. These days the fish is
mainly imported from Norway and Iceland and stored as what appears to
be ossified gray cardboard, with its high smell. Home storage needs to be
made in layers of plastic bags to lock in the smell. It needs a good
overnight soaking before it can be cooked. The most famous dish is
*bacalhau à Gomes de Sá,* though many claim there are at least 365 cod
dishes, one for every day of the year. But this cod is not to everyone's taste.

Julie Myerson remained pretty adamant on what she did not like
about Lisbon: the cod. "This time I made sure I avoided the dreaded
bacalhau, the absolute worst thing I've ever tasted. I am not alone. Two
years after I tried it I was walking down a Suffolk street when my six-
year-old asked me to name my worst food. I told him it would have to
be salt cod and immediately the stranger in front of me spun round to
agree." I mention it here so as not to spoil your meal later on.

If the delights of cod are not to your taste, when you are on the
other side of the Baixa, pop into the Conserveira de Lisboa in the Rua
dos Bacalhoeiros and buy all manner of tinned sardines and other fish
that are stacked high on the shelves. You can also watch the women in
the corner hand wrapping with colorful labels, sealing them with two
pieces of cellotape.

## In the White City

In Alain Tanner's *In the White City* (1983), the lead role, having had his
wallet stolen by a mugging in the street, ventures into the market and
tries to steal an apple. Tanner's film is filled with Lisbon locations, but
the predominance, as with any film about a sailor in port, revolves

around the docks, bars and hotel. For this film, the main bar and hotel are within a fishing net's cast of the market.

Tanner came to Lisbon to make the film following an invitation by the then young Portuguese producer, Paulo Branco. "(He) invited me to make a movie in Portugal. I had no particular story in mind but I felt sympathetic to the atmosphere and working conditions. Something about Lisbon intrigued me: it struck me as a distant city on the edge of a continent, facing the Atlantic and Africa and with its back turned towards Europe. A place to escape to and from."

The sailor, Paul (Bruno Ganz) is a German-speaking Swiss, who becomes a temporary exile in Lisbon, using the city as a place to reassess his job and his commitment to his wife at home in Basle, whom we see reading and responding to his mail in what appears to be a drab city, overlooking another river, the Rhine, which looks equally drab and dull, intentionally filmed in that manner.

Tanner admitted that the idea for the film came from his own sense of alienation in the far-off city of Lisbon; a lot of the *ennui* and wanderlust of his main character came from himself. He finds it difficult to work as a filmmaker in Switzerland: "So I'm condemned to wander, like Paul, who knows the sea is his only true home, in search of new visions."

Tanner said that he spent four months in Lisbon and "found an extraordinary absence of arrogance and aggression. When we were shooting in those narrow streets, there would be parked cars which we needed to have moved. We didn't even have to ask… people volunteered to move them, called out to their neighbours, and in five minutes there wasn't a car left. You wouldn't find that in any other city—quite the opposite."

A linchpin for the film was found in the light, the high contrast of light and dark, the whiteness of the city in the bright sun, as against the dark interiors and passages excluded from the sun. This was enough focus to give the film its title, with the repercussion Lisbon has since been regarded as "the white city." Even Portuguese writers note that this sobriquet can be traced to Tanner; José Cardoso Pires mentioned it, adding: "is it a color or a metaphor?" Cardoso Pires, like Paulo Rocha, sees the city in terms of other colors (as indeed does Tanner), but it seems that Tanner's presentation of the whiteness has stuck. Those who know nothing of Tanner's film seem to think that if you mention the "white city," you are talking about the houses, the view from the river, or the far shore, which indeed you are. But there is more. Machedo in *Taxi Lisboa* says that it is the reflection of the sun on the stones that makes it white, that the city is "paved with bright stones that shine as much as my car when I clean it."

Writing to his wife, Paul says he has left the boat, taken a room, but why he doesn't know: "I dream that the city is white, like the room, solitude and silence." A romantic solo saxophone wails on the soundtrack—this is 1983, we still haven't shaken off that lonely saxophone cliché—if we ever will. Tanner added in an interview that the white "signifies the color of the forgotten that his character searches for." An idea that seems to suggest more that Tanner was educated on the French side of his homeland with its cultural background, than the German-related angle of this particular film.

Throughout, Paul shoots with a Super 8 camera, documenting life, writing his diary, sending the footage back to his wife in Basle. Once ashore and involved in an affair with the chambermaid/barmaid Rosa (played by Teresa Madruga, already seen in Eduardo de Gregorio's *Aspern* the year before), he does not refrain from either filming her in his room, or in his bed, and sending the resultant images back to his wife, "a process that distills the experience into imagery he hopes will explain his state of mind to his wife back home."

At the end of the film, having sold his Super 8 camera to pay off his bills after the mugging, he returns to his wife, and "when he sees an attractive girl in the homewardbound train, I mix from a 35mm shot to the Super 8 image even though in reality Paul no longer has his home-movie camera. Romantic perception has become totally subjective by this point."

There is something about Lisbon that draws the idea of the hallucinatory from artists. Tanner here with *In the White City*, and indeed later with *Requiem*, although the hallucination is in Tabucchi's original book. Saramago too, with *The Year of the Death of Ricardo Reis*, and Cees Nooteboom with *The Following Story*. All concern themselves with the nature of dream and shifting time sequences. How much can be lain at the door of Pessoa is another matter. One senses that Paulo Rocha, and indeed others, think that this perspective has gone on long enough, and that other aspects of Lisbon and its artists need prominence.

## The British Bar

Tanner has a way to direct our attention to the time element. There is a shot in his hotel room that lasts eighty seconds, "just right both for the mood of the scene and the overall pace of the film." It shows the bright sun outside, as against the dark interior of the room, with the red curtains billowing in the breeze through the open window: "no camera movement, nobody in shot, just the open window and the curtain (…) This eighty seconds probably represents a whole afternoon." Or to take another example, at night, when Paul lounges at the bar, drinking, listening to the music, the shot rolling on. This is the mood of the film, slow enough to capture Lisbon and Paul's need to reflect on the path of his life, but not slow enough to let boredom take hold.

If one is not particularly film literate and able to notice that grammar, the British Bar situated in Rua Bernardino Costa, off the Praça Duque da Terceira, which Tanner uses as Paul's base, not only for drinking, but also for its room upstairs in the attached hotel, offers a pointed reference. The first thing Paul sees on his arrival at the bar after ordering a beer is the clock on the wall. It is a reverse clock. He inquires of Rosa, the barmaid, about it, points out that it's wrong, it goes backwards. She's says it's right. "It's the world that goes backwards." To which Paul responds that if all the watches went backwards, then the

world would go forwards, thereby indicating the heart of the problem he is trying to resolve in the film that is unfurling. Perhaps there is the added joke that it's a Swiss clock. Swiss clocks have traditionally been the most famous symbol of precision and quality. Tanner's character even sells his own Swiss watch later to raise funds, noting its pedigree when the price offered is poor.

The British Bar, despite its title, is far from being filled with the British. There are plenty of others locally, including Irish bars, which seem to attract them. In fact, while the British Bar has been a bar for sailors in earlier times, it is now a much quieter place. Literary people and artists undoubtedly did visit. Tabucchi in his novel, *Declares Pereira* (1994), has his character venture there: "He knew it was a place frequented by writers and he hoped to run across someone. In he went and sat down at a corner table. And sure enough there at the next table was Aquilino Ribeiro the novelist lunching with Bernardo Marques, the avant-garde artist who had designed and illustrated the leading Portuguese Modernist reviews."

In *The Following Story*, Cees Nooteboom takes his main character into the bar: "The back-to-front clock is still hanging there—and since I included it in Dr. Strabo's Travel Guide half the population of Holland has been to see it. Ninety-one correspondents have so far explained to me that you can tell the proper time on the clock by looking in the mirror." If there was a mirror in the place that enabled such a reflection, it is not there now.

The hotel above the bar is fictional, although Tanner filmed nearby. The perspective when he looks out the window of the hotel to gain his view of the Tagus would suggest a place close at hand, perhaps further down the street, or set back one street, to gain some height.

### Faces of Pessoa

Virtually next door to the British Bar is the Hotel Bragança, which Ricardo Reis stayed in on his return from Brazil. It is not there any longer, at least not as a hotel. Climbing into the taxi at the dock, Reis asks the driver to take him to a hotel:

> *To a hotel. Which hotel, I don't know, and having said, I don't know, the passenger knew precisely what he wanted, knew it with the utmost conviction,*

*as if he had spent the entire voyage making up his mind, A hotel near the
river, down in this part of the city. The only hotel near the river is the
Bragança, at the beginning of the Rua do Alecrim. I don't remember the
hotel, but I know where the street is, I used to live in Lisbon, I'm Portuguese.*

The first thing Reis notices on climbing from the taxi in the square
is the Royal, another haunt of Pessoa, where he ate, no longer in
existence: "The passenger got out, glanced fleetingly at the café, which
was named Royal, a commercial example of monarchical nostalgia in a
republican era, or of reminiscences of the last reign, here disguised in
English or French."

The book is filled with detail that tells us not only about Reis and
Pessoa, but also about Lisbon and the political mood of that era. Saramago
has based his Reis on the description that Pessoa outlined, along with the
poems that he wrote under that heteronym. Thus he creates a protagonist
"somewhere between absolute fiction and fictitious reality."

When Reis arrives at the hotel, Pessoa has been dead a month. He
goes to the cemetery to find him and pay his respects, but draws a blank.
That is, until Pessoa pays him a visit at the hotel. (Before I go further, I
should note that Saramago wrote *The Year of the Death of Ricardo Reis*
before Tabucchi wrote *Requiem*. Stepping on each other's toes, or just
clever dancing?) Pessoa explains why he is up and about:

*I have about eight months in which to wander around as I please, Why eight
months Ricardo Reis asked, and Fernando Pessoa explained, The usual
period is nine months, the same length of time we spend in our mother's
womb, I believe it's a question of symmetry, before we are born no one can
see us yet they think about us every day, after we are dead they cannot see
us any longer and every day they go on forgetting is a little more, and apart
from exceptional cases it takes nine months to achieve total oblivion.*

No sooner do we grasp this idea than Pessoa is standing before the
mirror, and recounting: "It gives me an odd feeling to look in the
mirror and not see myself there, Don't you see yourself, No, I know
that I am looking at myself, but I see nothing, Yet you cast a shadow,
It's all I possess."

Our immediate thoughts are to agree, to remind ourselves of
vampire films in which the vampire is discovered, unveiled, when he
casts no mirror reflection. I wonder whether this idea for the novel

originates from Saramago, or if he found a source in Pessoa's work? Pessoa's interests would have taken account of the fears of various cultures of mirror images, the feeling that the soul might get caught in the mirror after death while it stills resides in the house, particularly if the body and coffin are still in the house, leading to the custom of covering mirrors with cloths or turning them to face the wall, allowing the dead to find eternal rest. From this comes the idea that the vampire, as an undead without a soul, could not possess a reflection. Or perhaps further, with Mario de Sá-Carneiro, the young writer and intimate friend of Pessoa, who committed suicide in Paris. In *Lucio's Confession* (1913) there are scenes where Sá-Carneiro's characters Ricardo and Marta are seen to appear, disappear, or fade; at one point Ricardo recalls how he had looked in the mirror, "but I wasn't there!" I suspect Tabucchi was drawing from this source too, in *Requiem,* as much as from the comments by Pierre Hourcade, and probably others, about Pessoa's imminent vanishing act. Why that source when both were writing their novels in the 1980s and the horror genre has made it an everyday concept? Because both writers are threading themselves into Pessoa's work and references, using them as source material. The question is where did Sá-Carneiro get his ideas about reflection from in 1913? What was he learning about in Paris? The writer Fernando Guerreiro might take the discourse further and open onto a deeper Lacanian psycho-analytical level, asking of phantoms: "Are they deprived of the *mirror stage,* don't they experience narcissism?" An interesting question in terms of Pessoa and his work, centered as it is around the nature of being and the ego.

José Saramago himself is Portugal's first writer to be given the Nobel Prize, in 1998. He came late to writing novels, but not to writing, nor to literary life. His parents were farmers. He attended school in Lisbon, but spent most of his childhood in the countryside in the province of Ribatejo. Although he did manual jobs early on, he was self-taught and moved into journalism, editing and translation. He wrote some poetry, essays, stories and a play, but it was not until after the 1974 revolution that his full powers as a novelist came to the fore. At 55, in 1977, he published his first novel. Although very much a Portuguese, today he lives in Lanzarote, as a result of a literary dispute, when he discovered that the Portuguese Under-

Secretary of State, Sousa Lara, had his name withdrawn from the list of the European Union's Ariosto literary contest. Offialdom did not like what Saramago had written about "their prejudices and illiberal views," it seems. It just happened that the argument flared at the moment he was deciding whether to build a house near Lisbon, or to follow the encouragement of his relatives and build a home in the Canary Islands.

### Rua do Alecrim

Ricardo Reis takes the steep climb up the Rua do Alecrim, the road that runs from the Cais do Sodré up towards the Bairro Alto. It is a road that is distinguishable at its lower end, for it is bridged across two other streets, the Rua Nova Carvalho and the Rua de São Paulo, making it another recognizable landmark, as witnessed in countless films whether from visiting or Portuguese filmmakers. Many are fleeting shots, but a more enduring shot of the street is found in *Vertiges* (1985) directed by Christine Laurent, the French film actress, director and writer (one of those credited with scripting Jacques Rivette's *La Belle Noiseuse*). Her film, set in the world of opera, is mainly located in a theater, where the drama unfolds at the rehearsals, and away from the opera house at the hotel, whether in its foyer or one of its rooms. Returning each night to the hotel, the troupe takes to the streets, walking, stretching their legs. It is so late that as a group they can walk in the middle of the Rua do Alecrim, come down the street with barely any traffic to disturb them, as they search for bars in which to unwind. (Interestingly, in the cast is an early performance by Maria de Medeiros, a few years later to become Portugal's biggest female film star on the international stage.)

One time when Reis climbs the Alecrim he also takes another turn into the Rua António Maria Cardoso to attend a summons he has received to the police headquarters. The resultant scene reminds one of Kafka, only this inquisition is more pertinent as it derives from the very specific period of the Salazar dictatorship. It shows that whether innocent or not, it is all part of an atmosphere meant to unnerve Reis, or any citizen, setting him in an uncomfortable position before the eyes of those around him, who watch his every move, real or imagined.

## The Texas Bar

We'll steer clear of that route, and the police. Rather than take that road, we can slip alongside the incline at the foot of the Alecrim, and sidle along the narrow passageway, or, alternatively, go around the block to reach the other side. Whichever, one comes across the first of the arches, the first bridge of the Alecrim, this one over the Rua Nova Carvalho. Immediately one realizes a different world has been slipped into, another world, a seedy underworld. This road used to be filled with sailors, the bars around here still bearing the appropriate names that link it to places far and wide: Jamaica, Copenhagen, Hamburg... though nowadays it is for the pleasure of those in search of prostitutes and topless dancing, and probably more, that these sex bars are frequented. The German director, Wim Wenders, shot a long sequence here with Sam Fuller in his early acclaimed film, *The State of Things* (1982). The precise location was the Texas Bar. What other name would you expect? In the film the American director plays the cameraman in the film within Wenders' film. They have been shooting out at Sintra and there is a halt in production. Fuller comes into Lisbon en route for America to bury his wife who has just died in hospital in Los Angeles. He detours to the Texas Bar for a drink. Wenders has made it a suitable B-movie bar. It seems to be a regular haunt for the cast and crew of the film, as others coming in to Lisbon wander in and see Fuller at the bar holding court,

drowning his sorrows and trying not to contemplate what awaits him back home. (Fuller was to return some years later to film "noir" writer David Goodis' novel, *Street of No Return* (1989), shifting the location across the Atlantic to set it in Lisbon.) The Texas Bar exists still, but it is clear from the signs on the door that the world within is that of a sex bar, not a quiet watering hole.

Tanner's sailor manages to avoid the Texas Bar, finding more excitement just down the street in another bar where he can stagger in and drink, involve himself in a brawl and be accosted by various women with undertones of racism sliding into the picture. A picture that can be enlarged if one continues under the bridge, or goes around and under the next bridge, along the Rua de São Paulo, for they both lead to the same square, the Praça de São Paulo. Here, as in the surrounding streets, the prostitutes ply their trade, as inelegantly as in the poorest areas of most cities around the world. This is just one of the areas frequented by prostitutes, one we stumbled into, unlike the other areas. A report stated that around 1,200 prostitutes are officially registered in Lisbon today. That aside, it is almost possible to travel around Lisbon without being confronted by displays of gross sexual allurements, a situation probably deserving of some form of prize for a capital city.

This traditional docks nightlife district is the one alluded to in Fernando Lopes' film, *O Fio do Horizonte* (The Edge of the Horizon, 1993), at the point when the main character, in search of the answer to the mystery of the dead man on the slab in the morgue, ventures into the red-light area. In a jazz club he gains the attention of a woman, a prostitute, looking considerably better than those on the real streets, and later accosts her outside, accompanying her to a brothel, where he starts to unravel the mystery of the naked woman in a photo he has in his possession. This film is again full of time shifts, as the clock is rewound and the pathologist, Spino (Claude Brasseur), becomes the man who is murdered and on the slab before himself, thirty years earlier as a young man. If you are confused, read the novel, *Vanishing Point*, by Tabucchi, of course. The original title in Italian is *Il filo dell'orizzonte*, the direct translation of which shows in the French and Portuguese titles, but not in the English published form, meaning the edge of the horizon, the horizon within us, the horizon that cannot be crossed but that is always there in the distance, always beyond reach, evoking a postmodern sense of anxiety that is a hallmark of Tabucchi's writing. Though the novel was not set in Lisbon, but Italy, the film has been adapted and transposed to Lisbon by its Portuguese director Fernando Lopes. If it all sounds somewhat Borgesian, it is. Or Pessoan, it is. Pessoa also features as a subject, when the pathologist's partner, Francesca (Andréa Ferréol), a university teacher, gives a tutorial to her student on Pessoa, discussing heteronyms and the need to disappear. Francesca says: "There are many ways of not living, of opting out of one's place. We can play at being or we can divide ourselves, always dreaming and trying to disappear. Like Pessoa." The student asks: "So as not to die?" And Francesca replies: "Or not to live." She could equally have pointed out, like Spino, her partner, for it is the main thread of the narrative, the need for the central character to find a way to confront the death of his parents, and the sister he doted on, all of whom died as a result of a car crash many years before. He is effectively swallowed up by the murder and the unidentified body presented to him on the slab at the morgue.

While it makes good theory to set the film in this area, it was in fact shot elsewhere, relocated further along the docks, towards Santos or Alcântara.

## Alto de Santa Catarina

Walking along the north side of the square there are alleyways and steps north that can take us up parallel to the Alecrim, through the area they call Bica. Like the Alfama, it is filled by steps and narrow streets, often impassable to cars. Although the famous funicular, the Elevador da Bica, climbs steeply up here, the streets and *largos* (squares) either side make it a pleasurable walk, particularly by night. Rather than climb to the top and make a circuitous trip, we cut across the valley trough and climb directly to the *miradouro* we are aiming for, the Alto de Santa Catarina.

This *miradouro* appears to be one of the favorites for *Lisboetas* themselves, including the young. There is a kiosk that provides food and drink, so people can sit all afternoon in the sun watching the river or nothing in particular. There is little rubbish or destruction to cause distaste. All is geared to encourage lounging. In the summer one can stay late into the night, as the kiosk remains open. The only daunting sight is the edifice of Adamastor, a crude sea monster to be found in Camões' *The Lusiads*. But one doesn't have to look at it. Or fear that it will rise behind one's back, its voice to horrify as it did the sailors who rounded the Cape of Good Hope, or, as it was then, for good reason, the Cape of Storms.

Ricardo Reis also favored the area, and after walking up the Alecrim came round to the height via the Praça Luís de Camões:

*The palm trees look as if they have been pierced by the breeze coming from the sea, yet their rigid blades barely stir. He simply cannot remember if these trees were here sixteen years ago when he left for Brazil. What most certainly was not here is this huge, roughly hewn block of stone, it looks like an outcrop but is really a monument. If the furious Adamastor is here, then the Cape of Good Hope cannot be far away. Below are frigates navigating the river, a tugboat with two barges in tow, warships moored to the buoys, their prows facing the channel, a clear sign that the tide is rising.*

Once life at the hotel starts to become unbearable, suspicions drawn at his every move, Reis decides it is time to move. In the classifieds he catches sight of just what he wants: "Suddenly I come to a halt, Furnished rooms to let, Rua de Santa Catarina, deposit required. I can see the building as clearly as the photographs of the flood, its upper story decorated with inscriptions, it's the one I noticed that afternoon (...) how could I have forgotten it." He goes to view the property, looks around the rooms and crosses to the window. "From his windows bare of drapes Ricardo Reis watched the river's expanse. To get a better view he switched off the light. Gray light fell like pollen from the skies, becoming darker as it settled."

### Docks

After looking at the stretch of water for so long and so often, it feels as common as the sweet air we breathe. Perhaps it is time to work our way back down through the Bica and approach the docks, to see them at close call. These docks where Tanner entered Lisbon, where he walked and pondered whether it was the sea or not that was his future. These docks too, which encouraged the Chilean filmmaker Raúl Ruiz to substitute Lisbon for his homeland when making *Three Crowns of the Sailor* (1982). And while there is quite some breadth allowable when filming docks, Ruiz gave himself considerable poetic license, not worrying that he could roam as far as the Terreiro do Paço, even to show the two very recognizable Cais das Colunas, or that the tram looming down on his character was Tram 28, with the Prazeres destination clearly marked on its front for more than the discerning eye to notice. How ironic that a country that has created so many political exiles itself among its people and its artists, should serve as a haven for another exile. As Ruiz notes: "It's a small country, and, as Borges said, all small countries are connected, like mirrors."

But the image I see here on the docks is Tanner's camera walking off in the direction of Ponte 25 de Abril. The image I see is Tanner's sailor with his home movie camera filming what lies before his eyes and his feet, pacing along the quay. It is this traveling shot, mute Super 8 footage, without a shadow, without a shadow of a doubt, that we will rejoin later when it arrives at its destination, if there is one.

# 3. Elevadors

Snap. Another photo. The Elevador da Santa Justa on the edge of the Baixa, a celestial insert on the Rua do Ouro, is undoubtedly another much captured image to represent the city. Whether it be from afar, usually looking down the Rua da Santa Justa from across the grid, from as far as the Rua dos Fanqueiros, or whether from directly underneath, its head swimming against blue sky, the lift has a set of profiles that consumes rolls of film (unless working with a digital process) ready to be transported to all corners of the world. It is such a splendid object, "a machine to visit the Moon," as French writer, Valéry Larbaud observed, standing 136 feet high, a lattice of metal that has been endlessly credited to Eiffel, erroneously. Monsieur Eiffel did not build it. It was, in fact, the work of one of his disciples, the Portuguese-born Raul Mésnier de Ponsard.

Snap. Once inside the two alternating cabins that transport people up and down, cabins fashioned in a decorous varnished wood, almost as luxurious as those old Parisian hotel lifts except that this has a view as it rises that is not a stairwell wraparound. I use the word transport because the Elevador is part of the public transport system and a comparable ticket is required, or the flash of a pass that allows transference across the variety of city transportations on offer.

Snap. At the top another panoramic view of the city from its platform. Also a closer look at the intricate latticework of the circular staircase that ventures up another floor.

Snap. The lift won't snap. When it was opened in 1901, it was powered by steam, but now it is electrically driven, and well maintained. I've peeked through the door and inspected the workings. As has anyone who's seen Wolf Gauldlitz's *Taxi Lisboa*, in which his guide Josefina Lind, accompanied by her friend for the occasion, the exiled Prague Jew, Wajsberg, show us all aspects of this splendid structure.

There is a viaduct bridge across to the old Carmo church, except that since the great fire in the Chiado in 1988, the buildings have been weakened and, until some future date when the engineers have resolved the problem, this alternative to the street climb has been withdrawn. Snap.

## Art Deco Suicides

Snap, there goes a neck. Or some limbs. Instant death. In the last section of his book, *The Flying Creatures of Fra Angelico* (1987), the section appropriately titled, *Last Invitation*, Tabucchi welcomes us to another side of Lisbon:

> *For the solitary traveller, admittedly rare but perhaps not implausible, who cannot resign himself to the lukewarm, standardised forms of hospitalised death which the modern state guarantees and who, what's more, is terrorised at the thought of the hurried and impersonal treat-ment to which his unique body will be subjected during the obsequies, Lisbon still offers an admirable range of options for a noble suicide, together with the most decorous, solemn, zealous, polite and above all cheap organisations for dealing with what a successful suicide inevitably leaves behind it: the corpse.*

Means to die, and places for the accomplishment of that act. There are so many. Tabucchi does not want to deprive the prospective suicide of using his own sense of creativity:

> *However, one can hardly avoid mentioning the means which, given the city's structure and topography, would seem to be Lisbon's chosen vocation: the leap. I appreciate that the void has always been a major attraction for spirits on the run. Even when he knows that the ground awaits him below, the man who chooses the void implies his refusal of fullness; he is terrified of the material world and desires to go the way of the Eternal Void, by falling for a few seconds through the physical void. Then the leap is also akin to flight; it involves a sort of rebellion against the human condition as biped; it tends towards space, towards vast distances, towards the horizon.*

Back to earth. Lisbon certainly has a range of choices. "Hilly, constantly changing, riddled with stairways, sudden terraces, holes, drops, spaces that open all at once before you, complete with historic places for Historic suicides (try the Aqueducto das Aguas Livres, the Castle, the Tower of Belém)… and mechanical places for Constructivist suicides (the Ponte 25 de Abril)." And in there too are also "sophisticated places for Art Deco suicides (the Elevador da Santa Justa)." Though, naturally, Tabucchi forgot to advise that there is a mesh fencing to foil such a leap—but if one's determined… One other is his favorite but I'll leave that to a future moment for contemplation.

Snap, the lid shuts too. For Tabucchi observes that unlike many other nationalities, the Portuguese seem to take pride in their disposal of the corpse. Checking the Yellow Pages in the telephone directory for Lisbon, he was surprised to find that it had rather an abundance of funeral directors. Sixteen pages in fact. Rather a lot, "you will have to agree, especially if one considers that Lisbon is not an enormous city; it is a first and very telling indication of the number of companies operating in the area, the only problem being that one is spoilt for choice. A second consideration is that death, in Portugal, does not appear to belong, as it does in other countries, to that ambiguous area of reticence and 'shame.' There is nothing shameful about dying, and death is justly considered a necessary fact of life." It is not that there are sixteen pages of tight listings, but rather a series of boxed affairs, not surprising when one thinks about it. A display made "with show, with pomp, and undeniable charm. Sober or ornate, and using extremely pertinent slogans, they will often take out a whole page to illustrate their services." And then he expands, details and quotes some of those on offer. You can undoubtedly feel safe in their hands is his conclusion from the accumulated advertising.

There is a plethora of transport systems on offer, from ferries, trains, buses, taxis, the elevador, and the trams, both old and the latest streamlined models. And there is a fine collection of travel cards to select from. Snap. And another system, the funiculars, to reach those parts that other systems cannot reach—to climb the steep inclines that only feet can manage, or not. These lopsided trams have been heaving up and down since 1885, originally powered by water displacement, then steam, and now electricity. There are three, two lifting passengers onto the Bairro Alto, and the other onto the Campo de Santana.

The Elevador da Bica operates from the Calçada do Combro down to the Rua de São Paulo, plunging the straightest, presenting an eye-catching sight, so much so that it has its fair share of snappers. Or snappy Japanese if you see *Taxi Lisboa*, in which a group of Japanese pack the carriage and laugh the climb through the roof.

The Elevador da Glória, which ascends like a snake from one side of the Avenida da Liberdade up to the *miradouro* on the Rua São Pedro de Alcântara, is convenient, much used and consequently not so spectacular. And the third, which hides on the other side of the Avenida da Liberdade is so discreet that it is barely referred to. It's called… what is it called? You have to search to discover that it is the Elevador da Lavra, and it is squeezed like a lemon between the straightjacket of houses from the end of the Rua das Portas de Santo Antão up to where… it's hard to tell. Or why.

And then there's another transport system, the Metro, the one beneath your feet, at least on the flat part of the city. And, fortuitously, as a bonus, a new transportation has come into operation that beats the shank's pony system of climbing the steps or the steep road inclines from the Baixa up to the Chiado and Bairro Alto for the years that the Elevador da Santa Justa will not be doing that job. Phew! The route is to enter the new Baixa-Chiado Metro entrance just along from the Elevador, and, after first going down a couple of flights on the escalators, instead of proceeding through the cavernous space or chasm, as this station is in reality, to the train platforms, cross and step onto the escalators that take you out the other side. This is a system of five connecting flights that draw one not only up the other side, but carve a way through the hill beneath the Rua Garrett, until you emerge atop the Chiado, right outside A Brasileira, ready for *uma bica*. Or to have your photo taken seated beside the ever patient Pessoa. Snap.

# 4. Chiado & Bairro Alto

## Pessoa

Pessoa is still the contemporary writer of Lisbon, even though he died in 1935. Pessoa means person. And it is as if Pessoa is the person of Lisbon, the man in the street. The street sign for pedestrian, the man with the suit and the hat, is almost a symbol for him. The photos that abound mainly show him as such. Striding out too. Pessoa had 72 other names, heteronyms as they are called, although only a handful are spoken of as his major names. Yet with just a handful he expressed himself as different characters. It is as if Pessoa peopled a period of Portuguese literature, wanted to populate it, to give it body.

Fernando António Nogueira Pessoa was born on June 13, 1888, Santo António's birthday, the patron saint of Lisbon, hence the middle name. He was taken to Durban in South Africa when he was six and returned to Lisbon when he was seventeen. He only left the city a couple of times after that for brief trips to the provinces. His life in Lisbon was quiet. He worked as a writer of foreign correspondence for various firms, led a limited social life with only one love affair that is known about. Although he was a prolific writer and contributed regularly to various magazines, often ephemeral small-circulation publications, he only published four books of poetry in his lifetime, all but one in English. It was only after his death in 1935, from cirrhosis of the liver, that his life's work started to become public. He had been in no great hurry to publish. As he died young, at forty-seven, all his plans for Portuguese and English editions of his works had never materialized. A famous trunk that was discovered with his writings contained 27,543 documents, all now stored in "envelopes" in the National Library. It appears that he held onto all he wrote: poetry, prose, philosophy, criticism, translations, linguistic theory, horoscopes and various other texts, whether typed, handwritten or illegibly scrawled in Portuguese, English and French. Notebooks, single sheets, backs of scraps, letters, envelopes, adverts, all manner of stationery from places he worked and places he ate and drank in, in other words, almost anything. It appears that all was not necessarily haphazard in the trunk. But as it was never cataloged at an early stage, over the years manuscripts plucked from the trunk for publication have created a disorder. Also it seems that quite a lot has been stolen or lost. It was not until 1968 that an attempt to catalog was undertaken. Richard Zenith, an authority on Pessoa and one of the English translators, noted "that the researcher of E3, the Pessoa archives, had better approach them in the spirit of an archeologist." Since 1988 the editing of the complete works has been in progress.

The world of heteronyms is outside of all tradition, outside of all literary history, placing Pessoa in a new framework, making him not just a Portuguese phenomenon.

It appears that Pessoa was six when he created his first imaginary companion, Chevalier de Pas, whom he wrote to, posting the letter to his own address, replying in similar fashion. "Since childhood I had the tendency to create around me a fictitious world, surrounding myself with friends and acquaintances that never existed. (I don't know, of course, if they really didn't exist or if it was I who didn't exist. In such matters, as in everything, we should not be dogmatic.)"

Others quickly followed, like Dr. Pancracio and David Merrick. While still a teenager living in Durban, he wrote poetry and tried writing detective novels. Educated in English, it was reasonable that names like Charles Robert Anon and Gabriel Keene should be used. He also took on a French heteronym at an early age, Jean Seul de Méluret, and retained it throughout his life, which was not necessarily the case with most of the others.

Pessoa was clear about his intentions: "I divide what I have written into orthonymic and heteronymic work. I do not divide it into autonymic and pseudonymic work because those that I publish under fictitious names do not represent either my opinions or my emotions." There are three names that comprise the main heteronyms for the body of his poetic work, alongside those he wrote as Pessoa. "I saw before me in the colourless but real space of a dream the faces and gestures of Alberto Caeiro, Ricardo Reis, and Alvaro de Campos."

These inventions were fleshed out, so to speak. In a letter he explained, and I quote at length:

*I made out their ages and their lives. Ricardo Reis was born in 1887 (not that I remember the day and the month, though I have them somewhere) in Oporto, is a doctor, and is now living in Brazil. Alberto Caeiro was born in 1889 and died in 1915; he was born in Lisbon but lived nearly all his life in the country. He had no profession or any sort of education. Alvaro de Campos was born in Tavira, on the fifteenth of October, 1890 (at 1.30 pm, Ferreira Gomes tells me, and it's true, because it's confirmed by a horoscope I made of this hour). As you know, he's a naval engineer (in Glasgow) but now lives here in Lisbon, unemployed. Caeiro was of medium height and, though delicate (he died a consumptive), he didn't seem as delicate as he was. Ricardo Reis is a bit, though very slightly, shorter, more robust, but shrewd. Alvaro de Campos is tall (1.75 meters tall, two centimeters taller than I), slender and with a slight tendency to stoop. All are clean-shaven: Caeiro pale, without color, blue eyes; Reis a vague dull brown; Campos between fair and swarthy, a vaguely Jewish-Portuguese type, hair therefore smooth and normally parted on the side, monocled. Caeiro, as I said, had no education to speak of——only primary school; his father and mother died early and he stayed at home, where he lived on the income of some small properties. He lived with an old aunt on his mother's side. Ricardo Reis, as I said, a doctor; he has been living in Brazil since 1919; he became an expatriate immediately, because he was a monarchist. He is a Latinist by virtue of school training and a semi-Hellenist by virtue of his own efforts. Alvaro de Campos had a high-school education; he later went to Scotland to study engineering, first mechanical, then naval. On some holiday he went to the Orient, from which the "Opium Eater" is derived. An uncle, a priest from Beira, taught him Latin.*

He even goes further and talks about their abilities at writing: "As far as that's concerned, Caeiro wrote Portuguese badly; Campos, reasonably but with lapses, as when he would say *eu propio* instead of *eu mesmo*, et cetera; Reis, better than I but with a puristic streak that I regard as exaggerated. It's difficult for me to write the prose of Reis— still unedited—or of Campos. Simulating in verse is easier, because it is more spontaneous."

Pessoa wrote that his explanation for his many names, his heteronyms, was neurasthenic. The Mexican poet, Octavio Paz, who has written on Pessoa, does not go along with that. "A neurotic is a man possessed: if he controls his disorder, is he then sick? The neurotic suffers his possessions; the creator is their master and transforms them." As Paz saw it: "Pessoa, their first reader, did not doubt their reality. Reis and Campos said what perhaps he himself would never have said. In contradicting him, they expressed him; in expressing him, they forced him to invent himself. We write to be what we are or else to be what we are not. In either case, we seek ourselves. And if we have the luck to find ourselves—sign of creation—we will discover that we are an unknown. Always the other, always he, inseparable, alien, with your face and mine, you always with me and always alone."

Any idea that we should confuse the heteronymic with the pseudonymous is not acceptable. "The pseudonymous work is by the author in his own person, except he signs it with another name," Paz observed, "the heteronymic work is by the author outside his own person." And it is not the same as a playwright creating different characters. "He is not an inventor of character-poets but a creator of poets'-works." Adolfo Casais Monteiro, the critic, added: "He invented the biographies to accompany the works, and not the works to go with the biographies." Or, as Pessoa's semi-heteronym, Bernardo Soares, defines it: "In each of us there is a differingness and a manyness and a profusion of ourselves."

Perhaps part of what formed these branches of himself lies in the fact that Pessoa became a foreigner to himself, having been taken away from Lisbon and his language at the age of six to start with a new language, English, which he loved, and its authors. He then returned to Lisbon at seventeen, the city that he wanted to be in more than any other, only to find he was a foreigner there, and that he had to rediscover Portuguese with different eyes, as an outsider. As a result, the critic, Eugénio Lisboa adds: "he saw the 'obvious' in a new and different light. Taking nothing for granted, because he was never a natural part of it, he was free to question reality afresh. He even 'reinvented' Portuguese—because he knew English." The writer, Jorge de Sena, believes that Pessoa was "feeling out of place and thinking most of the time in English (his little notebooks were largely written in English except for lines of Portuguese verse)."

"Into Caerio I put all my power of dramatic depersonalization, into Ricado Reis all my intellectual discipline, fashioned in the music appropriate to him, into Alvaro de Campos, all the emotion that I allow neither in myself nor in my living." And then there was the other major name he adopted, Bernardo Soares: "He's a semi-heteronym because his personality, although not my own, doesn't differ from my own but is a mere mutilation of it." The tendency is to equate Pessoa with Soares too closely, but Soares did not have Pessoa's humor, nor was he self-deprecating. He was "a Pessoa with missing parts." The similarities are drawn because Soares is the author of *The Book of Disquietude*, the fragmentary notes of his life and reflections in the Baixa, an area where Pessoa himself spent much of his time either eating, drinking or working, though not like Soares as an assistant accounts clerk. "My semi-heteronym Bernardo Soares, who in many ways resembles Alvaro de Campos, seems always to be tired or sleepy, so that his powers of ratiocination and his inhibitions are slightly suspended; he writes prose in a constant daydream. He is a semi-heteronym because, not being a personality to me, he is not so much different from myself as he is a simple distortion of my personality. It is myself, less rational; and less emotional. It is prose, except for what reason attenuates in mine, equal to mine, and the Portuguese, completely the same."

The Lisbon that is Alvaro de Campos' is the one of the wharf, the one looking out to the sea. Whereas the one that belongs to Bernardo Soares is the one of the city as the village in which he lives, the streets of the Baixa that he sees from his window, or walks in each day. For Pessoa himself it is the Largo de São Carlos where he was born, and to which he refers in the "bell of my village" namely, the Igreja dos Mártires (Church of the Martyrs), in the Chiado. For Pessoa, Lisbon was a country in condensed form, more than a city. As one of today's authorities on Pessoa, Teresa Rita Lopes, writes: "it's impossible to walk through certain areas, certain streets, without hearing his fluttering steps at our side."

The world of his heteronyms was Pessoa's family. After all, he did have half-brothers who moved to England, and yet he never visited them, even though he was an anglophile. He never married, though he is known to have had one amorous relationship in 1919 with a young nineteen-year-old, Ophélia Queiroz, that lasted thirteen months and was rekindled some ten years later, albeit briefly. At one point, Campos interfered in the relationship, writing letters to Ophélia, drawing the comment from her that she did not like Campos.

Jorge de Sena wrote of Pessoa as a latent homosexual, noting that "he sublimated all sexual impulses in himself to the extent of killing, as far as we know, all possibilities of sexual activity or any attachment that could involve more than just an impulse." And thus he saw that when Pessoa wrote in defense of his gay friend, António Botto, he was "defending him from attack and writing about him at length and with a depth unsurpassed in his writings about anyone else, into still another heteronym standing for things he had repressed in himself." Jorge de Sena observed that in his private life, Pessoa was a charming man, with "a humour that was very British, though with none of the traditional grossness in it." He continued: "But this role was also that of a heteronym, which saved him from intimacy with anyone while allowing him to take a modest part in the normal feast of daily life."

This world of the others was noted by João Gaspar Simões, at the time a young editor of *Presença* magazine, to which Pessoa contributed. He related that when he and José Régio went to meet Pessoa in June 1930, rather than finding Pessoa, the writer had "sent someone else, we might say, in his place—a third person, none other than Mr. Alvaro de Campos, Engineer!" He presented himself in character, which did not seem to go down well: "Régio, who was quite subtle and even Socratic when dealing with intellectuals, was not sufficiently so on either account to accept with pleasure the ostensibly histrionic façade of a comrade toward whom he had behaved magnanimously and who was from Lisbon to boot." The relationship between Régio and Pessoa soured, while it remained warm with Simões, who was to write the first biography of his friend.

At some point he probably considered retaining some form of secrecy over his heteronyms, or at least some of them, but as he told Simões: "It is already too late and therefore absurd for the absolute disguise." Jorge de Sena saw in the "Pessoa-Himself" poems not so much the principal poet, "with the heteronyms being only clever games, albeit games of genius," but that "Pessoa-Himself was as much a heteronym as all the others were. More accurately, he represents the void left within the man as poet after the flight of the other selves. None of those selves, not even Alvaro de Campos in his hours of blackest despair, is as much the poet of the specific 'nothing' as Pessoa-Himself is."

Although he disliked having his photo taken, there are a number in existence, and they seem to be reproduced and more available than those of many another poet. Most show him very formally, in an English fashion, with white shirt, bow tie and suit, wearing a Homburg hat. He wore spectacles, as he was myopic, and a little mustache. He smoked eighty cigarettes a day, and drank quite heavily.

Pessoa worked, ate and drank in the Bairro Alto and Baixa areas predominantly, but the rented rooms he lived in were scattered around the city, whether staying with aunts and relatives, his mother, or alone. In all he is said to have stayed at 24 addresses. His final house on the Rua Coelho da Rocha, in Campo de Ourique, has been turned into a library, work center and performance space called the Casa Pessoa, where his own personal library, which moved continually with him and comprised mainly English books, is also housed.

Pessoa died in the Bairro Alto, spending the last couple of days of his life in November 1935 in the São Luís dos Franceses Hospital on the Rua Luz Spriano, a French hospital, which is ironic as Simões says, because he never showed much interest in French literature: "It would have been more appropriate for him to have died in an English hospital." Buried in the Prazeres cemetery, he was later moved to his current home in the Mosteiro dos Jerónimos (Jeronimos Monastery) at Belém.

"But when did he live?" Jorge de Sena asked, replying: "He never did live, in the romantic sense that had been and would again become so fashionable. Not having servants to live on his behalf (…) Pessoa created a group of people to do it for him."

### Café A Brasileira
At the top end of Rua Garrett is the old Café A Brasileira, where Pessoa is cast outside, seated alone, the accompanying chair vacant, at best occupied by a tourist smiling for the camera. If you have not arranged to meet someone before going out for a meal in the Bairro Alto, or elsewhere, you can just as easily stand at the bar with *uma bica*, or perhaps something stronger, and, why not, a *pastéis de nata*, and look around the darkened wood and big gilt-framed mirrors and think of its

earlier days. Although this old-style coffee house was opened in 1905, its real fame is attached to the 1920s and 1930s, with its literary clientele, particularly Pessoa and his friends. But that is to take away from it all its other connections, its use by politicians, lawyers, policemen... for all these people came here to talk over a drink.

The last time we were there, the lights went out. Not personally. I only had *uma bica*, but the electricity. And not just in the bar, but outside, in Lisbon, across Lisbon, and as we were to find out, across the whole of southern Portugal. The official line blamed a large bird nesting on the electricity cables that had short-circuited the system. For two hours or more the city was thrown into darkness, except for the banks, whose generators came into operation to protect their interests. For the rest of us everything stopped. Tills and machines electrically operated curtailed business. Our guests arrived, found us by our profiles in the dark, and we negotiated our way out. It was meant to be a late night tour around the modern sights of Lisbon, with our final destination, the Lux. We all laughed. A good start! Eventually we found the light. Or was it the light that found us?

It is for José Cardoso Pires with *Ballad of Dogs' Beach* to remind us that the clientele was not comprised of only famed artists, as his inspector Elias tails the lawyer into the Brasileira. "He sat, smoking, at a table of well-known faces. (Not that the inspector knew them; they

seemed to be from the ranks of the Law and the political opposition.) A neighbouring group, of artistic appearance, were probably dancers from the São Carlos theatre. Elias took a chair at the door, with his man in sight." A few lines later he begins to identify some of the clients: "...as usual, the Brasileira had its patrons from the PIDE, whom he recognised from their business-visits to the Criminal Police. They were not dawdlers here—they were in and out 'on the way to the office', their establishment being round the corner—but Henrique Seixas, of the PIDE, was prominent at the table where Dr Soares da Fonseca and a selection of Deputies were accustomed to drink their morning coffee." Cardoso Pires gives us a footnote to show whom we are dealing with here: "Henrique Seixas had been a guard in the concentration camp at Tarrafal in the Cape Verde Islands. José Soares da Fonseca was a government Minister, Managing Director of the Colonial Steamship Company, and an adviser of Salazar."

The Brasileira gained one aspect of its fame as the *café des artistes*, the role that is most remembered, from its writers and artists. When the place was redesigned in the 1920s, the architect José Pacheco had the place transformed into "the museum of modern art that Lisbon did not yet have," as he succeeded in gaining commissions from the artists of the day to contribute their work, controversial as they were, placing the café firmly on the map. They included Eduardo Viana, Jorge Barradas, António Soares, Bernardo Marques and Almada Negreiros. One of the most referenced paintings is *The Self-Portrait in a Group 1925* by Almada Negreiros. It is a somewhat disturbing painting, for although it comprises two couples seated at a café table, there is no sense that a conversation is in progress. In fact, the two women appear to be elsewhere; at best one of them could be looking at the drawing one of the men appears to be holding for all to see. But there is no discussion, there is no look of involvement. The painter himself, who holds a sheet with another portrait, seems to be even further removed from the group. It has been suggested that the men are deep in thought. As if the women are not, as if their looks are vacant, or more frivolous! One wonders what three of them are looking at, outside the frame of the painting.

José de Almada-Negreiros (his full name) was one of the most important artists of his day in Portugal. He was also a poet, playwright, novelist and essayist. Along with Amadeo de Souza-Cardoso, he formed the first generation of modern artists. His acquaintance with Pessoa was to remain for the rest of his life.

The difficulty in talking about that period of modern art in Portugal is that there are no schools as such, not in the way that other countries had them. Most Portuguese art is discussed in terms of individual artists, many of whom went abroad, mainly to Paris, and either stayed or returned enthusiastic to work on what they had experienced. Thus, Amadeo de Souza-Cardoso, Eduardo Viana, Sarah Afonso, José de Almada-Negreiros, Carlos Botelho, Mário Eloy and Maria Helena Vieira da Silva, all trained in artists' studios somewhere between Montparnasse and Montmartre. Berlin was another favorite for some, including Bernardo Marques and Mário Eloy. Amadeo de Souza-Cardoso, José de Almada Negreiros and Eduardo Viana had met Robert and Sonia Delaunay in Paris, and for a while during the war, the Delaunays came to Portugal, staying in the north in Vila do Conde, a stay that was beneficial to their Portuguese friends, who regained some of that flavor of the cosmopolitan life that they had begun to miss. Sonia Delaunay later wrote that the stay was one of the most marvelous times of her life.

While many of them were more concerned with importing the foreign for their own needs, as they saw nothing to grapple with in the visual arts, Pessoa was concerned to export Portuguese culture and make it known abroad as part of his fight against the country's "demotion from European status."

## António Ribeiro, Camões and Eça de Queirós

And while the past slipped by, Elias, the inspector sat in the café watching the lawyer, having placed himself in "such a way that he could watch the outside world, draw on memories of his childhood, his first memories of the poet Chiado, whose statue was within sight." Pessoa's figure outside is a more recent addition. A few yards further stands Chiado, the *nom de plume* of the poet António Ribeiro, "a verdigrised, unremembered statue, finger raised to admonish the passer-by: Ignore me, sinner passing by, but I shall have the last laugh soon enough, when you are where I am; and *Pax tecum*."

This statue was part of Elias's childhood: "The bohemian, celibate poet, the satirist—who could be more typical of Lisbon? A monk, what's more, and ideally sited in this square, between churches and bookshops, sacred and profane." He recounts the memory of an old toothless "dotard" in his home town of Elvas, who squeezed "wriggling white worms from his nose," and whose laugh reminded him of "the statue's malevolent smile and blackened tears," frightening him.

Further up the road one comes to the Praça Luís de Camões (Camões Square), with the statue of the great poet in the center, erected in 1867. Only at this time there is no statue, and indeed there is no square. There is actually a cube, for the square has been excavated and the hole is as deep as it is long and wide. The intention is to make an underground car park, and when the surface has been restored, to return the statue—"perhaps"—as the residents say.

Luís de Çamões is the national poet of Portugal, although for centuries he was virtually ignored. He wrote the first European epic poem, *Os Lusíadas* (The Lusiads), which is principally about the exploits of Vasco da Gama and the discovery of the sea route to India, giving it depth with a richness of mythology. Much has been surmised, but little is known of his life. He was born in 1524, or 1525, of parents who lived in the Mouraria district by the castle. He was a scholar and attended Coimbra University before becoming a soldier. Following an ill-chosen romance with Caterina de Ataide, a lady-in-waiting to the queen, as the story goes, he was banished from Court and served in Morocco, where he lost an eye in a battle with the Moors. On his return to Lisbon he was involved in a street brawl that ended with a year in jail and departure for India. He was away for sixteen years, experiencing the full range of adventures to be had by the Portuguese of the sixteenth century. Although it appears that he lost much of his poetry, he managed to rescue the manuscript of *The Lusiads*, reputedly swimming ashore from a shipwreck holding it aloft with one hand. On publication his work was recognized by Dom Sebastião I and he received something of a pension, though he lived in poverty and died a pauper. Three hundred years later, what were assumed to be his remains were re-buried in the Mosteiro dos Jerónimos at Belém.

Earlier, when we were walking up the Rua do Alecrim with Saramago and Reis, we passed the statue of Eça de Queirós near the top,

set in the Largo do Barão de Quintella. As Pessoa points out in his guide to Lisbon: "The chief figure, in marble, represents Truth—a naked woman whose body is imperfectly veiled by a gauze covering. Above and behind it is the novelist's bust." Engraved on its base is a phrase taken from the novelist as inspiration by the sculptor: "On the strong nakedness of truth the transparent veil of fancy." At various times others have added, by hand, other pearls of wisdom.

## Chiado
Not far away, the Teatro Nacional de São Carlos (São Carlos Opera House) and the Museu do Chiado, formerly the Museu Nacional de

Arte Contemporânea, almost face each other across the Rua Serpa Pinto. The opera house began construction in 1792 after the previous one was destroyed by the Great Earthquake. It was designed by José da Costa e Silva along the lines of its namesake in Naples, and its rococo interior with the draped, columned, mirrored royal box flanked by satyrs is similar to La Scala in Milan. It has seen better times, however, previously attracting great international performers from opera, theater and ballet like Maria Callas, Sarah Bernhardt and Margot Fonteyn, as well as many other top musicians and composers. Even today it struggles, and at one point went into such decline that it closed. It stood in as a substitute for the Kirov in St. Petersburg when the American director Taylor Hackford was filming *White Nights* (1985) with a galaxy of stars, including Mikhail Baryshnikov, Gregory Hines, Jerzy Skolimowski, Helen Mirren, Geraldine Page and Isabella Rossellini. According to the story, it was here, during his visit to Lisbon, that Byron was struck by the irate husband for making advances towards his wife.

Pessoa was born at 4, Largo de São Carlos, on the fourth floor, directly opposite the main entrance to the opera house. At that time grass grew in the middle of the square, giving it the feel of a village square, but these days it is jammed as a parking space. Any idea of the view Pessoa had of the Tagus in his childhood went long ago with the building of taller buildings, although the childhood memories lingered with the poet. Later he wrote:

*The dining room windows and those of my room*
*Overlooked the low buildings, and gave on the nearby river,*
*On the Tagus, this very same Tagus, but much lower down.*
*Were I to arrive at those windows now, they would not be those windows at all.*
*That time has passed like the smoke of a steamer upon the high seas.*

One of the great delights of walking around Lisbon is suddenly to see between the houses, along the downsloping roads, a view of the Tagus, always spectacular, always a surprise and delight. As one of today's most renowned poets, Sophia de Mello Breyner, wrote in her poem, *Lisbon*:

*Tagus*
*Here and there as we walk Lisbon's streets*
*In a hurry or lost in thought*
*Turning the corner we suddenly see*

*The shimmering blues of the Tagus*
*And our body becomes light*
*Our soul is winged*

The Igreja de São Roque (Church of St. Rock) which is found further up the hill into the Bairro Alto does not look much from the outside, a casualty of the Great Earthquake too, but inside there is one of the city's most splendid chapels. Virtually a folly (though one shouldn't say that too loud), the Capela de São João Baptista (Chapel of St. John the Baptist), demonstrates the use and abuse of power and wealth of its time. Dom João V ordered it in 1742 from the papal architect, Salvi e Vanvitelli in Rome, where it was built, taking five years. It was then consecrated by Pope Benedict XIV—for a gift of 100,000 *cruzados*—before being dismantled and shipped to Lisbon, at a total cost then of more than $375,000 — making it one of the most precious chapels of its size ever built. On arrival it was reconstructed near the high altar. When it had been crammed to capacity with Carrara marble, lapis lazuli, amethyst, alabaster and gold, everything that was left over found its way into the museum next door. The trouble with the luxury of abundance is that one delight drowns another, until they all drown: the richly decorated vestments, a mitre encrusted with Brazilian rubies, a cope with 33lb of gold, silver plate, medieval paintings…

On August 26, 1988 at 5AM a fire that began in one of the historic Art Deco department stores, Grandella, in the Rua do Carmo, devastated a section of the Chiado district. It took six hours to control, during which time it killed two people, injured another thirty and destroyed countless old and historic buildings. One of the great losses for fans of Amália Rodrigues were all the files relating to her career since 1939 in her manager's office, as well as the record label Valentim de Carvalho's archive of sheet music, catalogs and records, for their premises were gutted. Some 2,000 people in all lost their jobs. Lisbon was thrown into shock and the world media covered the disaster as one of the major events of the decade. For years the area was a series of holes and buttressed façades, and many wondered whether it would ever be restored. This was a fashionable part of Lisbon, its shops, boutiques and department stores making it an equivalent of London's Bond Street.

Overseeing the rebuilding are the ruins of the Convento do Carmo, which was founded after the Battle of Aljubarrota in 1385 by Nun' Alvares Pereira, the great military leader, in honor of a vow made at the battle. The foundations twice gave way, delaying completion until 1423, at which time the founder himself entered the monastery for the remaining eight years of his life. Later it was shaken to its foundations by the Great Earthquake, and the roof collapsed on the congregation. Some of the walls, nave arches and five apses are still standing, and over the years it has been put to various uses as a graveyard, a refuse tip, a chemical factory and a stable for the neighboring barracks of the Republican Guard. Today there is also an archaeological museum incorporated into the site, stocked with everything from Bronze Age pottery and oddments discarded by the Visigoths to assortments of coins and ancient tombstones.

Another overseer of the area is João César Monteiro, who pays attention both to the ruins of the convent as a place for evening concerts as well as documenting the devastated shells of the burned-out buildings in his *Recordações da Casa Amarela*. Monteiro, who regularly features in his own bizarre films, dresses up in the outfit of a general and parades the walkways of the Chiado, looking down on the ruins. This particular footage is in almost documentary style, as if desiring to commit to film a record of this terrible disaster. The choice of army uniform fits well with the location, a comment on the earlier use of the Convento do Carma perhaps.

Monteiro began his film career in London, at the London School of Film, afterwards taking five years to finish his first film. One of the actresses on another film *Silvestre* (1982) was a young woman called Maria de Medeiros. She became an actress by accident, but impressed quickly because of two features: the intense gaze in her eyes, and a sense of otherness. In 1984 she went to Paris to study philosophy, but acting featured in her life, both on stage and film. Chantal Akerman's episode for *Paris vu par... vingt ans après* (1984), and Michel Deville's delightful spur to reading, *La Lectrice* (1988), were two roles, but her international fame came with two American films, Philip Kaufman's *Henry and June* (1990)—as Anaïs Nin—and Quentin Tarantino's *Pulp Fiction* (1994). She has returned to Portugal to film, particularly with the young Portuguese director Teresa Villaverde in *A Idade Maior* (Alex, 1991), and *Três Irmãos* (Two Brothers, My Sister, 1994). As a writer and director herself, she has made a film based on Pessoa, *A Morte do Príncipe* (The Death of the Prince, 1991).

## Bairro Alto

The Bairro Alto is often referred to as the bohemian area. Certainly it has a grid of streets, not unlike the Baixa, although set on a hillside so that the pattern is not really organized or elegant. "Nothing is in a straight line, not even time, which mixes centuries and cultures, races, creeds, rites," writes the novelist Teolinda Gersão. The narrow streets are filled with *tascas* (little taverns), bars, restaurants and *fado* houses, as well as bookstores, art galleries and fashionable boutiques—not fashionable in Bond Street terms, but more Soho or Covent Garden terms. For many years the discos and noisy clubs went on well into the night, but today the music has been encouraged to move to the docks and to occupy the converted warehouses, where revelers can continue until dawn.

At the beginning of the 1970s three women met regularly to talk about common interests, particularly the relationship of women to men. Determining to commit their ideas to paper, sending each other letters between their weekly meetings, a project emerged that became *The New Portuguese Letters.* For the three women this brought celebrity because it invited the censors of the time to confiscate the book on its appearance in 1972, and to charge the women and their publisher with "offending public morals and abusing the freedom of the press." After two years of the judicial process the case was abruptly quashed in April 1974 at the time of the coup, but not before support from abroad brought translations and attention to the book.

The Three Marias, as they became known, were Maria Isabel Barreno, Maria Teresa Horta and Maria Velho da Costa. The book took its title from a seventeenth-century classic, *Letters from a Portuguese Nun,* a book purporting to be written by a woman, trapped against her will in a convent, writing to her lover, a French officer, who had deserted her. With this book as the focal point, a series of essays, poems, letters and various fictitious texts were collaged together to present the issues that beset women as the authors saw them at the time. Although particularly relevant to the Portuguese, in their socially, politically, economically and culturally repressed society, it also struck a chord internationally with women's groups around the world.

One of Europe's more radical writers today, in political exile from her native Croatia, Dubravka Ugresic set a section of her novel, *The Museum of Unconditional Surrender* (1996) in Lisbon. Her character accepts an invitation to a two-day literary gathering, decides to go earlier, and asks her hosts to book her into a cheap hotel room: "It turned out that the hotel was not so cheap. Instead of the small, romantic, decrepit *pensão* (that I had imagined), I ended up in a newish hotel of indifferent appearance which resembled East European ones in every way." It is her first time in Lisbon and she recalls Remarque's novel *The Night in Lisbon* because, like herself a refugee, "Remarque's novel is concerned with the already forgotten time when 'a man meant nothing' and 'a valid passport everything.'"

In the evening she goes to the Bairro Alto, for a meal "in one of the small, cheap restaurants warmly recommended by my guidebook." At the back of her mind is the thought that a romance might be found. Not unnaturally, she makes a "pick up" who seduces her and then proceeds to fleece her, promising repayment, and although she does see him again, he does not repay her or refer to his debt. She describes her first night:

*My memory of that night is nightmarish, a series of disjointed images, a rapid, intoxicating night drive. I remember a homosexual behind a bar, his strong, bare arms, port in little glasses, the sound of fado which coated the visitors, like dew at dusk, there was a drunken Dutchman, a Polish Portuguese man or a Portuguese Pole who looked like a greyhound, into whose hand my companion thrust some money and received a little lump of hashish in return, then an Englishman, a desperado, and his friend, a local prostitute. I remember the speed and ease with which my companion rolled a joint with one hand...*

Eventually there is the return to the hotel, the unpleasantness of the receptionist and the night together... and the realization of her aging, something she was to revive on another night out:

*I broke away from my invisible leash and hurried to Bairro Alto. The old city district was pulsating to the rhythm of my excited heart. I walked through the narrow streets, stopping by the little black taverns. In the dark holes the local people were watching television, playing cards and drinking wine. In one bar, where some older women were sitting, lit by a dull light, my eye was caught by a large oil painting of a young beauty. A dried-up old woman noticed my gaze and, just like a ghost from a nightmare, came towards the door, looked at the picture, and then sighed, nodded her head and pointed to a stout old lady who was staring absently at the television. She was the girl in the portrait. That sorrowful pantomime, that brief lesson on the transcience of life, that old woman pointing the way like a grotesque stewardess in the spaceship of life, cut me to the quick like a vague intimation of loss.*

The area is still a hotbed of experimental music and visual arts. Tucked away in a side street you might hear disjointed new musics, and seek the source. Perhaps it's a record shop that only opens at night, or a one-room club with a guitarist seated before a handful of people. Rafael Toral is one of today's young Portuguese guitarists and sound artists, making what he calls "soniscapes," or others "waveform." A musician who has broken onto the international circuit, abroad he might play with members of Sonic Youth, but at home his audience will probably be no more than a handful, unless, as he says, John Zorn is in town and asks to play with him. Then the audience is larger, because they are there to see the American.

Talking on his music, Toral explains: "Since to me sound is the source of music, I can make a single sound and the changes this sound goes through become the music. I don't like traditional playing because people always have to stop a sound to make the next one, and the faster they do it the more annoying it is. I like to make only one sound and keep it going—then it's like traveling, many things can happen with it." Ambient music is one term that is used in relation to Toral's music. Indeed, one of its prime exponents, Brian Eno, was one of his initial influences: "The kind of ambient I'm looking for is one that sets a mood of tranquility while having embedded in itself elements that disturb it." His prime influence is John Cage, and the composer's notions of silence, which Toral feels that people take far too much for granted.

When one walks anywhere near the Ponte 25 de Abril one cannot fail to notice the noise, the hum of the traffic. It is immediately there when watching a film like Wenders' *Lisbon Story*. Wenders does nothing to hide this background noise; indeed, it could be said he brings it to the fore. It is part of Lisbon, particularly in this film in which Phillip

Winter, the sound engineer, is collecting the sounds of Lisbon. Toral also appreciates this particular noise. He has a project called *Bridge Music*, in which he records different bridges in the world, including his own in Lisbon. "The idea is to make music out of vibrations of large bridges with metallic structures, recorded with contact microphones. The thing is to listen and tune into the bridges' resonant frequencies. There are many sounds, rattles, drones, metallic harmonies, impacts... it's heavy traffic that activates them. Bridges look like huge instruments to me."

Although the discos might be moving down towards the docks, with their modern décor, greater parking spaces and lack of real atmosphere, (or perhaps the atmosphere that is exactly right for them), the Bairro Alto still retains that feel of the pulsating heart of Lisbon nightlife. There are always bars to venture into, boutiques, record shops and galleries that live by night. ZDB (Galeria Zé dos Bois) is one such alternative venue that is always worth checking out as a gallery, spot for improvised musics or a cultural meeting point.

## Foreign Considerations

Back at A Brasileira, the music we might expect to hear is from Bévinda, a singer who has taken *fado* and South American music and edged them forward. Perhaps it would be more appropriate to listen to her album of sung Pessoa poems, the Pessoa as Alberto Caeiro, a more mellow sound with cellos as accompaniment.

We drink *uma bica* and eat another sweet pastry (*bolo*). The day is well under way, the floor is littered with crumpled paper napkins and empty sugar sachets. Dentists must do good business. One down the road, a first-floor surgery, has large images of various teeth, molars and incisors, painted on its windows, outlined, advertising as if the British-based artist, Michael Craig-Martin, was exhibiting his conceptual work in an upstairs gallery.

Cees Nooteboom has passed by, and is now sitting by the river, reflecting:

> But try as I might, the seat beside me remained empty, just as empty as the
> chair in front of Café A Brasileira by the statue of Pessoa in the Rua Garrett.
> His solitude at least had been self-imposed. If anyone had been sitting beside
> him it would have been himself, one of his three alter egos come to join

*him in drinking himself silently and deliberately to death in the dark shad-
ows beyond, among the high-backed chairs with black leather brass-stud-
ded upholstery, the distorting mirrors of the heteronyms, the Greek temples
floating across the walls, and the massive clock (by A.Romero) all the way
into the back of the narrow space, drinking its fill of time just like the
customers sipping the black, sweet liquid of death from small white cups.*

No dentist needed there, nor for the French poet, Bernard Noël, who
noted in *Le Reste du voyage* (1997) that "only the body of the poet
remained intact, alcohol preserves better than memory." While the
American poet Armand Schwerner squeezes Pessoa between Whitman
and George Oppen, and squeezes Lisbon between London and San
Francisco in his *Old Dog Sermon* (1983), and the British poet and
translator, Michael Hamburger, unable to sleep, talks of the noises that
keep him awake in his hotel room in *Lisbon Night* (1975):

*… The cacophonous throb*
*Of competing juke boxes in the pinball saloons has ended,*
*The cabarets down in the square have closed their doors.*
*Only motor bicycles rev and clatter; and all over the city*
*Still the twenty-one revolutions and counter-revolutions take place*
*On the walls. I begin to extract a silence, a privacy from*
*The repeated yap and whine of a dog in a nearby year,*
*When not later than two or two-thirty, long before dawn,*
*The false alarm clock, a denatured cock*
*Shrills, irresistibly shrills again and again,*
*Ripping me out of a quarter-sleep filled with the alleys,*
*The pine, eucalyptus, cedar and fish smells of Lisbon,*
*Glaze of tiled housefronts, the slippery marble of paving-stones,*

Only dream could rid him of it, "thoroughly pulping the stuff." But
in the end he is resigned to defeat when he cannot dream the dream:

*… There's nothing for it*
*But to live, as the poor do here, on credit, making the best*
*Of expecting the worst, and where other energy can't,*
*For the moment, be drawn upon, keep going on coffee.*
*Insomnia, television—they're much the same,*
*After all, apart from the missing knob.*
*So, resigned, I wait for the kinder blankness of morning.*

It is as if Hamburger has become a Pessoa, back to witness the revolution and its aftermath, this poem written a year after.

In 1922 *The Anarchist Banker* by Pessoa was published. Fifty years later when it was translated into French, the American poet Lawrence Ferlinghetti discovered it on a visit to Paris. The facts of Ferlinghetti's family tree came late to him, discovering that while he was the child of an Italian father, his mother was a Portuguese Jew, her grandfather descended from Sephardim Jews from the village of Monsanto before emigrating to the Caribbean. The story inspired him to write a novella *Love in the Days of Rage* (1988), and to ask Edwin Honig to translate the Pessoa story from the Portuguese so that he could publish it at his publishing house, City Lights, based in San Francisco. Later Ferlinghetti was to visit Lisbon, that city that has uncommon bonds with San Francisco, with similarities of bridges, hills and trams, and the underlying tremors that threaten with faultlines, which have already brought devastation famously to both cities.

## Mário de Sá-Carneiro

There might be others who would like to see themselves as worthy companions of Pessoa, to seat themselves next to him once the chair outside A Brasileira has been vacated by the stream of tourists. Jorge de Sena tells us that Pessoa's "daily companions for conversation and congenial talk were not drawn from the lists of the greats of history but were rather undistinguished, if sometimes charming, beings." There were a few exceptions, and perhaps the main one was Mário de Sá-Carneiro, "whom he really accepted as his peer." Not that Pessoa had a long life with his friend, for Sá-Carneiro committed suicide in 1916 in Paris, aged 26, his death a botched affair with strychnine. Pessoa became his literary executor, although many of his writings disappeared. We might note, too, that one of Pessoa's heteronyms, Caeiro, is derived from Carneiro.

The young poet Sá-Carneiro had an unhappy childhood, his mother dying when he was two, followed by problems with his father and the nanny, and later with his stepmother, a former prostitute. At school he witnessed his friend's suicide, committed in front of teachers and students, something that Sá-Carneiro thought was courageous, leading him to describe his own life as "existing without living." To escape from

Lisbon was a prime objective, and though he went to Paris feeling that life would change for him, it was in fact just a little less boring. His stories are threaded with suicide and madness.

In *Resurrection* (written in 1914) his character, a writer (as are many of his main characters), says: "Lisbon was a narrow yellow house, old parents who refuse to let their daughters out in the streets, oil lamps, harsh voices, the smell of lavender..." He was in Paris by this time, for he was able to continue: "In mundane Lisbon there were no sumptuously dressed women wearing audaciously revealing clothes out of the latest fashion journals, nor were there honking cars cramming the avenues; there were no museums or vast libraries, no nude bodies in the finales at the theatre, and the cafés were empty; lovers did not walk along holding hands or stop to kiss in the middle of the street; one was not surrounded by magnificent buildings, great palaces, huge department stores, towers, churches, heraldic columns!"

At first sight it might seem surprising that Pessoa had such an intimate friendship with a man whose characters despised the ordinary person leading a healthy decent life. For it is such a person who is the scoundrel in Sá-Carneiro's eyes, not the criminals and drug addicts, those who have the courage to transgress the limits of society. This was the position that Sá-Carneiro also saw for the artist, a transgressor who has no comfort in the world, for whom, ultimately, death is a release.

# 5. Fado & Food

*Saudade* is a word in regular use and, as mentioned earlier, has come to mean a feeling of nostalgia for the past, as the future can never offer better. There are all manner of extra nuances to this definition, as people try to define something that appears indefinable, such as a longing for, a yearning for something that cannot be attained. Or a sadness for something that might have been. It is a specifically Portuguese term, there being no equivalent in other cultures, because it is a feeling, an attitude as much as anything that is woven into Portuguese culture. It is used in everyday conversation, as well as in relation to the arts and particularly music.

*Fado* is often regarded as the music by which one expresses *saudade*. This is probably why outsiders frequently refer to *fado* as comparable to the blues, a term that can be applied to an everyday feeling, and also to a very specific type of music. The idea is not without its merit.

*Saudade* is at the heart of *fado*, or, more correctly, is probably best described as the soul of the music, if one is to use such metaphors.

While often presented as *the* traditional music, *fado* is not. There is plenty of folk music around Portugal, as in other countries. *Fado* is regarded as a music particular to Lisbon, its probable place of origin. (There is another variation of *fado* centered on the northern city of Coimbra.) To use an analogy with jazz, one would not say that jazz was *the* music of America. It is a music, a form, and it is a form more often associated with a certain area or district of a city than another. At least that was so in the past. Jazz has its origins in the brothels of New Orleans, for example. Likewise with *fado*. It is a form of music that started and is associated with the old working quarters of Lisbon, among people who had a need for it, although now it has been transformed and used as a popular entertainment, or a popular entertainment has been derived from it. Many purists, of course, can be heard to mutter when *fado* is being sung that it's not the real thing, that it's just for the tourists, as if they each held the key to the one room where it can be heard in its purity. *Fado* has also been likened to flamenco in Spain, again an incorrect analogy, as flamenco is a wilder music. It goes to show that as one doesn't compare flamenco to anything else, or tango for that matter, one has to accept that *fado* is simply *fado*.

*Fado* is found in particular areas of Lisbon, most often in *Casa de Fado* (*fado* houses) in the Alfama area or the Bairro Alto, although there are other districts too. Again, there are varying stages or types of *fado*, some being more for the tourist than others. Some establishments have all the trappings of a *fado* house, where you are entertained and pay more for the meal that you eat, whereas others are in less salubrious surroundings. In the latter the feeling and atmosphere of the place may be better, it being more a place to drink than a restaurant. Thus there are *fado* houses where only the locals go, and others where only tourists go, sometimes by the coachload. And there are those in between, which are hard to find.

But what does "entertained by a singer with a better voice" mean?—for that is how the expensive *fado* houses are qualified. *Fado* is not about perfect pitch, *fado* is about feeling; no trained voice is required. There is an *adega* (tavern) at the bottom end of the Rua do Diário de Notícias, a street in the Bairro Alto that has a number of *fado* houses both on and just off it, where the cook is likely to come forward and sing along with the three regular singers. In this *fado* house there is usually a singer who will come in off the street and sing in return for a meal. This is called *fado vadio* (tramp *fado*). Last time we were in this *adega* one such singer, a man, sang such a mournful pair of songs that everyone was brought to total silence, if not tears. He had the look and passion that I best associate with Jacques Brel. For all the derision poured onto *fado* by the younger generations, there are such moments that we experienced where labels are of no value. Here was a singer who moved an audience with a level of cathartic release that generated intense emotions, as pure and as simple as that.

Where *fado* comes from is a matter of contention. People are agreed that it is a music originating from the poor, and that its home is in the Alfama and other old districts like the Mouraria or the Bairro Alto, but no one is really sure whether its roots are in African, Brazilian or Moorish cultures, or whether it is something sparked by a mixture of cultures. But since the nineteenth century it has been consistent. To link it to other countries suggests a part played by mariners, a popular theory. *Fado* at root comes from the sea, from sailors singing of their loved ones at home, or their loved ones at home singing for those away. For when the boats went out fishing they often had to go far away and there were long periods before they returned.

The *fadista*, the *fado* singer, who can be male or female, is usually dressed for the occasion. Although a woman is usually dressed in black, there is no fixed rule, but she will always pick up her black shawl, which might be hanging on the wall, and draw it about her shoulders before she starts singing. This suggests a parallel with attending church in a Catholic country such as Portugal. The musicians are two, and almost always male. One plays a Portuguese *guitarra*, also called an English guitar, from where it originates (a relation of the Renaissance zither), which is a pear-shaped guitar with twelve strings (double-coursing) and a distinctive shaped tuning head called a "turkey's tail fan," the strings resonating, the player improvising with embellishments. The other guitar, the *viola da França* the Portuguese call it, although we would term it a Spanish guitar (not such an acceptable name in Portugal), holds the basic structure of the song.

The lyrics are important. Almost entirely comprised of four-line stanzas, the one thing all note is that they must be "poetic," otherwise they are not *fado* lyrics. *Fado* means "fate," which gives the tone, as they are always mournful songs, of loss, absence and other forms of despair. They can have any subject matter, although often they are above love, jealousy, homesickness…

There are general rules around which *fado* is played and sung. People sing in the order in which they arrive. Usually a set comprises three songs, not longer than three minutes each. Thus if you do not particularly like one singer, you know that the set will not go on forever. On the other hand, if you enjoy one singer, you might have to wait some while before he or she sings again. It is also expected that no one should talk while the *fadista* sings. In some places people stop eating too. A *fado* house might be distinguished from others by how these rules are applied. Tourists drag their own culture with them like dirty socks and impose their smell on others—and singers do not take kindly to their chatter or rowdiness during the set, even if they try not to show it. This is more to do with the nature of Portuguese politeness than the need for tourist money—at least I hope so. For the minute or less between songs, mixed with the clapping, cheering, and appreciative comments, people talk briefly, eat another mouthful, and create a general noise, but it stops quickly once a new song commences, the guitars giving an introduction to lead the way.

## Amália Rodrigues

Amália Rodrigues, the best-known and most famous *fadista*, had lyrics written for her by the more celebrated poets and writers of the day. In that sense, there is an overlap with *chansons* in France, where someone like Juliette Gréco has had Jean-Paul Sartre and the poet Jacques Prévert write for her, let alone the very nature of *chansons* by poet/singers like Georges Brassens, Jacques Brel, Léo Ferré, Serge Gainsbourg and others.

Politics has also played its part. As with any art form that captures the imagination, politicians like to appropriate it for their own means. With the increasing popularity of *fado*, particularly with the rise of Amália Rodrigues, who not only popularized it but gave it credibility in a context away from the *fado* houses, the Salazar regime seized it. After the 1974 revolution it was a form of music looked down upon for some years until the bad taste had dissipated. Amália was criticized for apparently being supportive of the regime, and although it seems she never openly criticized it, she had recorded songs whose lyrics were written by poets banned by the dictatorship. Its appropriation by the dictatorship made it easier for others to criticize *fado*, with some credence, saying, like Maria Isabel Barreno, that its popularity had developed like a cancer that cloaked all musical diversity, until it was regarded as the national music, the sole

representative of its country. If there had been no Amália, perhaps this state of affairs would not have happened.

Amália Rodrigues shaped *fado* and made it a music that attracted attention around the world. Her voice is the voice of *fado*, the mark used by which others are compared. And yet her music opened up over the years, with full orchestral backings, performances in big theaters, films... Taking it to the world, the term "Ambassador of Fado" is an applicable title for her. When she died in 1999, the nation mourned, and the state funeral that was held in the Basílica da Estrela, not far from her last home in Rua de São Bento, drew worldwide attention and brought Lisbon to a halt as the streets were lined all the way to the Cemitério dos Prazeres. She was 79 when she died, and she had sung well into her seventies, even though ill health reduced her public appearances. Her life had had its ups and downs, with depressions, broken love affairs and attempted suicides, the subject of many a song, not only *fado*.

For Amália (to use her Christian name is enough, her status is such) the origin of *fado* "as far as I'm concerned, and I'm sticking to it, derives from people at sea becoming homesick for their families... a lament... this sadness... this *saudade* for home is *fado*."

She was born in 1920 into a poor family. She left school early, helping her mother and sister to sell vegetables at a stall in Lisbon. She wanted to go into the theater, but her voice led her into the *fado* houses, and at nineteen she was singing at the most famous *fado* house of its day, the Solar de Alegria. She was always a shy performer, and preferred the theater stage for its distancing in preference to the intimacy of the *fado* houses.

In 1945 on a visit to Brazil she made her first records, which were then imported to Portugal. While she opened up the range of *fado*, she was able to exert an enormous influence on the upcoming generation of female *fadistas*, who looked to her voice and style as the template for themselves. In a way this has not changed. The Amália sound is still the foundation of the female *fadista*, and it is the sound the tourists seek in the *fado* houses. And yet Amália was still held dear in the hearts of the Portuguese, because she was special enough to sing *fado* with an authenticity. "I don't sing *fado*, it sings in me," she once said. Unfortunately, it was the commercial aspect that strode the world, and which the world comes to Lisbon to hear.

Or the world can see it on film. Amália appeared in a number of films, both for the home market, and on the international screen. One of the latter is *Les Amants du Tage* (The Lovers of Lisbon, 1955) directed by Henri Verneuil, in which Amália plays the manager of a *fado* house, who sings while the stars eat. Not unexpectedly, no sooner have we warmed to the song than she is dropped into the background while the conversation continues. Not unexpectedly too, the sights of Lisbon are the usual tour of the city. And yet the film has its fame because it is a love story set in the city, a film whose intention appears to be to use *fado* as its motif. The story revolves around a French man (Daniel Gélin) who bears the scars of his wife's infidelity, having been acquitted after killing her in the arms of her lover on his return from the war. Living in Lisbon and working as a taxi driver, he meets a rich English woman (Françoise Arnoul) on the run after murdering her husband and tailed by a police inspector (Trevor Howard). The love between the man (Pierre) and the woman (Kathleen) is doomed, the tragedy hanging on the final decision of whether she should flee to Brazil on a boat with him (leaving a question mark over whether her intentions are love alone), or surrender to the police and thereby prove that she loves him. Decisions in those days were not as now.

In this film, and in another from that time, *Lisbon* (1956), directed by and starring Ray Milland, the *fado* houses are enormous caverns. Perhaps there are such places, but they come across as studio sets, rather than the small intimate places that most experience. In Ray Milland's film, the lead female, Maureen O'Hara, asks Milland for the title of the song, after the *fadista* has finished. *Lisboa Antiga*, he replies, "a kind of home from home for Brazilians," summing up *fado* and applying the Hollywood makeover.

## Espionage and Intrigue

It was not only Amália who drew international attention to Lisbon. The city's significance was also enhanced by events during the Second World War, when Portugal was playing the role of a neutral government, its long association with Britain being balanced by a Fascist dictatorship also willing to deal with the Nazis. Thus it became a playground for the world of espionage and intrigue through which the refugees weaved their path on the escape route through the free port.

Into this arena entered one of the celebrities of the time, Josephine Baker, the renowned dancer and entertainer who was based in Paris. The "Jazz Cleopatra" as Phyllis Rose calls her, was a member of the French Resistance, with official military status, something which many did not perceive, particularly the Germans. Colonel Paillole who directed military counterintelligence from Marseilles was skeptical about Baker's involvement, fearing echoes of Mata Hari, as well as the fragility of show business personalities in the face of such work. Baker was to prove him wrong. She made a journey to Lisbon, accompanied by Jacques Abtey, the head of military counterintelligence in Paris who needed to pass information to the British about airfields, harbors and German troop positions. Posing as her secretary and assistant, Abtey planned to travel to Portugal with the cover that South America was the final destination (an idea conceived by Baker). All the information was written in invisible ink on Baker's music sheets.

Wartime travel was all a matter of permits, and Baker had few problems for herself. As Rose said: "Baker was an excellent cover. Everyone knew her. Everyone wanted to see her close up. She was like Poe's purloined letter, so obvious as to be invisible." Consequently, the couple openly took the classic refugee route on the train through Pau in the Pyrenees and across to Spain at Canfranc. Baker played her part to perfection, drawing all attention to herself, wrapped in an immense fur, allowing no eyes or thoughts to settle on her assistant. What impressed Abtey, he later observed, was that she had asked to have written in her visa that he "accompanies Madame Josephine Baker," thus implicating herself if the ruse was uncovered.

In Lisbon, Baker stayed at the Hotel Aviz, and Abtey in a less expensive hotel. Lisbon was more like an amusement park, in comparison to Paris, with its network of spies working on both sides providing the atmosphere. This was not the only trip Baker made to Lisbon; the next time she came alone, the information again written on her music sheets. As a social person she met many people, picked up useful information and camouflaged it all by giving performances and attending parties. One of the small restaurants, the Primavera, just off the Rua do Diário de Notícias in the Bairro Alto displays a signed photograph above the table where she ate.

Not only films actually set in Lisbon told of its wartime activities, its port of transit. One of the most celebrated films of the period concerns the need to get to Lisbon. *Casablanca* (1942), directed by Michael Curtiz with Humphrey Bogart and Ingrid Bergman, revolves around those fleeing Europe for America who come via Morocco to gain visas to travel on to Lisbon. As the film ends, that is precisely what we see, the flight to freedom, via Lisbon. In one of his two essays on the film, the Italian theoretician and writer, Umberto Eco, suggests that there is "a real text-analytical" work to be done on *Casablanca*, citing the link of Casablanca-Lisbon, as well as their value as places of international intrigue.

Some like to claim that Carmen Miranda, another popular artist who gave a touch of South America to the northern part of the continent (more as a fruit salad, with her cornucopian head-dresses), was from just outside Lisbon, before she went to Rio de Janeiro aged two, and later to Hollywood and fame. But it is not true. She was born in Marco de Canavezes, which is much more to the north, near Porto.

### Delights for the Stomach

There are many places to eat, not only Portuguese food, but other cuisines from around the world, as one would expect from such a cosmopolitan culture. One of the most celebrated places to dine out is the Tavares Rico (rich Tavares) in one of the main streets, the Rua da Misericórdia on the edge of the warren that is Bairro Alto nightlife. Its lavish Edwardian décor is as gilt-ridden as the city's Madre de Deus church. It is the oldest restaurant in Lisbon, dating back to 1784. If Catherine Deneuve is in town she'll be dining there. And she does come to Lisbon, specifically to film with John Malkovich in *O Convento* (The Convent) for Manoel de Oliveira in 1994, just outside on the coast around Setúbal.

In *The Following Story*, attempting to believe he is not an apparition in the city, Cees Nooteboom returns to the haunt and its mirrors:

> *A thousand mirrors in a cabinet encrusted with gold. It is not out of masochism that I will go there again tonight. I will go for the sake of verification. I want to see myself, and sure enough, there I am, reflected in a forest of mirrors casting my shoulders further and further away, the lights of chandeliers sparkling in my thousand bespectacled eyes. A dense crowd of waiters hover around me as I am led to my table, dozens of hands light dozens of candles, I receive a dozen menus and fifteen glasses of Sercial, and when they finally leave me alone I observe myself in multiplied form, my detestable back, my treacherous profile, my countless arms reaching to my one glass, my countless glasses of wine. But she is absent. Mirrors are useless, they retain nothing, not the living and not the dead, they are mercenary perjurers, nauseating in their glassy deference.*

What makes the place more unusual is that on the floor above there is a self-service restaurant called Tavares Pobre (poor Tavares), which caters for those who cannot afford downstairs. Some perhaps work their way down, while others move upwards.

Another place of exception in the area, more for the place itself perhaps than for the food, is the Cervejaria Trindade, whose interior walls are filled with *azulejos* (tiles). It is large, formerly a beer hall that was converted from the refectory of the convent of the Frades Trinos da Redenção dos Cativos. As most restaurants are too small to accommodate a last-minute gathering of friends, this eating place can usually oblige. Or you might just want to experience the décor.

Yet another that has a faded glory, which we will return to as it is in another area, is the Casa do Alentejo, not only for its blue and white *azulejos*, but for its large interior courtyard with Moorish appeal. It is a feature of Tabucchi's *Requiem*, the book and the film.

As one might expect from a country that explored the world and established trade routes, Portugal introduced a variety of foods into European cuisine, namely coriander, pepper, ginger, curry, saffron, paprika, coffee, peanuts, pineapples, tomatoes, potatoes… and tea. It was the Portuguese princess Catherine of Bragança, wife of England's King Charles II, who popularized the beverage in England, with her afternoon teas. It comes as no surprise either that some of these foods are used in Portuguese cooking, a cuisine that is simple and wholesome.

As already mentioned, cod is not a local fish, but it makes the traditional fish dish. It has been observed that the Portuguese live on dreams and subsist on salt cod. *Bacalhau* is distinctly Portuguese. The idea of salting it came in the sixteenth century when the ships took so long to bring it back from the fishing grounds off Newfoundland, that salting was a way to preserve it, sun-baking it into the board-stiff form in which one finds it. Oswell Blakeston notes with humor that "if dropped before it has been soaked, (it can) make a dent in the pavement." The best-known *bacalhau* dish is Bacalhau à Gomes de Sá, the cod cooked in a casserole with thinly sliced potatoes and onions, then garnished with hard-boiled eggs and black olives.

If you are in Lisbon, you can at least try *sardinhas* (sardines), for there's little point in going to a country rich in fish and seafood and not tasting it. The sardines grilled here are regarded as the sweetest and fattest in the world, and you can find them during spring, summer and early fall, though not in winter when they are too bony. Or you could try seafood, which might be as expensive as anywhere, although squid and octopus often find their way into dishes.

When one comes to meat, there is only one king: pork. Its sweetness and tenderness are attributed to the leisurely life the pigs enjoy and their diet of acorns, truffles and chestnuts while foraging in the cork orchards through autumn. *Porco à alentejana* (pork cooked with clams), which originates from the Alentejo area, is the dish to eat. As described by food critic Jean Anderson, the "cubes of pork are marinated in a paste of sweet red peppers and garlic, browned in the very fruity local olive oil, then covered and braised with baby clams, still in the shell. The clam opens slowly under the gentle heat, spilling its briny juices into the ambrosial red muddle."

Something that seems unusual to the British or American visitor is soup on a daily basis. Many cultures could not survive a meal without it, and Portuguese culture is no exception. The main one is *caldo verde*, which is finely shredded green cabbage with potatoes, onion, garlic and a little olive oil.

To drink with your meal, Portugal has its famous names, known worldwide, from the Ports and Madeiras, those wonderful appetizers, known only too well to the British who have direct investment in the trade, to the equally famous thirst-quenching green wines like *vinhos verdes*, just right for a warm-weathered city. Perhaps not so known is the Moscatel de Setúbal, which comes from just outside Lisbon, a dessert wine that is very sweet—and will come as no surprise after days of eating *doces* (egg sweet things).

This national palate for sweetness is thought to originate from the five hundred years of occupation by the Moors. In the seventeenth and eighteenth centuries, visitors to Lisbon told of visiting the convents to talk with the nuns, attend poetry recitals, and be tempted with sweet dishes. It seems that many of the egg-and-sugar desserts came into existence in the convents, some betraying their origins in their names: Toucinho do Céu (Bacon from Heaven), Papos de Anjos de Mirandela (Angel's Double Chins), Barriga de Freira (Nun's Belly)… all extremely sweet, of course. With names like that, who couldn't face the day without getting their teeth into such delights. (To temper the humor, I should add that during this time many of the convents were more like "aristocratic brothels," the inhabitants "more or less" nuns.) Personally, I try the *pudim flan* (crème caramel) regularly when out eating, judging its consistency, whether it melts in the mouth (though some are made with small crunchy bits in them), and the caramel, the art of burning the sugar just enough to make caramel and not turn the dessert into a total ruin of bittersweetness.

Cinnamon is probably the most used spice, a discovery by Vasco da Gama, who sought black pepper and found cinnamon. Cinnamon is sprinkled across so many of the egg sweets, whether the nun's belly or the famous *pastéis de nata* (custard tart) that are the staple diet on all true seekers of palatal pleasure in Lisbon.

It is worth keeping one's eye open for *marmelada*, perhaps at the breakfast table, not to be confused with marmalade (though the English marmalade of bitter orange jam may well be derived from the same idea). *Marmelada* is made from quince, and has a taste that relates to pear, though a stronger perfume. It is in reality a quince jam, although its firmness also allows it to be cut into slices and eaten in that form, providing it with a somewhat distracting name, quince cheese.

One of the pleasures of Tabucchi's *Requiem* is the attention he affords to food and drink throughout the book, often detailing the recipes. I can understand that preference in an Italian, my own family background on my mother's side pointing me in that direction. Hence, when sitting on the castle walls, or walking through the cathedral cloisters, it seems such a sacrilege to me to observe the amount of fruit from the orange and lemon trees that have fallen to rot on the ground, fruit that could have been savored. I guess something of *saudade* comes into play here, not a feeling I necessarily experience at home when neighbors squander their apple trees, or abandon the wild blackberries in abundance along the pathways. Probably the relating of oranges and lemons to warmer climes and the desire to remain there are the underlying reasons. Edite Vieira in her book on Portuguese food, *The Taste of Portugal*, talks of her *matando saudades* for Portuguese food. She means that living abroad from her homeland, if she is to relieve her painful feelings she must "*matar saudades* (*matar* means to kill, hence to kill that deep nostalgia) by doing whatever is needed for the purpose. In this case... cooking."

# 6. Tram 28

## Cemitério dos Prazeres

Unless visiting the Cemitério dos Prazeres (Pleasures Cemetery), or rising from it, not so many will start the Tram 28 ride at this terminus. Not that the cemetery is a morbid place. No Lisbon cemetery is that. Prior to the place becoming a cemetery, it was an area for celebration, hence the name, and it appears that rejoicing and merry-making continued among the graves until forbidden by law. Today the color is maintained by the remarkable quantity of flowers piled on and around graves, evidence of serious remembrance going on here, the flowers being not only for the recently deceased.

Many of the famous reside in these grounds. It is regarded as *the* Lisbon cemetery, even if not the biggest. Amália Rodrigues is here. And Pessoa was here, until he was removed to be part of a national monument at Belém.

Saramago puts in an earlier appearance with Reis in *The Year of the Death of Ricardo Reis.* Barely a month after Pessoa's funeral, just after Reis' own arrival from Brazil, "he starts to descend the road lined with poplars, in search of the grave numbered four thousand three hundred and seventy-one." At that time there was a predominance of chapels. "On either side, the chapels of the family tombs are locked, the windows are covered with curtains made of lace, the finest linen like that of hankerchiefs, the most delicate flowers, embroidered between two plants, or in heavy crochet made with needles like naked swords, or saying *richelieu* or *ajour*, Gallicisms pronounced God alone knows how." And then he finds it: "These are titles of property and occupation, the tomb of Dona Dionísia de Seabra Pessoa inscribed on the front, under the overhanging eaves of this sentry box where the sentinel, a romantic touch, is sleeping. Below, at the height of the door's lower hinge, another name and nothing more, that of Fernando Pessoa, with the dates of his birth and death, and the gilded outline of a funeral urn that says, I am here." Reis ruminates on the mad old woman, grandmother Dionísia, "she keeping vigil with eyes wide open," and her grandson Fernando, "he with eyes averted, looking for a gap, a breath of air, a glimmer of light..."

Tabucchi visits too, in *Requiem*, but in a more circuitous way; after all, his hero has arranged to meet Pessoa later that day. His arrival at the gate by taxi is to buy a fresh shirt, as he has been pouring with sweat, and being a Sunday it is not easy to purchase another until the taxi driver reminds him that the gypsies have a stall outside the cemetery. He buys a Lacoste polo shirt, two in fact. Once the purchase is secured, the Old Gypsy Woman proceeds to explain to him why he is sweating profusely, grabbing his left hand: "Listen, my dear, she said, this can't go on, you can't live in two worlds at once, in the world of reality and the world of dreams, that kind of thing leads to hallucinations, you're like a sleepwalker walking through a landscape with your arms outstretched, and everything you touch becomes part of your dream." Then she grabs the right: "I see that you have to visit someone, she said, but the house you're looking for exists only in your memory or in your dream, (…) the person you're looking for is right here, on the other side of that gate." And so in he goes to the cemetery and inquires of the keeper the location of the grave of the person he is looking for. And we think he'll say Pessoa. But it's not Pessoa, but another friend, for a parallel course is being pursued, a game. "Tadeus Waclaw Slowacki. He was the son of Polish parents, I explained, but he wasn't Polish himself, he was well and truly Portuguese, he even chose a Portuguese pseudonym. And what did he do?, asked the Keeper. Well, I said, he worked, but he was mainly a writer." They locate him in the register at number 4664. A reversible number—another game. The gravestone bears a photo taken a week after his release from prison, for political reasons, Tadeus clutching the French newspaper that helped secure his release from Salazar's prison. The image is out of focus, and he thinks "time swallowed up everything." He calls to his friend, he needs to resolve a problem that has been niggling away for years inside, and his friend is lying in wait, so to speak, ready to take it a step further.

Going deep into the cemetery, walking at its boundaries, any prospect of silence is broken by the sound of a humming, a sound like a hive. It's possible to look over the wall at various points, to realize that the cemetery ends sharply, the slope falling fast away towards the main feed to the Ponte 25 de Abril. On further study one can see the shanty town slum, the one known as the Casal Ventoso, its proximity to the cemetery appropriate given the reputation it has for drug overdosing.

## Tram 28

Tram 28 awaits outside in the Largo. Whichever way one looks at the cemetery experience, French writer Olivier Frébourg's note that "the tram is time suspended" doesn't fall short, even before we depart.

Ahead lies a six-mile ride across the heart of the city, from one high spot to another, from the cemetery across to Estrela, then clanking hard into the Bairro Alto and on down, screeching to the Baixa and up the other side, skirting around the castle in search of the path across the Alfama fringes and up to Graça, and, if indicated, further, to wind back down looping to the Martim Moniz behind the Rossio. This takes the good part of an hour and a half, not that the clock is ticking, for this is not a taxi.

Tram 28 is the main tram ride in the city, or one of the main tram rides in Europe, many say. Even in the world, others add. Better to climb aboard and flash our pass, which means we can step on and off if we desire, or go all the way and then turn round and come back again. We've all the time in the world.

Where before there was a whole system of these trams, the *eléctricos*, that criss-crossed the city, many have now gone to pasture, the tramlines being a danger to other traffic and pedestrians. Thankfully, the enthusiasm of the city authorities did not get out of hand and remove all; they have held back on the breaker's yard with a few, particularly the most known, like number 28.

Although they look old, like something from the past, there is an elegance about them. Perhaps it is to do with our nostalgia for our childhood toy cars: Dinky Toys, Matchbox. Not that the latter existed yet as a brand in 1930, but I mention them to give more resonance for us to appreciate Pessoa's lines: "They look like giant yellow mobile matchboxes, in which a child has stuck a slanted used match to serve as a mast. When jerking into motion, they give a loud, iron whistle."

The frame might be of steel, but the timberwork paneling is what is on view. And there is a sense of color about them too, most being two tones, one of yellow, the other a form of white, with smatterings of other colors, like red for the Coca-Cola advertising. All have advertising on them, some with style rather than brashness. The British had a hand in their building, or their re-fitting according to another source, acknowledged with cast-iron little plaques, quite visible, in this case with the phrase "Made in England" emblazoned on it.

These trams are not a tourist trap, but an everyday part of the transport system, a necessary facility for going up and down the steep hills. What else can effectively clamber up the impossible gradients, or squeeze through some of the narrow streets offered as posers? These carriages, or cars, are not large. They are agile. And yet they hold a good number of passengers. Many people can stand inside (they have to, particularly on the busy sections of the route), but there are at least two dozen seats, and one of the memorable city sights is to see the tram pass in the street, with its passengers seated by their lifted windows, elbows on sill, watching life progress at its leisurely pace. It is probably for some of these reasons that the handful of survivors has been retained, for they are still effective on this landscape, even if "quaint." That they enhance the atmosphere of the city is a bonus.

There is not a lot to look at once we set off from the Prazeres but a wide avenue. Things are not into their stride as yet. Only when we turn into Rua Domingos de Sequeira, on the hill down towards the Basílica da Estrela does something attract attention, for there is the derelict Paris cinema that has aged a little more since Wim Wenders used it as one of his symbols for the dereliction of cinema today in *Lisbon Story*. In 1982 he used the Texas Bar in *The State of Things*, and later in 1994 he filmed in the Paris cinema, both in Lisbon. And in between he made the film that sealed his international standing, *Paris, Texas* (1984). Wenders likes these little points. His films

a dor de cabeça sai ,a na prox'ma.

hold together as an *oeuvre*; there are threads that weave their magic, not just a length of common string to tie films to the Hollywood stake.

## Estrela

The tram halts at the Praça da Estrela, before the huge Basílica with its large white dome, another feature of the cityscape. Some trams in fact stop here when coming in the opposite direction, never going as far as the cemetery, their main ride through the center accomplished. Stop right outside the gates to the gardens. A walk through this park brings one to the Cemitério dos Ingleses (English cemetery) on the other side, where among the cypresses Henry Fielding is buried. Whether it is actually Fielding beneath the monument is anyone's guess, after the shenanigans performed by various people over the centuries. "The bones it covers may possibly have belonged to an idiot," Dorothy Quillinan noted. And nearby too, just along the Rua Coelho da Rocha stands the house where Pessoa lived for his last fifteen years and that has now been made into a functional literary center, rather than a mausoleum. Walking back, I swore I saw Ophélia Queiroz, the only love of Pessoa, sitting on a bench in the park, where they met, watching the children play, dreaming. Or was I?

For preference I would rather have sat with Maria Gabriela Llansol, for real or her phantom, who writes in her diary of coming here: "Grows the panic that one speaks of me when I'll die. To be dead for me and living for others, ontologically what does that mean?"

## From Bairro Alto to Baixa

From here the tram is about to start accumulating passengers, and to be tested for its metal, for the next stage is to go from the Estrela hilltop down and up to the Bairro Alto, the inclines not so much the problem as the narrowness and the traffic of the streets.

It will be somewhere along this stretch that the tram is first taken by the horns, or at least that we notice the screeches and grumbles of the grinding steel. This music will become a more complete accompaniment as the journey progresses. Along this section too, the children start to hop on the back, hold on for a few blocks and then jump off. This is not to be copied. They are competent at what they are doing, they know the ins and outs, when the angled turns give a sudden jolt and they have to hold tight, not to be left sprawled in the road at the mercy of the following traffic. Adults grabbing on for a free ride are not welcomed, indeed the driver is likely to stop the vehicle and climb down to admonish them. Only children have free carriage. It is almost as if the handrails are there for the benefit of these young outriders.

Coming down the Calçada da Estrela one sees a high wall and what appear splendid gardens hidden from view, only to discover at the bottom that it is the rear of the Palácio da Assembleia Nacional (National Assembly). Originally, like many buildings, it was connected to religious usage, as a convent. First used as a parliament in 1833, it has been considerably altered since.

As we pass along the Calçada do Combro, looking at the bookstores where we have spent pleasant hours, at a restaurant we have visited a few times (enough to warrant free drinks to end our evenings), we pass the Elevador da Bica. At its height the funicular is disgorging a group of Japanese tourists, just as in *Taxi Lisboa*, these too with laughing faces, seeking a fresh adventure. Jammed in the traffic at the end of the Rua Loreto, peering into the cube that was formerly the Praça Luís Camões, finally we edge off again and negotiate the junction, smiling at the Japanese who have overtaken us on foot and flock like pigeons over Pessoa outside A Brasileira. And then we are grinding and swinging, on a rollercoaster ride, heading down towards the Baixa, with metallic groans as the driver holds its steel wheels hard, switching his lever, trying not to let the car run away with itself.

It is the tram ride that places Pessoa in a different frame from most: *I don't need fast cars or express trains to feel the delight and terror of speed. All I need is a tram and the astonishing capacity for abstraction that I'd been given and that I cultivate. On a tram in motion I'm able, through a continual and instantaneous analysis, to separate the idea of the car from the idea of speed, separating them completely, until they're different real-entities. Then I can feel myself riding not in the tram but in its mere-speed. And, should I get bored and want the delirium of inordinate speed, I can transfer the idea to the Pure imitation of speed, increasing or decreasing it at will, stretching it beyond the fastest possible speeds of trains.*

## Sé Catedral

With Pessoa on board, we start our climb up towards the Castelo de São Jorge (St. George's Castle), swinging round the Madalena and pulling hard to tackle the climb; first port of call the Sé Catedral, heaving the hairpins.

Most old cities are built around their cathedrals, but not Lisbon. This one appears as an inconvenience in the road up the hill, an obstacle to be steered around. Sé is the abbreviation of *sedes episcopais*, the Sé Patriarcal de Lisboa. The Sé, as it is known, is somewhat disappointing for a cathedral. It was built for the crusader-priest Gilbert of Hastings, when he became the first bishop of Lisbon, by Dom Afonso Henriques, although much has been done to it since that time as a result of earthquake damage, not only in 1755, but earlier quakes from 1337-47.

In 1383 a riotous crowd flung Bishop Dom Martinho Anes unceremoniously from its north tower, because he was Castilian, "owing to his partiality to the policy of Dona Leonor Telles" is how Pessoa explained it. His death unknown to Pope Clement VII in Rome, he appointed him a cardinal seventeen days too late.

In the sacristy is a museum, which includes a casket containing the relics of St. Vincent, although others say there are none since the 1755 quake when they were scattered. Legend has it that two ravens escorted a boat containing the body of St. Vincent into Lisbon from Valencia, where he was martyred. Ravens became one of the city's symbols, and the image of a sailing boat with a raven fore and aft can often be seen in unexpected places, including street lamps or pavements, as well as in the city's coat-of-arms. Though he never saw Lisbon alive, he was made patron saint of the city. Later he was displaced by St. Anthony of Padua, who was born in Lisbon in 1195, a little further down the hill, but finished his life in Italy. To commemorate his birthplace a little church, Santo António da Sé, has been built over the spot. St. Anthony of Lisbon, as he is known locally, was a missionary who performed miracles in Italy, entering the newly founded order of St. Francis of Assisi and dying in Padua. He was canonized within a day, which is the quickest anyone has made it to sainthood. He is often regarded as the patron saint of lost things, which is appropriate in Lisbon, at least with bearings if you believe in using the maps as your guide. The festival of his birth is the occasion for Lisbon's biggest celebration each year in June, with the grilling of *sardinhas* and dancing in the streets.

The Sé also boasts a fine Baroque organ, "a blaster" as one friend informed me. A recent performance can be heard by the contemporary group *Osso Exótico*, half of their series of church organ works recorded in the Sé, though at times I feel the spirit of the American minimalist Terry Riley is lurking behind the pipes once they progress from the ambient to ramblings akin to awaiting the bride's arrival or the deceased's departure—strange how often it's the same style of improvisations.

This side of the city, this hill, is the setting for another book by Saramago, *The History of the Siege of Lisbon* (1989), in which his main character finds himself drawn into studying the history around him: "I have lived in Lisbon all my life and it has never occurred to me to come and see with my own eyes things described in books, things that I have often looked at time and time again, without actually seeing them, as blind as the muezzin." And so he begins his search:

> *Perhaps if we were to remove this modern paving in the Largo de Santo Antonio in front of the Cathedral, and dig deep down, we should discover the foundations of the period, the rusted remains of ancient weapons, the stench of a tomb, the entangled skeletons of warriors, not lovers, who shouted in unison, Dog, and then proceeded to kill each other. Cars pass up and down, the trams creak round the bend of the Madalena, they are on the 28 route, particularly esteemed by film directors, and yonder, turning in front of the Cathedral, goes another bus full of tourists, they must be French and imagine they are in Spain.*

## Around the Castelo de São Jorge

The tram does not go all the way up to the castle door, it is not an invader, you have to do that under your own steam. It skirts around the base, taking a breather at the Largo das Portas do Sol before going on. We will return later to admire the view from one or other of the spots. All we see at the moment is that solitary palm that rises from among the streets below. It is as if the tram drivers do not want to stop too long because they know that delays are about to become part of the journey as we approach the single-track section. Here are the possibilities of cars blocking the way, or gentle confusions of cars unable to turn the sharp bends and having to wriggle back and forth to get into a suitable turning circle. Inside the tramcar, everyone looks out without a care, it's all a usual feature of the ride.

Rose Macaulay, who undoubtedly lived in a different world from me, admired "the trams, which were as pretty as wasps humming on their way." The image that comes to my mind seems more connected to the art work of Jean Tinguely, the Swiss sculptor, creator of those kinetic machines that function in their own way, not necessarily a function that relates to productivity. Machines made from ready-made pieces of iron junk, chaotic frameworks, welded playtoys from an age of obsolescence, with series upon series of geared wheels that waste their potential, joyfully, "an aesthetic out of 'mal' function," as art critic Guy Brett stated. Although not so much the self-destructive machines, *for an end of the world*, but machines that grind and groan, back and forth, shudder and judder, making every effort to attract our attention, watch them in all their mechanical glory as they pass us by. And this tram is going somewhere. It is about to snake downhill and find a way across the fringes of the Alfama before climbing again to the Graça heights and perhaps beyond to Martim Moriz, as I had forgotten the destination on the front, it being so long ago.

Picking up on Saramago's reference to film directors' use of this route, this is the section of the ride that is most captured on film. Tanner and Wenders have favored this area, mainly because the track is reduced to one line at times, with all the attendant problems for two-way traffic. And also because the streets become so narrow that if you lean out at the slow points you can almost stick your head, or hand, inside someone's window. But the idea that "you are so close to the shops that you could almost take a can of sardines off the shelves," is something of a fiction on that friend's part, as no shop I've seen would leave itself so vulnerable, even in relaxed Lisbon.

As we start the slide down from the junction where a large Mercedes proves that it has no place in these small streets, we recognize a spot where Wenders set up to capture the trams crossing the screen, and each other, as his couple run up the steep Alfama street, escaping Winter, and vanish in *Until the End of the World* (1991). It is another favorite Wenders shot, always including transport, always on the move, on the road. And Winter is a joke, relating to Phillip Winter, the character Wenders has used in three films to date, with the same actor, Rüdiger Vogler, his arrival at the house in *Lisbon Story* being announced with: "Winter's here!"

Another time at this spot on the short flight of streets, having ourselves emerged from that same Alfama street and crossed the Rua das Escolas Gerais to rest on the steps up to the next street, the Rua de São Tomé, we watch Tram 28 swing down the incline and turn abruptly along the straight. It is a corner that offers a ruminative view of the trams in action in addition to views into the Alfama, the long winding street just climbed. Once I noticed that someone had scratched, if not etched, into the wall the initials WW, perhaps a marking by one of the crew, or an enthusiast after the fact. A little later, re-reading the American novelist Paul Auster's *City of Glass* (1985), I recalled that William Wilson is the crime-writing pseudonym of Auster's character Quinn, in the same way as Paul Benjamin was the pseudonym for Auster in his own less successful attempts to write crime novels at an earlier stage. Not that it matters now. All is assimilated, and the mystery goes into the other novels. And Benjamin becomes the actor William Hurt and another film unrolls in *Smoke* (1995). What has this to do with a wall in Lisbon? More than one thinks. Wenders and Auster are friends. Auster wrote a script for Wenders, to be shot in Lisbon, according to an interview I found with the Belgian critic Alain Delaunois in a pamphlet published in Liège, although the project came to nothing, as is frequently the case with so many scripts. Wenders went on to develop the idea in another way and make *Lisbon Story*, while Auster himself determined to use the script, making it later as *Lulu on the Bridge* (1998). Was it all just another chance, or should we bear in mind that some years earlier, in *Wall Writing*, the title of Auster's book of poems collected in 1976, the title poem ends:

*Or the whiteness of a word,*
*scratched*
*into the wall.*

This is the point when the clanging of the bell is heard most often, with blind alleys, cars clogging the streets or people wandering in the road, as the driver hangs on the metal bell to warn of his arrival, as if one hadn't heard the tram's grindings. But what other form of revenge have the tram drivers on the modern car and its horns?

Once upon a time, and not so long ago too, men were employed to regulate the trams when reduced to single track along this stretch and similar stretches. They used a system of ping-pong paddles, which went into the night, when oil lanterns with red and green glass took over the procedure. The system had a stop-go nature, human traffic lights, all at the whim of the man with the paddles, if not on a first come first served basis. Today traffic lights have brought the trams into the modern era.

Snaking its way through the narrow streets, Tram 28 finally heaves a sigh as the road widens slightly and aims up the Rua Voz do Operario towards Graça, which was once a wealthier area than today, with its worker's area stamp, almost a town in itself. But before we reach the top, we alight with other passengers.

### Feira da Ladra

On Tuesdays and Saturdays there are always extra passengers destined for the Feira da Ladra (fleamarket) that clutters the Campo de Santa Clara. There are times when a visit has an edge of interest, there are others when everything seems pedestrian. Some visits bring forth treasures while others leave one cold, but it's probably the same with most markets. Perhaps one has to be in a market mood. Anything can be bought here, whether books, various crafts, or shoes—there is a large gathering of shoe stalls, with prices that make you wonder how you ever bought them

elsewhere. The fleamarket side is more an amusement, much of it what most would have termed discarded rubbish and disposed of accordingly (perhaps at New Year, out the window). Or there are characters selling tiles of uncertain provenance, always fragments, mementos for the tourist. Almost daily on one's travels one finds tiles lying at the bottom of a wall, always broken bits as if the person who had tried to prise them off during the night had snapped them, abandoned them. Feira da Ladra is regularly translated as Thieves' Market, but *ladra* also means "chattering" and "din," which is more how it is these days. Ghettoblasters fill the air, sometimes with *fados*, although predominantly with music from former African colonies, from stalls selling their crafts.

With little purchased, the area is always worth seeing for the tiles on its walls, whether whole façades of patterned tilework or elaborate images, particularly on the street as one walks round to the large white church, the Igreja e Mosteiro de São Vicente de Fora (Church and Monastery of St. Vincent Outside the Walls). Fora means outside, because the church was built outside the medieval walls of the city, and thus outside the jurisdiction of the Bishop of Lisbon. Although the story of St. Vincent's arrival in Lisbon was related earlier, it was not until hundreds of years later that the Spanish King, Philip II took it upon himself to build the church in honor of the saint.

It was built by Filippo Terzi and Baltasar Alvares, between 1582 and 1627, over the old cemetery of the Teutonic Knights, inspired by the Jesuit church in Rome, its large white limestone façade being one of the features of the skyline of Lisbon, along with its two square corner towers. The Great Earthquake of 1755 brought down its dome, and another was built. The great *retábulo* of the Infante by Nuno Gonçalves that also stood there was later transferred to the Museu Nacional de Arte Antiga.

The refectory of the monastery was selected as the Bragança Pantheon in 1855 by Dom Fernando II, and since then the remains of several members of that dynasty of kings and queens of Portugal, from Dom João IV through to Dom Manuel II, the last king, who died in exile in England in 1932, rest there. Earlier the coffins had glass tops to enable the embalmed bodies to "spy on the world." Catherine of Bragança returned from England after her husband's death and was later entombed here. There is little presence in this pantheon.

## Graça and Beyond

Back at the Largo da Graça is another *miradouro* at the Esplanada da Igreja da Graça that provides the locals with a space to sit and ponder, better than the castle with its hordes of tourists. Or there is another spot a bit further up the road, called Miradouro da Nossa Senhora do Monte. Unlike man's gradual change, even if slow in these parts of Lisbon, nature usually doesn't change that quickly, and Aubrey Bell's description of the sunset from the Graça must have been almost the same then, a hundred years ago, as now:

> When the evening light is on the windows and the sun "lance son dernier adieu" (casts its last goodbye) in flame of gold on every pane, while the clear blue sky forms a background to this mass of houses, the effect is most weird and beautiful; as the afterglow dies, white and yellow lights appear here and there along the hill in street and window. Everything in Lisbon, the sky, the air, the colours of the houses, the lamps at night in narrow streets or shining through leaves of trees, is soft and beautiful.

Below stretches what used to be called Mouraria, although there is not much left now, nor the pottery works and the olive oil refineries. The Mouraria was the old Moorish quarter where the Moors settled once driven from the castle walls in 1147. At its base is the Martim Moniz (in tribute to the soldier who held the city gate open at the cost of his life during the siege), which has had years of upheavals in recent times as planners destroyed and rebuilt, now leaving it as rather an inglorious, albeit modern-looking, square—a city hall disaster location. To reach it in a roundabout way is to get back on the tram and take the long loop round. A rapid pealing of the bell indicates that the journey is over, everybody out. Whether you wish to stay around is another matter. Best to rush off in any direction, though it's perhaps not best to do this at night, as it's not an idea of paradise that all would choose. From pleasures to disasters, from death to life!

If the day is over, you could ask the driver whether you can hitch a ride to the depot, where the *eléctricos* are jammed together, nuzzled down for the night, one depot almost directly beneath a concrete pillar of the Ponte 25 de Abril on the Rua da Junqueira.

# 7. Castelo de São Jorge

While the castle is not the highest point in Lisbon, it does occupy the complete top of a hill. Other hill points that are good for viewing are just points, *miradouros*. The castle, as one would expect, was built to be the city's protector, to be fortified against attack. These days the only attack it receives is from tourists clambering over its towers and battlements to view the city in all its panoramic glory, or from the builders who rejuvenate the walls, making them not so much whiter than white, but seeming to take away any sense of antiquity. They look far too presentable, only fit for dignitaries to visit, or as a background for gentrified apartments. The restaurant in the castle is indeed an expensive place to come to eat, although the pleasure is to be surrounded by a variety of birds that indicate they own the place, the latest invaders, including peacocks, pheasants, flamingoes, pelicans, swans, geese and ducks. As the colors of the city are black and white, there is an emphasis on birds of that color—hence black swans, I believe, and ravens, though they also have a further symbolic value for the city.

The castle presides over the old areas of Lisbon, the Alfama spreading from the southwest to the south, between it and the river, the Rossio at its eastern foot, Mouraria and Graça to its north. It was constructed by the Moors, but prior to that it had been inhabited by the Phoenicians, then built upon by the Romans and the Visigoths, who raised the first fortifications. In 1147 Dom Afonso Henriques besieged the castle and drove out the Moors, who had been established for four centuries. The history of that action is not as glorious as many would like to think.

Afonso Henriques, who had taken to calling himself King of Portugal after his defeat of the Moors at Ourique some years earlier in 1139, determined to take Lisbon. To help him in this task he persuaded a band of crusaders en route for Palestine to detour and assist in the attack. With promises that all the enemy's loot was theirs if the city was taken, the bunch of adventurers, comprising English, Flemish, French and Germans, set about the assault in June 1147. At first the Moors were not worried, proclaiming: "How many times within your memory have you come hither with pilgrims and barbarians to drive us hence?" They managed to hold off the attack for seventeen weeks. Eventually, in October, the Christians (described by another observer as "plunderers, drunkards and rapists... men not seasoned with the honey of piety") took control and set about pillaging the city, murdering all, whether Muslim or Christian, ignoring all pledges of leniency that Afonso had held out to the losers. The only one who seems to have shown any mercy was Gilbert of Hastings, an English priest with the party, who was later to become the Bishop of Lisbon. Another English priest, Osbern of Bawdsley, wrote a full account of the episode. The siege is depicted in *azulejos* (tiles) on the walls of the nearby Igreja de Santa Luzia (Church of Santa Luzia).

Afonso rebuilt the defenses and added further fortifications. His statue stands at the entrance today. Although the main citadel was a palace, the kings only lived there until the fifteenth century, when Dom Manuel preferred grander accommodation adjoining the Terreiro do Paço at the edge of the Tagus.

### Beyond the Walls
With a view from the walls that stretches across the Baixa to the Bairro Alto, or down to the Tagus with the Ponte 25 de Abril, and further to Belém and across to the banks on the south of the river, this has traditionally been a place to sit and look. There is little else to do. Others watch children march along singing "I'm the king of the castle" or variations on that theme in several languages. Many a visitor's photograph has been taken, and not only by amateurs. Henri Cartier-Bresson on his trip to Lisbon in 1955 took a famous photo of three old men seated there, taking their daily constitutional, one with an umbrella as shade, backed by the classic scapes of city and river. There are still many old people, mainly tourists, but one feels that the old people who live locally and who might have come here are getting fewer as they pass on to another world. Their houses are rejuvenated and sold to a younger generation, who might be more interested in getting on with life, with being upright European citizens.

Vergílio Ferreira's narrator, in his novel, *Na Tua Face* (1993), would like to visit his daughter more often. She lives near the castle, but it's

"further and further because it's less and less easy to go there." By which he means that tourism makes it more and more difficult to find a place to park. But the view is splendid, "the views are light and airy, like a smile."

Over the plunging walls, which the Christians tried to storm all those years ago, one peers down into the gardens of the houses, and their fruit-laden trees, many of the splendid oranges and lemons rotting, as previously mentioned.

In *Lisbonne, dernière marge* (1990), the French novelist Antoine Volodine's couple look over the parapet of the castle at the vast space of the city below them: "and everywhere tens of thousands of roofs, mainly covered in tiles, and houses tinted somewhat roughly." They wonder why it could be called the "white city." And the question is valid from this angle, with the waves of red or rose terra-cotta. Volodine's novel is a more recent addition to the genre that sees Lisbon as escape route, as a passage through to another continent, but this time for a member of Germany's Red Army Faction. The choice of Lisbon is bound in with the manuscript of a book that Ingrid Vogel is carrying, written under another name, the loose tie-in with Pessoa another link with the city.

Within the *intramuros* of the castle was the medieval quarter of Santa Cruz, now mainly a few touristic shops and restaurants. Coming away from the castle is easier than going up, although the rule for finding the place has always been to just keep going upwards. Up the wall, I imagine. Unless it is meant that once you reach the wall, you have to go around it, which is quite a way, to find the entrance. As one comes away from the gate, the Pátio de Dom Fradique is directly before you along the Rua do Chão da Feira, which you can either go through, or turn sharp right and keep to the road.

## Palácio Belmonte
Outside the Pátio (or Yard) there is still an old street urinal, its smell indicating usage, although tourists brave a stupid face, hold their breathe and pose for the click. In the Pátio is housed a luxury hotel, the Palácio Belmonte. The transformation occurred a few years ago when a Frenchman took over the building, fallen into decay, and decided to renovate it and reinstate some of its glory. It appears to be a large building, virtually a palace, with staircases, large rooms, tiled rooms and a big patio. Wenders' *Lisbon Story* was filmed there before the conversion, and those not willing or able to pay for the accommodation can see some of its inner sights and size in the film, as Winter, the sound engineer, sets up camp among the absconded director's belongings and begins to work on the film within the film, while upstairs the local group, Madredeus, rehearse their music. Not all of the interior shots were accomplished here; others were shot in an old abandoned convent across the river in Sesimbra. Unable to foot the bill, even for one night, we walk on through the arch and into the open area beyond, where many of the old houses have been tumbled. Enough is left to recognize locations both from *Lisbon Story* and Tanner's *In the White City*. The latter, shot a decade before, includes a scene where Paul goes to visit Rosa's parents in search of her new Paris address, a tight shot designed to exclude some of the area's dereliction.

Raúl Ruiz also returned to Lisbon to film *Dark at Noon* (1992) with John Hurt, using this large building, pre-conversion. On this occasion he had enough time and money to spend setting up complex shots, such as furniture on tracks that move in the opposite direction to the traveling camera, giving a spatial dislocation, an effect repeated in his more recent adaptation of Proust, *Time Regained* (1999).

## Pessoa and Crowley
Within the network of streets around the castle we chanced one day upon a small bookstore that specialized in the occult, the only one in

which I ever saw Pessoa's writings on the occult for sale:

> *I wasted nights of terror pouring over tomes of mystics and cabalists,*
> *which I was never patient enough to read in their entirety except with an*
> *intermittent trembling and... The rites and tenets of the Rosicrucians, the*
> *symbolism of the Cabbala and the Templars ... I suffered from their prox-*
> *imity for a long time. And they feverishly inundated my days of poisonous*
> *speculations, with demonical logic of metaphysics — magic... alchemy —*
> *and I extracted a false vital stimulus of painful, prescient feelings of always*
> *being on the edge of discovering a supreme mystery.*

So wrote Pessoa in *The Book of Disquietude*. Pessoa had an interest in the occult for most of his adult life, these other writings and notes collected in a volume. The occult, astrology, theosophism, freemasonry, table tapping, magic... had a substantial following in parts of Europe during the early twentieth century, mainly as a result of quakes in religious belief, advances in science and increased attention to material wealth. At one point Pessoa also had plans to set himself up as an astrologer. In 1915 he undertook translations of the works of Amy Besant, C.W.Leadbeater and Mme. Blavatsky. Aleister Crowley was another who loomed into sight. Pessoa corresponded with him, although Crowley only knew him as a student of the occult (in particular the shared interest in the Great God Pan), until he decided to visit Lisbon in September 1930, bringing along a young female companion, Hanni Jaeger. When the steamer *Alcântara* docked, Pessoa was there to welcome the couple. They stayed at the Hôtel de l'Europe. Crowley was unimpressed with the city: "God once tried to wake up Lisbon—with an earthquake; he gave it up as a bad job." There is a recently published photo that shows Crowley and Pessoa seated across a chessboard in a Lisbon café. It looks extremely sedate, not the image one might expect. It is undoubtedly Crowley, but is it Pessoa? There is a question mark here. The man is seated with his hat and coat, but it is a side profile and does not appear to convince entirely.

What seems more appealing is the story that Crowley faked his suicide in the Boca do Inferno (Hell's Mouth) just outside Lisbon, along the Cascais coast. The Crowley-friendly location site occurs where the Atlantic waters crash and resonate in the cave, or as Paul Hyland has it: "gulps, throbs, sounds airy bass notes, spews water from blow-holes and, when the sea withdraws, sighs spookily and takes a panicky breath." Pessoa aided Crowley by enlightening the Press about the suicide, providing the note found, signed "Tu Li You"—not Crowley as a Chinese sage, but simply the farewell sign "toodle-oo". Of course, not long afterwards, given a suitable lying low period, more than three days, Crowley re-emerged, risen from the dead it seems, to continue with his life. Some say his female companion Hanni (known affectionately as Anu) left him because the "sexual magick" was too much for her to endure, and that the fake suicide was a ruse to win her back, as noted in his diary. Another less-publicized story is written by Pessoa's friend, the poet Roy Campbell, whose opinion of Crowley is quite clear: "the fatuous impostor, Aleister Crowley, the diabolist, dogmatic immoralist, sadist, and black-magic expert." This tale is somewhat different:

> ...and if I had not (in complete ignorance of Pessoa's dealings with this idiotic monster) shortened the latter's stay in Portugal, in my role of an épateur de bohémiens (flattener of bohemians), by planting a pair of explosive banderillas in his enormous posterior on the cliffs at Cascais, so that he beat an ignominious retreat home to England where he had to lie doggo for fear of ridicule, and to sleep face-downward for weeks—God only knows to what lengths of credulous self-mystification Pessoa might not have gone!

### Around the Castle

The French writer Guillaume le Blanc draws on the artist Vieira da Silva for his book, *Lisbonne au coeur* (2000), for not only does he acknowledge the title and section headings as inspired by her paintings, but names his character Héléna after the artist. His story is set around the castle: "The castle is like a lover who brings calm and majesty to the world." Il Gato Preto, the café-restaurant in the nearby Rua de Saudade is his precise focus. This is a road that also serves Tabucchi in *Declares Pereira*, his journalist living in a flat in the street, although the address turns out to be a non-existent number, 22, the author playing with numbers as is his regular habit.

One of Eça de Queirós' translators, Richard Franko Goldman, notes in his introduction to *The Mandarin* (1880) that "Eça was a fluent writer, but an indefatigable polisher, revising and correcting his work through all the stages of proof-reading and final publication."

He makes this point because some of the other stories in the collection he has been translating "abound in evidences of unrevised hasty writing, and, strange to say, in typographical errors perpetuated from edition to edition." Goldman adds: "Eça remarked that there is no criticism in Portugal; he might have added that there seems to be little proof-reading." The translator and proofreader are two readers of a text who are in a position to notice the errors; the translator is often left to tear hair out over what might appear a small error to some, but which can have far-reaching consequences for the whole text, particularly if no-one is available (or alive) to confirm if it is indeed an error. It is this line of thought that Saramago pursues in his novel, *The History of the Siege of Lisbon*, which follows the protagonist, Raimundo Silva, a proofreader who decides to insert a "not" in the text he is proofing, to say that the crusaders did "not" help Dom Afonso Henriques to lay siege to the castle. The consequences of this decision do more than affect the book, they take life in a different direction, as Raimundo's relationship with his superior at the publishing house, Maria Sara, develops into a love affair on the one hand, and Raimundo steps into research of the historical facts, on the other. He realizes that he himself lives within the outer walls of the castle, along the Rua do Milagre de Santo António, but that he has never explored it in the light of its history, only watched the tourists. "The idea, which came to him as he watched the roof-tops descending like steps as far as the river, is to follow the lay-out of the Moorish fortifications according to the scant and rather dubious information provided by the historian." By deduction he realizes that he is "on the outer side of the city, he belongs to the besieging army." Then "he realizes for the first time that he lives at the very spot where the Porta de Alfofa stood, whether on the inside or outside it is no longer possible to tell, so we cannot be sure whether Raimundo Silva is one of the besieged or an assailant, a future conqueror or hopeless loser." Using the image of the watch-tower position, Saramago has a way within the same sentence (paragraph-length sentences, akin to streams of consciousness) to swing from subjective to objective, from past to present, enabling him in this case to draw a new story through the parallel of his present love affair with another drawn from the time of the siege.

Raimundo determines to walk the area, to trace the remains, looking for something to transform him "into a Moorish soldier watching the shadowy forms of the enemy." He "hopes to receive, as tangible evidence, the detail missing from the narrative, namely, the indisputable reason for the crusaders' departure after that decisive *Not*." Once it occurs to him, he decides to write his own book of *The History of the Siege of Lisbon*. Saramago's interest is to pursue the slippery slope of historical truth, the way that history slides over, or finds ways to cover the unexplained or gaps in known facts, and to compare it with historical fiction, finding the overlapping areas of these different forms of writing.

Further along Raimundo's street, after its name changes to Costa do Castelo, stayed one of France's most radical writers in recent years, Pierre Guyotat. The outpost, in the shadow of the sloping walls, is called the Pensão Residencial Ninho das Aguias, commonly known as the "eagle's nest" because of its octagonal tower rising above the hotel into which you can climb and sit, looking out over the Mouraria as well as other aspects of the city. No surprise to find Guyotat here, a writer who sees himself outside all literary circles and who sees his work outside the terrestrial space where he molds his "written matter"—also a challenge to any proofreader no matter how conscientious. Guyotat's latest fiction, *Progénitures* (2000), is partly set on the slopes of this hill, although the nature of the writing clarifies little more than that. An earlier book, *l'Histoire de Samora Machel*, completed in 1979 but not published in book form as yet (extracts have appeared in magazine form only), almost led to Guyotat's death: "I went to the limits of aberration. I lost myself, uprooted myself, disinherited myself. I was completely dispossessed. I felt myself being taken over by an evil sickness. I had violated a limit I shouldn't have violated." The book opens in Lisbon, where a child is stolen by some pimps, then moves through North Africa, Marseille and into Paris. "The work treats prostitution on a grand, visionary scale: the total prostitutional existence."

# 8. Alfama

## The *Miradouro* and Light

At the start of a poetry reading, the American poet, Jerome Rothenberg, will often joke by saying that first he will tell you what he is going to do, then he will do it, and then he will tell you he has done it. Jerome's humor relates to the mixture of poems he presents, whether his own, or others, predominantly North American Indian in translation.

Thus I make no apologies for starting a trip through the Alfama from above the Alfama, from a *miradouro*. It is perhaps better to start above the old quarter and to work one's way down until one appears at the bottom on the esplanade before the Tagus, than to perpetually climb steps, working upwards, catching breath more than anything else.

The Miradouro de Santa Luzia on the Largo do Limoeiro is another of the best-known in the city, partly because it overlooks the Alfama, the area of old Lisbon not destroyed by the Great Earthquake as it is built on solid rock. It has retained a look that has changed little since medieval times. The *miradouro* itself also has a pleasant ambiance, with its trellised walls overrun with bougainvillaeas, its tiled walls and tiled benches. There is also a rose garden and the exterior walls of the Igreja de Santa Luzia, with their *azulejos* depicting the siege of the castle in all its bloodthirstiness. Here the locals come to sit and talk or play cards, young lovers to dream across the stretch of the Tagus, or film crews to seek out a romantic backdrop. I think of Eduardo de Gregorio's *Aspern* (1982) as one example, or a writer like Olivier Frébourg to reminisce, taking a journey towards forgetting. Or the Spaniard, Arturo Pérez-Reverte, whose bookdealer, Corso, in *The Dumas Club* (1993), rounds off the night singing *Grandola vila morena* drunkenly at the top of his voice with one of his "business associates," with only the moon to illuminate their encore. And, of course, the tourists to cast their eyes every-which-way (or perhaps one should say antennae, like the field of wire pointing into the sky across all the roofs, though satellite dishes are now starting to land among them).

At this time the *miradouro* itself is in the process of an overhaul, the trellis being replaced, fresh vines to be installed. Over the wall, which is the remains of the old Moorish ramparts, the Alfama has been obscured by a vast spread of tarpaulin and scaffolding that spans the roofs of a row of adjacent houses as they welcome their regeneration, albeit at the temporary cost of the view of others.

In that case, it is best to go around to the next *miradouro*, around the corner on the Portas do Sol (Gateway of the Sun). It is a *miradouro* stripped bare in comparison, more like a platform with a view and a telescope. There is no seating, just leaning across the rails to admire the sights. On film, its best-known appearance comes in *The Russia House* (1990), directed by Fred Schepisi with Sean Connery, when the British secret agents, after a briefing, stretch their legs here, in sight of the Alfama flat that Connery has as his hideaway. As noted in another scene, the view from his room cuts across the same view, though in John Le Carré's original novel all these scenes take place further along the river by the Museu de Arte Antiga, equally splendid but perhaps less captivating for Hollywood cliché requirements.

Before we take our first steps into the Alfama, beside the Portas do Sol, and let gravity do the rest, we might do well to survey the tiled map on the wall at the top, which gives possible routes, or just an appealing image of a locale in tiled form.

And again, before we take that step into the dark alleyways, a few words on the light and the way artists capture it. We noted earlier that Alain Tanner saw his film, *In the White City*, as a "noir" film once he grasped the nature of the contrasts of light and dark in the city. The light of Lisbon is a constant reference point. Undoubtedly most observers are struck by the brightness of the sun, a cut-diamond brilliance. Luísa Ferreira, a contemporary photographer, says of the light: "Here in Lisbon the light is very thin and also very hard. You see so sharply that sometimes it hurts. You need to cultivate, educate, your sight or you can remain unaware of its transparencies." Pedro Baptista, another young photographer, agrees: "People keep saying it and of course it's true: the light in Lisbon is very special and I don't believe even now I've ever seen it properly captured. It certainly encouraged me to start and to keep experimenting, though it's hard to translate into actual images."

What of the artists? Paula Rego, today's outstanding Portuguese artist, lives mainly in London, but has been going back and forth all her life, and is thus ideally placed to note what makes Lisbon's light special. In fact, as always, she has her own way of expressing it:

*Portuguese light is like looking into a pool. It contains you. It's green, yellow, warm. At sunrise and sunset we have something called "the golden hour." In England the light is more hazy and it's colder. You are on your own. It's more brittle. In Portugal you see a long way, far away—forever really. The horizon of the sea is clear, far, far away—it goes on. But the horizon of the sea in England is hazy.*

The artist most often cited when talking of an ability to capture Lisbon's light on canvas is Carlos Botelho. For the second half of the twentieth century it was Botelho who was the chronicler of Lisbon, who found a way to use color to present the brightness, observers often pointing to the corners of his buildings to show how he conveyed the contrasts of the light. Botelho died in 1982. He had studied in Paris, like many others, before returning to take a studio near the castle, using the location and its view of the city and the river. His interest was not its historic glories, but the ordinary houses and vistas of the working city, with the Miradouro de Santa Luzia and its vantage over the Alfama as one of his main viewpoints.

## The Warren of Dark Alleyways

Finally we trip into the Alfama, by now perhaps expecting something from Alice's Wonderland with ideas of its "warren of alleyways" and "precipitous staircases." It is another world, but not in the same way. Unless you live in the area, it is no use attempting to find specific streets. It is best just to roam, hoping that eventually you will turn a corner and come across a familiar name or landmark. The two main landmarks are both churches, Igreja de São Miguel (St. Michael's Church) and Igreja de Santo Estevão (St. Stephen's Church) and they might help to gain bearings. Otherwise it is a labyrinth of alleyways, even though some are referred to as *ruas* (roads). You might think that a road only qualifies for such a definition if a car can drive along it, but most here are no more than half a dozen feet wide, suitable only for a moped, though at times a little van bringing building material might be wedged in, blocking off pedestrians, local or otherwise. Other names used in abundance in this area are *beco* (alley), *travessa* (lane between two streets), *calçada* (cobbled street),

*escadinha* (small flight of steps), *largo* (small square), *boqueiro* (large mouth, hence court or passage), and *calçadinha* (little paved way). However they name themselves, it makes it no easier to find one's way. Some are so small that I wonder whether there is a map of them all, or at all. Perhaps it hides on a shelf in the city surveyor's offices. Many of the houses are so close together that they almost touch at the top. It is not an illusion. Remarque wrote of them "as though leaning on each other's shoulders." In some of the alleyways one can easily believe it possible to climb across from one side to the other, or to ask your neighbor to bring in the washing (hanging outside the window) if it rains.

People sometimes suggest that it is dangerous to wander through the quarter, that more attention should be paid at night, for there's a possibility of being robbed. Perhaps it's true, but it's equally difficult by day, because you can easily step into someone's front room thinking you've entered a tiny bar. Or slip and fall through a doorway. It is a network of intricate passages, "climbing and twisting in search of an outlet to the air," as Aubrey Bell observed. With the buildings so close together, there is little light in some of the alleyways, except at noon, when the sun might come down directly through the crack for a brief respite.

After a while you will want a drink or to eat. There are plenty of *tascas* (little taverns), no bigger than a front room. Inside you are as likely as not to find the locals all staring at a niche in the wall, or a shelf high on the wall. Perhaps in former times a religious icon might have caused heads to turn, but now it's television. There are only two things to watch: soap operas and football. (I am reliably informed, however, that there is a third way, for when cable/satellite TV has a regular free showing of pornography "as a taster" in the early hours, it's surprising how many televisions are all flickering in unison down a street.) Not only in the Alfama, but in most bars and restaurants where the locals eat there is this same menu. The insatiable appetite for soap operas, almost exclusively from Brazil, has taken over prime-time schedules. With such a diet it is only to be expected that a reverse colonialism is in operation, with Brazilian expressions being absorbed into the Portuguese native language. *Tudo bem?* (everything okay?) is ousting the more usual *como está?* (how are you?) as the Portuguese form of greeting. Portuguese is indeed ranked the fifth language in the world, in terms of the number of people speaking it, but it is being led by a Brazilian Portuguese, in the same way that the English language adapts to Americanizations in both spoken and written forms, or indeed in its computer "spell checks."

In the evening the men gather to watch football. If you don't mind the football commentary, it makes for a quiet meal, for the men watch, but do not appear to be overly animated by the goals or lack of them. Besides television, the other sounds to be heard are music, day or night, filtering through the doors or windows, whether from a radio or record player, or a woman singing in her home. And despite what people might think, the dominant form seems to be *fado*. Late at night, when the music has stopped, the only sounds one hears as one climbs the steps, emphasizing the intimacy of the neighborhood, are the sounds of the breathing and snoring of people asleep.

Despite the rebuilding, there is still decay, paint peeling from walls, and holes in walls with new pipes coming through, as plumbing has been installed, although the finer points of cementing the holes rarely seem accomplished. Perhaps it is a precautionary measure, as some bad plumbing seems in evidence, with leaks abounding, the water trickling down the alleys on its way for a day out by the river.

In these streets Richard Zimler, the American writer who lives in Portugal, has set his novel, *The Last Kabbalist of Lisbon* (1998). The year is 1506, the period when the Jews were being persecuted, when 2,000 or more were slain in a series of riots and *auto-da-fés* that took place not far away in the Rossio, which "opened like an infected wound maggoted with swarms of shouting people." The main location of the novel is set in the Jewish quarter of the Alfama, on the corner of the Rua da São Pedro and Rua da Sinagoga. This is no ordinary novel, but an attempt to do with Lisbon what Umberto Eco achieved in *The Name of the Rose*, in the process also becoming a work of history, filling in with details what no other book has done, there being no study written to date on the Portuguese Jews in the sixteenth century. The story follows a young manuscript illuminator, Berekiah, who sets out to solve the mystery of the death of his uncle, a renowned kabbalist, who is found in his cellar, which serves as a secret synagogue, his body naked alongside a young girl, traces of semen suggesting sexual activity. To unravel what is in effect a "locked-room mystery" requires research not only in, but under the alleys of the Alfama, tracing the paths of former times through buildings that have since changed their usage.

Pessoa only mentions the Alfama in passing in his guide and does not appear to venture there. Others find it unsavory or, seeking history, find that the lives of the area's working people do not match the adventures of the powerful or their historic buildings. Because this area has changed so little, clambering up and down the flights of steps and wandering back and forth through the maze of narrow passages and alleys gives one the sense of how it was years ago. This is a sense that many other cities cannot give because of the removal of old housing to provide more modern homes. Not that it was always so in the past. This area was inhabited by the Visigoths right back as far as the fifth century, and remnants of their wall still remain. But it was the Moors who gave it its appearance and atmosphere, as well as its name: *al-hamma* means hot spring, in reference to the spring near Largo das Alcaçarias. Earlier, some of the grander places housed the wealthy, but after the earthquakes they moved away, leaving the area effectively for the fishing community.

The main street, if one can call it that, lies near the bottom, the Rua de São Pedro, where in the mornings the fish stalls are out and the fishwives are at work, with cats skulking to see what can be salvaged. Towards the bottom, before one emerges at the Largo do Charifariz de Dentro (fountain within the walls), one can still see an inner court along the Beco do Mexias, where women come to do their communal washing.

This is the idea one has of the area: washing hanging above one's head across the narrow defiles, canaries singing in their cages, children playing on the stairways, balconies overflowing with pot plants and, at night, bright lighting housed in wrought-iron fittings, all helping to provide the images and memories. Dubravka Ugresic adds: "The hum of noise reaching me from everywhere, the swarms of flies and hot haze made me feel faint. It seemed to me that I was in the very heart of the Mediterranean, extended, admittedly, to the shore of the Atlantic. And, dazed, gasping for breath, I was crawling through one of its ventricles."

## Wenders and Madredeus

As with such areas in many cities, some old trades survive longest, like the knife grinders. Wenders captures one in the Alfama area in *Lisbon*

*Story*, his main character Phillip Winter rushing with his microphone to record him at work, recognizable from a distance by the sounds of the pan-pipes. According to Sitwell, the knife-grinders are Spaniards (*Galegos*), originally "coming from two small villages in Galicia."

*Lisbon Story* is shaped around a film within a film, in which the sound engineer, Winter, responds to a request from his friend, Friedrich Munro, the director, to travel to Lisbon to work on a film he has been shooting. On arrival, Winter finds an empty apartment with the film abandoned on the editing machine. He views the footage already shot and sets about providing the soundtrack, recording effects to accompany the images, and collecting together a store of useful sounds. The irony is that the film *Lisbon Story* itself was constructed in the opposite way, the soundtrack being provided before the story, let alone the filming, was conceived.

"I wanted to make a film in and about their city," said Wenders, "and from the beginning I thought there should be a band in my story. The musicians should play the music of the film, hopefully also compose it, and they could appear in the film as well. But I had no script yet, so my ideas were rather vague." He had heard the music of Madredeus and had the idea that they might be involved. He had never met them, had no idea of their looks or their stage presence:

> When I came into this recording studio on the outskirts of Lisbon late one night, a few weeks before our shoot, I saw them and heard them live for the first time. I remember I had goosepimples when I entered the place. They were playing Milagre and I knew that very moment that they just had to make the music for the film. Half an hour later I knew also that I had to write a story that involved a band. This band. I really wanted to shoot with them while they were playing. They were playing with so much pleasure, intensity and integrity, and Teresa's voice filled that little space with so much emotion that my goosepimples just worked overtime.

No sooner had he met them than Madredeus went to London to record their new album, returning two weeks later:

> When they came back from London they had not only recorded a great album, but had also recorded nine additional songs they suggested for the film, two of them instrumental. They were fantastic, all nine of them. It felt like a great present: I hadn't even started shooting the film, but could

*already listen to the soundtrack! And that was "not just" the music, but turned out to also be some sort of guideline through the city. When we shot the film, we always had the music with us. It was playing on the set, it was playing on the car stereo when we drove home, and I heard it in my earphones late at night when I continued writing the script. The city certainly had inspired this band and their music, now their music helped us to enter the city and find our way through it, and through our story. I have never made a film before that had been inspired so much by its music from the beginning.*

Madredeus do not play traditional Portuguese music, and yet it is not like other musical forms. It is as if elements of *fado* had been developed in the light of contemporary music, in the light of the color washes formerly created by bands like the Cocteau Twins or Dead Can Dance, suggested not only by the ethereal voices of their singers, matched by Madredeus' Teresa Salgueiro, but also by the melancholic soundscape. There is no direct similarity of instrumentation, however, as Madredeus work mainly with the more traditional Portuguese *guitarra* and accordion, enhanced with cello and keyboards.

In the film, Winter, having moved into Friedrich's base, hears the sound of music from upstairs and sets off in search. There he discovers Madredeus rehearsing. The role that Wenders gives the band is to allow them to perform uninterrupted, to make a concert for us, as well as to provide a soundtrack of music that talks about the Alfama and the Tagus as much as about Lisbon. Teresa Salgueiro, as the female lead in the film, enchants Winter as a siren (with echoes of Calypso and the myth of Lisbon's origins); her voice seduces him on that first climb of the stairs (as indeed it had initially when the other members discovered her doing *fado vadio*—tramp *fado*—and invited her to front the band they were forming).

"The Tagus is the only witness of our lives, not the city," is how Pedro Ayres Magalhães, Madredeus' leader, explains the lyrics to Winter as they stand on the patio looking over the river. Madredeus, whose name is taken from their former rehearsal space at the convent further along the river, have a deep affection for the city. Today they are perhaps ambassadors for the city across Europe and Latin America, if not quite yet in the English-speaking countries.

As already noted, although the house used as the base is set a little higher, just below the castle, giving more extensive views over the Alfama, the river and all of Lisbon, Winter's days are spent recording in the Alfama as much as in other parts of the city. *Lisbon Story* is a low-budget film, a personal film for Wenders that allows him to extend an approach used earlier, but also to reflect and make a film that is something of a statement about cinema at the end of the twentieth century, at a time when others were also preparing accounts and statements about the first hundred years of cinema. The nostalgia, the *saudade*, comes from a variety of sources. Manoel de Oliveira, the Portuguese film director, appears in the film. He is almost as old as cinema itself. Wenders presents him not only talking about Lisbon, a voice-over for his film within a film, but takes him back to the early days, acting in imitation of Chaplin walking in the street. The idea of doing a short anthology of film and its genres, of encapsulating the history of cinema is at the heart of the film. Thus romance, detective story, action, documentary, road movie, symbolic fable, slapstick... all become part of it. Friedrich is filming a personal film within the personal film, using an old camera, trying to crank his way like Dziga Vertov, the *Man with a Movie Camera*, into film itself, looking like Buster Keaton in *The Cameraman*. But when he abandons the project to re-question his course, he uses video as a contemporary development to notate his ideas, as well as to place cameras in the hands of local children to film as they wish.

Within this approach Wenders has drawn on two characters from his earlier work. Phillip Winter, played by Rüdiger Vogler, appeared as Winter before, notably in the early film *Alice in the Cities* (1974), and pertinently again as Phillip Winter in Lisbon just before in *Until the End of the World* (1991), where he came through Lisbon as a private detective. (And also in *Farewell, So Close* (1993), the sequel to *Wings of Desire* (1987)). As a different Winter, Bruno Winter, he was also in *Kings of the Road* (1976). "Winter's here," his opening comment when he pushes his head around the door of the house in *Lisbon Story*, is as much a joke on the freeze-up of cinema, as on Wenders' own sense of "goosepimples" on hearing Teresa Salguerio and Madredeus. Friedrich, too, is a former character, dating back to Wenders' earlier film in Lisbon,

*The State of Things* (1982), where Friedrich Munro, the film director for that film within a film, is played by Patrick Bauchau, the son of the Belgian writer Henri Bauchau (author of *Oedipus on the Road*). There are as many alleyways and aspects to this maze as in the Alfama itself. Friedrich, who is also heard being called Fritz and Frederico in the film, playing with Lang and Fellini in name, and implications, adds to the image of the film. Though Frederick relates to whom? And indeed what role does F.W. Murnau play, or should we say Friedrich Murnau?

Some Portuguese think that because Wenders showed unsavory aspects of Lisbon he was not well disposed towards them. But, in fact, the film is a love story, a romance for Lisbon, Wenders feeling at home enough there to show his passion for the place through its good and bad points. But then the main subtext is the state of film, the nature of things at the end of the century, and from an art cinema point of view (leaving aside ideas of commercial filmmaking) things are not all good, quite the opposite. In any case, Wenders says it all this time when he lines up his camera to skirt directly over the Texas Bar, passing on up the Rua de Alecrim.

Before Wenders found the new ambassadors, Madredeus, for *Lisbon Story*, he had Amália Rodrigues play a cameo in *Until the End of the World*, laughing in the tram as the couple kiss and celebrate their escape from Phillip Winter. The role for Oliveira is more an homage.

## Oliveira and Portuguese Cinema

Manoel de Oliveira has been making films since the early 1930s, although he is little known in Britain or the US, and then almost only for showings at film festivals. In fact it was not until the 1970s that he was noticed outside Portugal when countries like France and Italy acknowledged his mastery. For many years he made shorts and documentaries, and it was not until late in life that features started to flow more regularly, today at the enviable rate of almost one a year. A reluctance to compromise slowed his early progress, and the Salazar regime slowed not only him but all of Portuguese cinema for years. "That terrible expensive industry" is how Salazar described cinema, leaving it mainly to its own devices, barely using it even for propaganda purposes, unlike other Fascist regimes. In the mid-1930s filmmaking sank to a low, with barely a film being completed from one year to the next.

And although the industry rose after that to 25 films in 1952, by 1955 "the crisis gripping the national production reaches its trough: not one feature is completed during the year," writes film critic Don Ranvaud, editing a major feature in *Framework* devoted to Portuguese cinema.

Most of Oliveira's work has been based around Porto, his home city, rather than Lisbon, although in 1982 he was asked by an Italian production company to make a film about the culture of Lisbon, called *Lisboa Cultural,* which was shown on television, but appears not to be available now. A fully documented book has been published in Paris of the script and images, however, which indicates the approach, with experts commenting on various cultural highlights while the camera illustrates, alongside dramatizations and music from Rodrigues and others. *A Caixa* (Blind Man's Buff, 1994) is his most recent film to be set in Lisbon, not far away, near the castle, the story revolving around a blind man and the loss of his alms box.

Strangely, most home-produced Portuguese films are what we would call art-house films, not commercial products. This owes perhaps to the fact that throughout the Salazar years foreign films were not allowed to be dubbed, only sub-titled, even though the degree of illiteracy, particularly in the rural communities, was extremely high. Thus cinema was never allowed to evolve as a popular entertainment to the same degree as in other countries.

Also, since 1979, Paulo Branco started to produce films, developing a policy of creating films that appealed to him, films that were part of a European art context rather than aimed at making a commercial killing. In this way he worked with not only the Portuguese filmmakers of the time, but encouraged outsiders to come and film in Portugal. If it were not for him, Wenders, Tanner, Ruiz and others would not have made such distinctive films, films that attracted attention to both Lisbon and other Portuguese filmmakers. The list of filmmakers involved is extensive as his list increased dramatically with some like Manoel de Oliveira heading the roll-call, and others included João César Monteiro, João Botelho, Christine Laurent, Teresa Villaverde, Eduardo de Gregorio, Pedro Costa, Andrzej Zulawski and Werner Schroeter, besides the three named earlier. What is important is not that he does not separate the Portuguese from the others, but that he makes the

Portuguese part of the European collection. With offices in Lisbon and Paris, he is able to take the films out into the world. Back home, when Branco found that difficulty in distributing the films had sunk to a low, he expanded into distribution, acquiring theaters to show the films. Today he has a video section too, both these arms also promoting films that he has not produced, but which give wider context to the cinema that he feels is more than entertainment and an excuse to sell popcorn.

Indeed it is no joke to say that there probably would not be a Portuguese cinema today if it were not for Branco's years of activity, or if there was, it would be much poorer. At any one time he can have a handful of films in production, for he does not feel that he needs to be involved in the day-to-day details of each production to the degree that he could be called a meddler, as is often the case elsewhere. With someone like Tanner, for example, he knows that the director knows what he is doing and has no need of him looking over his shoulder, whereas others might require him to visit on location and offer practical help.

Because of someone like Branco, Portuguese cinema seems intent on avoiding the path of other cultures, "either to cut their cloth to the American pattern or getting locked into production packages and aesthetic decisions dictated by television co-funders," as film critic Chris Drake puts it. Portugal's idiosyncratic ways allow someone like João César Monteiro to exist, a man whose films have their own pace, and seem set not only to cause mischief, but to find a way to irritate in the manner in which they go against the grain. In *A Comédia de Deus* (God's Comedy, 1995) Monteiro himself, as he often takes the lead roles too, is an ice-cream artist, who, in Patrick Süskind fashion, creates new *parfums* for the ices. He is always seeking the perfect one, although ironically he chain-smokes throughout the film, something that would annul anyone's taste buds from having the required acuteness. Or perhaps this trek down the roads of excess is just an excuse to get his hands on young women (a recurrent activity) and acquire pubic hairs, for which he has a large "Book of Thoughts," a form of photo album where plastic bags hold the prized hairs, all neatly labeled. This vampiric approach is acknowledged by the cadaverous presence that is Monteiro, echoing Murnau's *Nosferatu* at points, as he prepares to pounce. But there is something extremely comic throughout, and the humor is perhaps summed up in what has to be one of cinema's classic images. With what looks like an oversized cream-horn that has been filled with eggs, and in which a young woman's naked bottom has been sitting, presenting a chalice into which Monteiro can plunge himself head first, the long shot shows him as if an insect, limbs flaying, his head stuck in a Venus fly-trap. An image that in itself could make him a contender to film French writer, Georges Bataille's *Story of the Eye* or perhaps *The Dead Man.* Monteiro's comeuppance is to be taken to death's door, almost by the short and curlies.

## Casa dos Bicos

You know on emerging from the Alfama that you would never live there. You can understand why the children of those who do have to escape. Rents might well be controlled and as low as $25 a month, but that is still no reason to stay. The one incongruity among this poverty is the sight of mobile phones clutched at so many ears, here as elsewhere.

When one emerges onto the main road, a guide to the location is offered by two points: the first, the Chafariz d'el-Rei, a façade-fountain integrated into the wall along the Rua Cais de Santarém, that has been in use since the thirteenth century; and second, further along, the Casa dos Bicos (Pointed House), another architectural façade curiosity with its diamond shaped stones, on the Rua dos Bacalhoeiros.

As promised, and in the tradition of Rothenberg, we are at the bottom, not quite on the riverfront, but tired enough to want a rest. Though Tabucchi sets the hotel in *Requiem* where he goes for a few hours rest, to sleep off his meal, elsewhere, in Tanner's film version the hotel is situated almost next door to the Casa dos Bicos. Tabucchi's main character has wanted a rest, but his friend Tadeus has mischievously sent him to a "guesthouse" that only takes couples. "This is a serious guesthouse, my friend, we don't take single people here," said the Porter, "do I make myself clear?" He hasn't understood, and asks to see the owner, Isadora, as Tadeus had told him to do. Tadeus was a client of the establishment, when he was alive, as becomes obvious. Finally he obtains his room and declines the offer of company. "I'm very clean and quiet, even if you want to sleep I won't bother you, I'll just lie next to you really still," pledges the young woman.

## The Lux

After oversleeping and feeling switched on again, despite the late hour or because of the late hour, for there's no point otherwise, you can go back along the road, down the front for a drink in the Lux. This bar/club has appeared in recent years just over the road from the Santa Apolónia rail station, which connects the city to Paris and Madrid, in fact to Europe. If it should seem strange for the main international station to be located here, its credentials are about to be reduced, for along the line the new Oriente station, part of the Expo complex, is destined to be the new center and showpiece for Lisbon terminals to Spain and beyond. Thus the Lux, by coming here, is also choosing an area that is about to be degraded further, but which it will in its turn lift up by attracting other nightlife to join it, if early indications are proven. It is owned by the actor John Malkovich and the "nightlife baron" Manuel Reis, who earlier ran the Frágil, an infamous night haunt in the Bairro Alto. One to set trends, not to follow them, rather than go west to the docks near the Alcântara like the others who've decamped, Reis has taken his new club east into uncharted territories, even taking a shape of building different from the old regular warehouses inhabited by the others. The Lux is half raised on concrete stilts, and stands out by itself at the end of the quay buildings. Inside it is awash with colors in its lighting and its décor, something from the Sixties and Seventies. This is a place for celebrities in town to unwind, whether on its disco floor or in the expansive bar areas, if they can gain admittance (door policy has its own rules). "I have succeeded in mixing what, in Paris, or London or elsewhere, is always scattered. Gays, Africans, suits, trendies... The night has seen two generations pass through since the revolution, the city has barely recognized it," says Reis, its owner. For our part, we have become fully acclimatized to belonging to the trio of dots.

# PART THREE

# *THE EAST*

*"There are several vanishing-points, but they are all at the same height."*
Paula Rego

## 1. Azulejos

### Museu Nacional do Azulejo

*Azulejos* (tiles) are one of the pleasures of Lisbon. They are found on the exterior, as well as the interior, of buildings. They cover complete façades as imaginative patterns or as decorous embellishments. They lend color and vibrant light effects to spaces. They can create scenes depicting historical, religious or mythological events, or they can be humorous sideshows. They are of the past, but also of today, an art form the Portuguese have expressively made their own.

The Igreja da Madre de Deus (Church of the Mother of God) and its adjoining Museu Nacional do Azulejo (Tile Museum) are found east along the river in the suburb of Xabregas. The museum is part of the convent of the church, being housed partly in earlier extensions around the cloisters. It was founded as a Poor Clare convent by Dona Leonor, the widow of Dom João II in 1509. Additional building came later as a result of earthquake damage and flood risk from high waters.

The church itself is crowded with so much gilt woodwork that even the official documents term it "drenched in gold," and the *coro alto* (upper choir) as a "richly jewelled box," with gold baroque reliquaries and a series

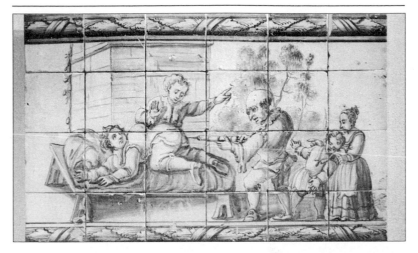

of paintings depicting the life of St. Francis attributed to André Gonçalves. After years of waiting, restoration work is currently in progress.

The tiles are displayed in buildings around the cloisters, although the highlight, the panoramic view of the Lisbon waterfront pre-earthquake, which is 100 feet long, is displayed along a cloister wall. Made in 1738, seventeen years before the earthquake, it shows many buildings that no longer exist, including the smoking kilns of factories in the Mocambo district where the very tiles themselves were probably made.

There are something like 12,000 *azulejos* in the collection, which ranges through the last four centuries, narrating the history of tiles right through to duplicates of the most recent tile extravaganza, the luscious display on the Metro system. A handful of other notables includes the grotesque Bacchus, with hairy breasts and a cluster of grapes at his crotch, some witty modern tiles of grasshoppers and crabs, and another panel of a doctor hard at work with his syringe.

Tiles are not peculiar to Portugal, but they have been used for a greater variety of purposes and more extensively than elsewhere, making them one of the main features of its artistic heritage. *Azulejos* date from Moorish times, the word itself probably deriving from the Arabic *al zulaycha*, which means "polished stone." It almost certainly has its roots there rather than in *azul*, the Portuguese for "blue," which traces its etymology back to the Persian term for lapis lazuli, the blue gemstone.

This misnomer seems to have occurred in relation to the blue glazes that predominated in earlier periods.

The Portuguese learned the technique of making tiles from the Moors, who had themselves picked it up from the Mesopotamians and others in the Middle East, although the practice can be found initially in ancient Egypt. During the reign of Philip II of Spain, when Portugal was reduced to the sidelines as a dominated country, there was no building and luxury items were in short supply. Determined to do something, Portuguese craftsmen chose the *azulejo* as their replacement for the tapestry or mural, and later, when Portugal regained its independence, it became a national art form.

The invention of the *majolica* technique by the Italians in the sixteenth century enabled colors to be applied more directly. The Portuguese forte was never the development and techniques of the craft, but the use of the materials. At first, the designs were geometric, like tapestry patterns, but interest soon turned to a taste for panels with religious imagery and landscapes. After the earthquake of 1755 a simpler style was adopted to suit the neo-classical architecture and also to meet the need for a larger quantity of tile work for the rebuilding process. Not only was it an economical way to cover wall areas, but it required less maintenance.

In the late nineteenth century there was an influx of agricultural labor into the city in search of work. To house the "laboring classes" accommodation was constructed, mainly by industrialists and businessmen for their employees. Some of these large buildings, for example in the Bairro Estrela de Ouro, built by Agapito Serra Fernandes, are distinguished today by their tile façades. Some are found in streets with names such as Rua Virginia, Rua Rosalina and Rua Josefa Maria that correspond to the names of members of the owner's family. The Golden Star sign, as the name Estrela de Ouro suggests, can be seen in the tile designs and elsewhere on the streets.

Lisbon today displays a variety of tiles from across the eras, many from the late nineteenth century. Larger surfaces are covered in Lisbon than elsewhere, although there are still a good number of friezes or borders, not only in a decorative role, but integral to the architecture. Many of these relate to the Art Nouveau and Art Deco movements, embellishments that caught the public's eye, particularly when they were used around doorways of shops, restaurants, kiosks, cinemas, bakeries, banks, hospitals, schools and railway stations. Their value lay not only in their decorative aspects, but also as a medium for advertising, or as street signs and maps.

There was a lull in their popularity for a number of years, particularly at one point when Salazar's regime virtually eliminated their use, but artists such as Jorge Colaço and Maria Keil created some wall mosaics and murals that helped to stimulate a resurgence in interest. Jorge Colaço was the first painter to use the technique of silk screen painting, which is now the most widely used process. Maria Keil was one of four artists (the others were Júlio Pomar, Rolando Sá Nogueira and Carlos Botelho) to create large tile ensembles on a building complex on the Avenida Infante Santo in 1958–59. Keil's work was judged to be so successful in the way she handled her rhomboid shapes to produce three-dimensional effects, that she was asked to create further designs for the first Metro stations, a system that has now created an underground tilescape second to none.

## Cemitério do Alto de São João

Overlooking the Madredeus is the city's other cemetery, the Eastern Cemetery, the balance to the Prazeres in the west. The Cemitério do Alto de São João is huge. If anything deserves the term "white city," it is this place. Here there are streets, main streets and side streets, numbering almost a hundred, many named after sculptors and architects, as seems fitting. Streets that are filled with mausoleums, little temples and a vast amount of marble. Both cemeteries were constructed in the early 1830s when it became illegal to bury the dead inside churches.

It is a more pleasant cemetery than Prazeres, even if not blessed with celebrity in quite the same way. "Beach huts for their eternal holiday," as Catherine observed when we walked along the streets, a grid system that enables many of the slopes to cast a view over the river. As with most cemeteries some tombs are well maintained, others not. Glass doors with lace curtains enable one to look in and see the shelves where families are tiered, or where decay has caused shelves to collapse, coffins to tilt or spill onto the floor. Only when deterioration has gone too far, and the broken glass and flapping lace have given way to wildlife occupation have boards been added to the doors, some sealed further to block admittance other than by forced entry.

And, as before, flowers are everywhere, waves of color. And among it all, a square of grass with a water display, the Jardim da Saudade. A place of quietude with a few benches to sit and contemplate, where our presence seemed misplaced among the women in black tending their thoughts.

On the skyline to the east a new landscape is emerging, a series of towers in various colors: white clusters, pink clusters, a red/turquoise/blue block. These are the social housing projects, the urban developments of the peripheries, though one sees them only as a stark contrast, an unacceptable face of modernity when one is standing firmly rooted in the past, among the dead. Only when one discovers the latest Metro line links to these outlying places, that a new breadth to the city is being offered, does one start to concede a positive attitude towards them, for these developments in Olaias, Chelas and Olivais are there to replace the corrugated sheds of the *barracas*, or shanty towns, that swelled from 1974 as more and more immigrants came in from the former colonies. As with all estates, lessons have to be learned. To build new housing blocks does not necessary mean they will be treated well. All the other facilities have to be offered, though the future seems to be geared to more than shopping centers and cinema complexes, with access opened by the Metro system. It makes this area part of the latest realignment of Lisbon, which could see its inhabitants as a vital organ of the new body that the city seeks to be.

# 2. Expo 98

In the aftermath of Expo 98, staged in Lisbon, what has become of the site? Pina Bausch and her troupe of dancers from Wuppertal in Germany might have walked through with their special commissions, as have many other international dancers, musicians and theater groups. Not that that is the end of it for them. They can return, the facilities are in place today.

But, as with any major exhibition, whether cultural, commercial or sporting, whether Expo or Olympics or any point in between, the promises always look great (as great as the bills), but afterwards the promises turn sour. Often the sites become derelict or not properly employed, and finally salvage work takes place, more to save face for those politicians involved—if not already out of office.

Proposals to hold a big celebration were intended as a means of urban redevelopment at a particular point in Lisbon's history. Not all stands three years later. The pavilions from the other countries are slowly coming down to leave the permanent structures as the basis for what is intended as a new shift for the city, indeed for a new city to emerge.

Expo was situated upriver of the center, in the eastern part of the city, past the cemetery, past the hills on the horizon, further along the many miles of dockland. What was once an area of oil refineries and docks going to waste, a semi-derelict space in decay, has been reclaimed and transformed. To ensure (at least that's the hope) that it is a permanent fixture, two major pivots have been put in place. The first is a large new bridge, a massive feat and feast of engineering, the Ponte Vasca da Gama (Vasca da Gama bridge). The second is a major new train station, the Gare do Oriente (Oriente Station), which is locked into a new Metro station, and indeed a new line, all tied in with bus terminals. Both are close to the city airport, Portelo, with a suggestion that a second city airport will be located south of the river to slot in with this grand plan. In other words, it amounts to a new shape and orientation for the city. And it looks splendid, very impressive.

Expo 98 was staged to celebrate the 500th anniversary of Vasco da Gama's discovery of the sea route to India, providing the maritime slogan: "The oceans: a heritage for the future." That was the pretext for the project, but part of the rationale for such redevelopment can once again be traced back to the Salazar regime and its interest in heritage and the restoration of particular historic monuments rather than the evolution of the general framework of the city. Although subsequent governments have planned to regenerate the city, with so much needing to be done and finance lacking, projects have been postponed, repeatedly. Portugal was one of the poorest countries in Europe until recently. But with an improved economic situation and finance via Brussels from the European Union, plans went ahead for the Expo. The 350-acre site that was cleared saw the removal of an oil refinery, slaughterhouse, refuse tip, arms factory and gasworks. In their place rose the Parque das Nações (Park of Nations), billed not only as a new artistic and sporting heart, but also a site with homes for 40,000 people and work for 30,000. Of these 18,000 would be completely new jobs.

**Garo do Oriente**
When you see the Gare do Oriente, whether from above by overland railway or arriving at the Metro terminus, you know that there is every intention to forge a new center of life. The station has been designed by the Spanish architect Santiago Calatrava, and true to form, it is a feast of steel and glass, fanning steel blades, an interlink of palm trees with glass leaves, the air allowed to circulate around its stems and sides. (The design appears partly as a foil to the palm columns and ribbing in the church at the Mosteiro dos Jerónimos at Belém.) When you come down from the platforms, you enter a walkway of concrete arches, a rib cage with light pouring in from above between the ribs, giving it an eerie futuristic look.

Below and down further towards the Metro is another network of concrete arches before we arrive at the Metro itself, a treat to be savored later.

Directly outside this monumental terminus, between it and the Expo site, is the shopping mall, one that you have at least to pass through. With water as the theme for all the designs of the main buildings, the shopping mall has not been neglected. The glass roof ripples water either way from its central rib, like a sea ebbing on the shore. For me it is a good enough distraction from the shops themselves, cubicles that can be slotted into any other monstrous mall around modern Europe.

**Parque das Nações**

The main buildings of the site all have impressive designs, all determined to exhibit their cultural permanency. The Utopian Pavilion, now renamed Atlântico Pavilion, which looks like the hull of an upturned boat, a caravel as used by Vasco da Gama, is a smooth silver skin supported by Glulam-laminated timber trusses and adjustable louvres, with photocells to control the amount of daylight. It is the biggest auditorium, with room for 17,500. It is specifically destined for sports events, a future Olympic Games bid in mind as one major usage.

The most stunning feat is the Pavilhão de Portugal (Portuguese Pavilion) with its canopy of concrete that sweeps as a wave from one wall, a series of rectangular, marbled arches, across to the building that earlier housed Portugal's own exhibition, today a government office. Designed by the Portuguese architect Alvaro Siza Vieira (who had earlier restructured the Chiado district after the great fire of 1988), the concrete canopy is strung like a sheet of paper, reinforced by rods across the open plaza. Weighing 1,400 tons and measuring 150 by 200 feet, it is a most awe-inspiring concrete sheet, its suspension only secured to the tops of the walls, creating a sight that one cannot imagine until one is physically beneath it and contemplating the sheer spectacle above one's head.

Most people feel the Oceanarium, designed by the American Peter Chermayeff, is the most striking feature, whether it is the biggest in the world to date or second biggest. Situated on an island in the site, it has four stone towers that surround the large central tank, each tower with a different marine habitat, "a declaration about the fragility of the planet," the architect says.

Other buildings retained include the Teatro Camões, mainly for concerts, and an exhibition center, the design of which suggests an architectural marina, with rigging and masts flying at angles, echoes of ship decks and a collage of maritime imagery, right down to the inverted sunshades, like wind-blown umbrellas.

Two towers stand at either end of the site. One is the Vasco da Gama Tower, which creates a new form of *miradouro*, with its bowed frame curving away from the central tower in contrast to the Monument to the Discoveries at Belém, also bowed and standing like the prow of a ship

with its discoverers line up to peer at the horizon. No statues here, only the ever-changing pattern of visitors who freeze atop the tower. The other, in the south, is called the Petrogal Torre de Cracking (Petrogal Cracking Tower). It is isolated at the moment as the temporary pavilions have been removed, but will in time be surrounded by other projects, as the new city continues to be built with further homes, hospitals, schools, cafés, restaurants... The Cracking Tower is functional, although it looks like a giant sculpture. On the one hand, there are the remains of a petrol rig—which indeed is part of the intention, a memorial to the history of the area (Petrogal being Portugal's biggest oil company). On the other hand, it acts as a further *miradouro*, which the city favors as its sign of existence.

The Ponte Vasca da Gama, which graces the end of the site, is another feat of engineering. British-built and comparable to the times, it spans more than ten miles, seven of which are above the water. Only for part of the span does it rise high enough for boats to pass beneath, through the suspension bridge construction near the north side. Most of the middle sections are on legs that give little berth or height for any water traffic. This monumental way to span the river at a wide point enables a long and undulating link to weave across the river, from north to south, and divide up the growing car congestion on the Ponte 25 de Abril at the other side of the city. At night its lighting tilts inwards to avoid confusing the fish, it is suggested, although Elizabeth Nash notes that the lighting also succeeds in "offering drivers a sense of protection from the vast expanse of water." That seems the more likely intention, for it is the drivers who need greater protection. Portuguese drivers are reluctant not to drink and drive, or to show bravado at the wheel, making them the most accident prone in Europe. All this splendor will mean nothing if reckless driving habits are not curtailed. A bridge is only a bridge if you can get from one side to the other alive.

# Part Four

# *THE NORTH*

*"How many loves, how many mysteries, perhaps crimes!"*
Eça de Queirós, *To the Capital*

## 1. Rossio

If you are coming from the Rossio station, you are not at first aware of the late nineteenth-century romantic style of neo-Manueline arches, "profusely dentelée, with great windowed doors of horse-shoe shape" (Pessoa). But if you are approaching it, to enter from the side, you cannot but be taken by them. It gives the impression you are about to enter a Gothic palace, whereas in fact you are entering a railway station. As you step through the doors you come down to the reality of a general mix of unpleasantness and split-level shopping, until you climb to the platforms themselves, which are two levels up. The station is built on the side of the hill, as you become aware, for once on the train, no sooner do you leave the platform than you plunge into a tunnel, cutting beneath the botanical gardens, emerging down the way in the suburbs, en route for Sintra.

Of course, if you come at the station from around the corner you can drive up the hairpin incline or walk up steps, losing the outside splendor, but avoiding the tackiness of the inner lower level. The platforms themselves offer another pleasure. Again the features are the tiles—along one side, images of fruit, along the other, tributes to writers of Lisbon and Portugal. As always, art has a public space in Lisbon.

Not that everyone is taken by the station. Ann Bridges and Susan Lownden declare it "one of the most grotesque railway stations in the world, with enormous Moorish horse-shoe-shaped entrances, decorated in the Manueline style. It rather reminds one of the station façade at Kiev, which is built like a Russian crown."

The Rossio itself, or to use its correct name, the Praça Dom Pedro IV, is something of a crossroads for the city. In the middle stands the statue of Dom Pedro IV, who was also Dom Pedro I of Brazil. The story goes that the statue of the king did not start out as his. It was originally cast in Marseilles in the image of Maximilian of Mexico, but by the time it was being transported to Mexico, stopping en route at Lisbon, news arrived that Maximilian had been assassinated. The Lisbon authorities seized their opportunity and struck a deal, acquiring the statue on the cheap, and after a few cosmetic changes erected it as Dom Pedro IV. As Pessoa reminds us: "This monument is one of the highest in Lisbon, being over 27 metres high." Perhaps its height deters close-up inspection of the likeness.

On the northern side of this large square, the only grandeur (Pedro faces the opposite way) is the Teatro Nacional Dona Maria II (Dona Maria II National Theater), its façade crowned by the statue of Gil Vicente, the most important playwright of Portugal, from the sixteenth century. At night some of the voicings from the stage might have a resonance with the past, for on this site—or "almost" as Pessoa notes—was an old palace, the Paço dos Estãos, later occupied by the Inquisition. Here horrific deeds were carried out in the name of religion: public hangings and the notorious *autos-de-fé* every three years, at which time if the prisoners did not repent, as the British writer, Charles Brockwell recorded, they were tortured by "pressing their thumbs in a Vice, Drawing the Nails from the Fingers, scalping the Crown, etc." After various of these unspeakable activities, the victims were chained to an iron chair and roasted before a fire. The Igreja de São Domingos, the church almost immediately next door, was where the Inquisition read out its sentences. As seems fitting, it has a history of disasters associated with it, the most recent in 1959 when it was blackened and gutted by fire.

In the nineteenth century, the governor of the castle set prisoners to work making wave-patterned mosaic pavements in the Rossio. Each cube, cut by hand, was around two and a half inches ("like a dragon's tooth") and either pale limestone or dark gray basalt. Knocked into a bed of sand, they have the advantage of being easily removable for underground repairs, and enable water to be absorbed. But over the years the pavement has also become uneven and can be quite hard on shoes walking across it.

The Tabacaria Monaco, situated on the west side near the Café Nicola, is small but worth seeking out for its humorous tile display both inside and around the doorway, by Rafael Bordalo Pinheiro, dating from around

1894. Using the technique of painting on stanniferous enamel, the Art Nouveau patterns relate to the shop's business, the main characters being storks and frogs smoking, lounging, drinking and playing guitars.

Blakeston emerged from the station onto the square, enchanted by the sight: "There were butter-coloured trams: some of them were of an old-fashioned open type with 'cow-catchers' for pedestrians, and others were sleekly new. There were shiny cars, glimpses of rather glittery cafés, vendors of lottery tickets, toothbrushes and razor-blades." But what he really wanted to know, and this was the Fifties, was what had happened to the traffic: "Where had we read that 'Lisbon is the noisiest city in the world'? And yet not a car was hooting. The pavements were crowded, the streets full; but numerous traffic police, in grey uniforms with white topees and black pistol holsters, saw that the pedestrians got across the roads with a minimum of noise, without frantic French shouts and whistle hysteria."

Not that you should talk about that to Virgílio Ferreira, writing in his novel *Na Tua Face*, where he sounds off about the traffic as his taxi grinds to a halt: "I would have done better to go on foot, the taxi is constantly halted by the aberrant traffic. Cars and cars. On the pavements on the squares in the alleys. One day the town, I see it from here paralytic. No room for a vehicle to remain on four wheels. Cars abandoned to rot."

Yet he is willing to climb into the back of the taxi with his guide Josefina Lind in Wolf Gaudlitz's *Táxi Lisboa*. He admits he wouldn't be doing so other than as the guest of his charming companion. For Ferreira the old taxi is too old, even though the driver Machedo might well be a nice enough man. Does it matter that Machedo's 1928 Oldsmobile is not the latest model? Despite its clumsiness, the city's traffic goes at such a crawl, a snail's pace even, that it's of no consequence. For Ferreira it is only suitable for the tourist, a romantic and nostalgic remnant.

The Rossio is also the location for a hotel where the French-American novelist Julien Green, returning in the early 1980s, remembers an incident from July 1940. A heavy memory. The hotel was called the Frankfurt:

*That name struck me then and appeared ominous. In the hall, I was seated when a young French boy came towards me, a little boy, who said:*

> *"I'm a Jew, can you help me?" I replied that I was broke, that I was waiting for the boat for America, but an idea came to me. I asked at reception for the Lisbon telephone directory and I looked at the list for Rothschild, there were many, I took the first, I called. A woman replied. I told her my name and I explained exactly what had happened. There was a silence, then she replied: "Send him to me, we will do the necessary."*

## Pictures of Poverty

Away from the riches, this is also an area that reveals the other side of the coin, not necessarily beggars, but those who ply their livelihood as sellers of lottery tickets or shoeshiners. They are all in abundance, on all four sides. One of the most remarkable and bleakest films of recent years is Pedro Costa's *Ossos* (1997). Filmed in the Lisbon shantytown suburb of Estrela d'Africa, it follows a depressing few days in the life of the young poor who struggle not only to survive with their newborn baby, but to attempt death. Not even able to commit suicide, not really determined enough, they are beyond despair. At one point the father ventures into the center with the baby in his arms and begs in the street for money and food for the baby in a scene filmed in the Praça da Figueira (Fig Tree Square), adjacent to the Rossio. The scene strikes hard because the camera is placed on a long lens and staged for real, the crowds coming from the Metro, the people out shopping, all milling, criss-crossing, sidestepping and ignoring the begging father with his child.

What comes across most remarkably in the film is that while other cultures would show a similar situation sliding into a world of sexual or criminal debauchery, a world of drugs and stealing, the world of these Lisbon young still retains vestiges of honesty and pride. The young women, who work as cleaners in an apartment, make no attempt to steal from or cheat their employer. Indeed, one of the girls, failing to do the cleaning, her time taken with an attempt at suicide before the gas oven, refuses the day's wage after being saved by the woman on her return. If she does not earn it she will not accept it. The despair is so low that there is no hope; the long stares on their zombie-haunted faces take us into a world that we previously experienced watching the films of the French master, Robert Bresson.

# 2. Sintra

Various trips out of Lisbon have been suggested at different points in the book, but perhaps the one that seems most relevant is Sintra. The Rossio station is our departure point.

Sintra, which is still sometimes written as Cintra, is about eighteen miles from the city. Its apparent desirability as a place to reside, or to visit, rests with its earlier attraction as the summer residence for the monarchs and its subsequent attraction for the wealthy of Lisbon, as well as rich foreigners, all of whom took to the area as a summer retreat. Sintra is dominated by steep mountains that create a microclimate, intercepting the rain clouds and bringing a moister and fresher air to the town and its surroundings than the summer heat of the capital.

Today's visitors appear not to be the Portuguese themselves, although, with the recent addition of a Museum of Modern Art, one wonders whether the *Lisboetas* will venture out to see the collection. Their lack of interest is almost hinted at by Pessoa, for even though a tourist guide, he scarcely wants to mention the town: "A few minutes more and Cintra itself appears, girt sometimes in a thin veil of mist, bathed, at other times, in a great splendour of sunlight." And that's it. His book ends there. Having attached an addendum entitled, "A visit to Cintra, via Queluz," on arrival he has no intention of saying more. And that is still how it seems today, three-quarters of a century later.

Many from abroad are drawn to the town as a result of the poets and writers from former days who have praised its luxuriant flora and its follies. A "glorious Eden," Byron was to proclaim in his poem, *Childe Harold's Pilgrimage*, a description that has been glued to countless mentions of Sintra since then. In a letter to his mother, Byron wrote that the village:

> is, perhaps in every respect, the most delightful in Europe; it contains beauties of every description natural and artificial. Palaces and gardens rising in the midst of rocks, cataracts, and precipices; convents on stupendous heights—a distant view of the sea and the Tagus... it unites in itself all the wildness of the Western Highlands with the verdure of the South of France.

Yet it is not letters or journals that others know, but the nine stanzas from the first canto of his poem that he started writing in

October 1809, a few months after his visit, along with a few choice snippets, particularly his phrase: "glorious Eden." Although Byron admired William Beckford as the author of *Vathek* (1782) and was filled with admiration for the Moorish palace at Monserrate where Beckford had lived, he was not enamored by his character and wrote rather scathingly of him, some of the stanzas being removed from the published version of his poem.

Another British writer, Robert Southey, wrote in praise of the town, though he too was given to continual complaints. In his case he thought little not only of the Portuguese but of his fellow Englishmen. "I go among the English no more than civility demands, and always return to my books with a better appetite," he wrote in 1800 to William Taylor, the translator of Lessing and Goethe.

Southey was staying at his uncle's places in Lisbon and Sintra, working on a book on Portuguese literature, as his uncle had a fine library. While Lisbon was fit for complaints, Sintra was a splendid world, "a cool paradise," as he wrote to Samuel Taylor Coleridge. In a letter to relatives he offers the best description:

*There is no scenery in England which can help me to give you an idea of this. The town is small, like all country towns of Portugal, containing the Plaza or square, and a number of narrow crooked streets that wind down the hill: the palace is old——remarkably irregular — a large, rambling, shapeless pile, not unlike the prints I have seen in old romances of a castle, —— a place whose infinite corners overlook the sea; two white towers, like glass houses exactly, form a prominent feature in the distance, and with a square tower mark it for an old and public edifice. From the Valley the town appears to stand very high, and the ways up are long, and winding, and weary; but the town itself is far below the summit of the mountain. You have seen the Rock of Lisbon from the sea, —— that rock is the Sierra or mountain of Cintra: above, it is broken into a number of pyramidal summits of rock piled upon rock; two of them are wooded completely, the rest bare. Upon one stands the Penha convent, —— a place where, if the Chapel of Loretto had stood, one might have half credited the lying legend, that the angels or the devil had dropped it there — so unascendable the height appears on which it stands, yet it is the way up easy. On another point the ruins of a Moorish castle crest the hills. To look down from hence upon the palace and town my head grew giddy, yet is it farther from the town to the valley than from the summit to the town.*

## Palácio Nacional de Sintra

The feature of the town itself is the Palácio Nacional de Sintra (National Palace), also known as the Paço Real, or Palácio da Vila. It is unmistakable, its silhouette topped by two giant conical chimneys, akin to Kentish oast-houses, or "not unlike champagne bottles" in the eyes of Hans Christian Andersen, the most famous Danish writer of all. Standing inside the kitchen, one can peer up these vast conicals and imagine the huge spits that must have stood beneath roasting a quantity of pigs or other beasts simultaneously.

This was a summer palace of Moorish origins that was initially taken over by Afonso Henriques when he pushed back the Moors in 1147. Though Dom Dinis first started rebuilding, it was not until later that it was extended and substantially rebuilt by Dom João I in the fifteenth century, later completed with further additions by Dom Manuel I. One of the inner highlights is the Sala das Pêgas, the room named after the flock of magpies painted on the frieze and ceiling, each clutching a rose in its claws and a scroll in its beak, bearing the words *por bem*. The accompanying story is told that Dom João I was caught kissing one of the ladies-in-waiting by his wife, Philippa of Lancaster, to whom he said: *por bem* (for a good cause). Another variation suggests that he offered a rose to one of the ladies of the court when his wife was not looking, and that a magpie stole it, drawing attention to his infidelity. The king consequently ordered the 136 ceiling triangles, each bearing a magpie, as a satire on the women of the court (136 in total at the time) in order to put an end to their gossiping. A more straightforward story that spoils the others claims that the magpie has the livery colors of the king's family, the House of Avis, namely, black, blue and white, and that the rose is the symbol of the queen's family, the House of Lancaster.

Another room, with a grille that looks onto the chapel, is where the disowned Dom Afonso VI was confined for nine years, the floor worn away by his incessant pacing, trapped like a beast.

Although the palace is something of a muddle architecturally, with all its additions, its main interest resides in its *azulejos*, which date back to the fifteenth century, all the various types of tiles from those times being the sole surviving examples on the Iberian peninsula. Manuel was the first to import the *azulejos* to decorate the palace. As one progresses through the rooms, inner courtyards and patios, each displays a different form of tile patterns and colors. The inner décor is the oldest, the outer mainly dating from the late sixteenth and eighteenth centuries. It appears that there is still much research to be done on the history of the rooms, because they have been witness to all the monarchs throughout the history of Portugal. The entire royal lineage resided there, each contributing in his or her own way, right through to Dom Manuel II at the declaration of the Republic in 1910. Only Dona Maria II and her husband Ferdinand preferred the Pena Palace that they built on the mountain, barely taking up residence in the town itself.

## Luxury Accommodation

Sintra is ready to cater to the wealthier visitor. The Lawrence Hotel where Byron stayed, built in 1786, was closed for fifty years, but today it is again open, refurbished by its new Dutch owners, who have spent some years researching the décor to restore much of its period charm—though they refused to erect a plaque to Byron (at the behest of the Byron Society), commenting that it is a hotel for the living not the dead.

The Tivoli in town is the hotel where the German writer Thomas Bernhard is known to have retreated to write some of his books. In his last novel, *Extinction* (1986), his character notes the pleasure he had in Lisbon:

> *Sometimes I've thought I could spend as long in Lisbon as I've spent in Rome, but then I always recall Uncle Georg's telling remark about Lisbon, which seems to me the most splendid city of them all. Indeed, Lisbon is more beautiful than Rome, but it's provincial. The pleasantest years of my life were spent in Lisbon, but not the best years; these have been spent in Rome. Lisbon has a perfect blend of architecture and nature, such as you find in no other city.*

If a lavish stay is your objective, then the Hotel Palácio de Seteais, on the Rua Barbosa do Bocage, west of Sintra on the way to Colares, is just the place. Built for the Dutch consul in the eighteenth century, it gained its name, which means "seven sighs," after the Convention of Cintra was signed there in 1808 with the French. The sighs were ones of relief, or exasperation, depending on the interpretation one gives to Portuguese sentiment on its signing—for the agreement between the British and the French excluded the Portuguese from the negotiations, allowing the French to retreat with the spoils of war, much to the disgust of the Portuguese. The hotel is notoriously snobbish. If you don't look right, you are not welcome even to walk in the place, let alone to stay, eat or drink.

In *The Dumas Club* by the Spanish novelist Arturo Pérez-Reverte, Lucas Corso, the rare book dealer, stays at the Hotel Central, just opposite the Palace, on his visit to track down the second of the three remaining copies of the seventeenth-century occult text, *The Book of the Nine Doors of the Kingdom of Shadows*, which is reputed to hold the key to summoning Satan. The house where he has arranged to see the copy is close by. It belongs to the collector Victor Fargas. With no taxi in sight, Corso takes the local horse and carriage transport to the Quinta da Soledade (House of Solitude), along the road that leads to the castle. "The Quinta da Soledade was a rectangular eighteenth-century house, with four chimneys and an ochre plaster façade covered in trails and stains. Corso got out of the carriage and stood looking at the place for a moment before opening the iron gate. Two mossy, grey-green stone statues on granite columns stood at either end of the wall. One was a bust of a woman. The other seemed to be identical but the features were hidden by the ivy climbing up it, about to take over the sculpted face beneath and merge with it." Once inside, Corso compares the copy he has brought with him with the second, noting the discrepancies in the engravings. The next day, on discovering the mysterious death of Fargas and the book smoldering in the grate, he departs for Paris.

The film version of the novel is entitled *The Ninth Gate* (1999) and is directed by Roman Polanski, who came to Sintra, using one of the villas very much as described in the book. He brought Johnny Depp as the book-dealer sleuth Corso to the location, along with Polanski's wife, Emmanuelle Seigner, as the enigmatic young woman whom Depp encounters on his journey. The film's title takes into account that the Alexandre Dumas aspect of the book's plot has been excised in the course of its adaptation.

## Palácio Nacional da Pena

In Ray Milland's film, *Lisbon*, he ventures out to Sintra, intent on displaying its wealth, framing the palace on the top of the mountain through the archway at the Hotel Palácio de Seteais. Seeing the Pena Palace from below is still not as astonishing as seeing the Pena Palace from eye level. It stands 1,400 feet above sea level, perched precariously atop the mountain peak, looking like all those images we've seen in fairy tales books. To reach it one can take a taxi or one can walk. The steep climb was our preferred path, never regretted, for periodically as one climbs the long, winding road, there are points where one can look down over the plain and village below, points where one can stand atop an outcrop of granite boulders, looking like styrofoam blocks that have been rolled down the hill, or even giant marshmallows that the gods have spilt from a packet.

As one climbs, one can see over the walls of the various *quintas* along the road, or peer down on those scattered near the base. These are homes for the fabulously rich, though not necessarily celebrities as some suggest, but more likely rich businessmen whose high walls and hedges are intent on excluding prying eyes, yet which cannot exclude when viewed from above.

On arrival at the park gates, we made directly for the Palace, aptly described by Oswell Blakeston:

> *(…) we plunged into a banshee tunnel to the foot of the castle that has every ogrish excess of Frankenstein tower and Wagnerian battlement and goblin castellation, and Mephistophelean passage-ways and grotesque ramparts; and on one ledge of coping there is a toy cannon and a burning-glass so that a salute to the spirit of wonder is fired automatically every day at twelve o'clock.*

It is the outside that is the sight one most remembers. Many find it hideous, completely kitsch, whereas others think it a folly that folds them in laughter. The Palácio Nacional da Pena (Pena Palace) was commissioned in 1840 by Ferdinand von Saxe-Coburg-Gotha, the husband of Dona Maria II, from the Prussian architect, Ludwig von Eschwege. The intention was to make a romantic baronial castle over the ruins of an earlier Jeronomite monastery that had been damaged by the Great Earthquake, only the chapel and cloister remaining. The result was a mixture of styles, from Gothic to Renaissance and mock-Manueline, a concoction of styles, an architectural cacophany as befitted the Victorian follies that were coming into vogue. It is comparable, in fact, to Ludwig of Bavaria's mock castles.

Entry is over the drawbridge, but one that does not draw up, of course. Gargoyles immediately watch your step, crocodiles jutting from the walls. The north facing battlements are the most frightening, for as one squeezes along the narrow walkway one is fully aware of the adjacent vertiginous drop, the place one needs to stand when a storm is lashing to test one's fear to the limit. In the sun, a stroll around this Disneyesque froth of strawberry mousse pink and banana yellow painted walls made me think of a contemporary comparison, the Amoreiras complex in Lisbon, designed by Tomás Taveira, which will appear a little later.

If one wishes to avoid vertigo, there are plenty of places to stand and cast one's eyes to the horizons, across to the Atlantic coast, or south to the Tagus estuary. The Estoril race circuit is at one's feet, certain to be heard at the appropriate times, and other famous landmarks are ready to be picked out, whether Montserrate, or the Mafra Palace. Hans Christian Andersen not only saw Mafra, but added: "The air was so clear that I thought I could count the windows in the building, although it lies several miles away."

Inside, the rooms are as they were left when the royal family fled in 1910. Rooms that appear to be made of wood are made of cement to look like wood. Rooms stuffed with vulgar decorations, crammed with furnishings. Each room is its own world, a kaleidoscope ride across the clouds to a Sultan's boudoir or a Far Eastern chamber. These are rooms ripe

for today's frivolities and gaudy collectors, fit for admirers of the fashion designer, Jean-Paul Gautier, or lovers of those paragons of kitsch, French artists Pierre and Gilles. One room contains paintings of naked women, one alleged to be the queen, but no one knows which. Rose motifs abound, explained by Dom Ferdinand's allegiance to the Rosicrucians. (Down in the valley the recently re-opened Quinta da Regaleira has a past with connections to freemasonry and other mystic bonds.)

On the way down there are ways off the road, ways to find paths down through the undergrowth, though one has to be prepared to be lost. "(It) is a garden, where nature and art complement each other," wrote Andersen. "It is the most beautiful walk one can imagine. It begins with cactus, plane-trees and magnolias and ends with birch and spruce among huge broken rocks. Geraniums of all kinds and colours flower here in profusion. Incredibly lovely thistles rise proudly by the myrtle bushes with their scented snow-white flowers; solitary paths twist up between ancient ivy-clad walls and natural arches of fallen rock." Little will have changed since 1866, when Hans Christian Andersen, aged sixty, made the trip to visit his old friend, George O'Neill. Though he spent time in the family home on the outskirts of Lisbon at Pinheiros, he enjoyed his stay at Sintra most. "Our house, with its many rooms looking on to the rock-face down which a stream trickled, had its own garden filled with lemon and figs, but so tiny that a tethered hen could circle it. From here on the tree-covered hills one could see, through the clouds, King Fernando's castle, half Italian, half Moorish in style."

Who better to relate this fairy tale view than the famed children's storyteller, even if we do tend to bear the image of him in our mind as portrayed by Danny Kaye: "It was really like Paradise here. I remembered my Latin grammar in school: 'There was a lovely valley in Thessaly called Temple'—could Temple offer anything more beautiful than Cintra?"

On the way down, one can sidetrack to the castle on the accompanying crest, lower down than the Pena Palace. This Moorish castle on the craggy mountainside was also captured by Afonso Henrique, and its ruins ordered to be partly rebuilt by Ferdinand so that his own view from above was not spoilt.

One could go the opposite way and seek out the Convento dos Capuchos, commonly called the Cork Convent, which was built among the thick vegetation in 1560. This monastery of spiritual peace for twelve hermits, hollowed into the mountainside, is noted for the cork lining of its walls, floors, ceilings, indeed even the benches and cupboards. All is cramped, small and damp. Byron found it ripe to mock the monk who lived in the cell he visited:

*Deep in yon cave Honorius long did dwell*
*In hope to merit Heaven by making earth a Hell.*

## Monserrate

What fascinated Byron when he went to Monserrate was the state of abandonment and the mysteriousness of the house and its gardens. The nineteenth-century French writer, L.F. Tollenare, found it in a similar state:

*I was surprised by the view of an elegant castle, constructed in Gothic style and surrounded by beautiful gardens. I went towards it with the idea of asking permission to visit it. The main gate was open and I entered without meeting anybody. The deepest silence reigned over the entrance courtyard. I climbed up to the landing at the top of the stairs… nobody. I entered the house: complete silence! I went into all the rooms, which were decorated with taste and magnificence, but in a state of abandonment and ruin capable of inspiring the coldest romanticism…*

As he added, while others would construct false ruins, here "the Portuguese let everything fall into ruin instead." None of the locals had stripped the place. The Portuguese lean towards the idea that what is gone is lost, thus that the garden is an oasis waiting to return to a desert, while the British, and some others, maintain notions of creating Romantic settings and landscapes.

The estate at Monserrate was first bought in 1790 by Gerard de Visme, a wealthy merchant, who set about building a palace that in essence stands today. An early engraving shows the structure with three towers, each with a domed roof, linked by lower buildings. It is built on a spur of rock in the center of the hundred acres, with views across the plain to the sea and with woods behind that climb up the slopes of the mountain.

William Beckford rented the property later, and when he decided to leave, it fell into ruin, the state in which Byron found it so appealing. Beckford had not liked the house, calling in a carpenter from Falmouth to make alterations. But he was captivated by the landscape and the garden. "I have been engaged," he wrote in 1795, "with the Royalty of Nature, with climbing roses and cork trees, with tracing rills and rivulets to their source and examining every recess of the lovely environs." He opened up several paths through the woods, thought to have become the basis for the later layout.

In 1856 Francis Cook, another wealthy Englishman, bought the estate and transformed the palace and grounds into something not unlike that found in Beckford's novel *Vathek*, with its oriental atmosphere. As Princess Rattazzi wrote in 1879: "the house seems to be a silver feather fallen from the turban of a sultan... an illustration from the stories of the Thousand and One Nights." Cook commissioned the landscapist William Stockdale to compose some scenic vistas that included tree-framed lawns, one down to the lake. Statues were added, brought from Rome, "some carved stone pillars and an Etruscan sarcophagus to make the chapel ruins look more picturesque."

William Nevill from the Botanic Gardens at Kew was commissioned to select rare and exotic plants to match the exoticism of the house. The effect created and which still holds today, even if somewhat shambolic and awaiting the hands of gardeners, was to take advantage of the microclimate so that the garden could sustain plants from all over the world in a mixture of tropical and temperate vegetation. The French novelist, René Bazin, wrote in 1875:

> The rarest of branches form a roof above our heads; vines run from branch to branch and purple bunches of grapes hang down everywhere. I began to walk slowly, for fear that this virgin forest would disappear with the strange sound of my footsteps, as in the fairy tales... it is a virgin forest, a wild garden unlike any other I have ever seen. I found myself living in Brazil for an hour, I searched for the golden-crested macaw, and I thought of tigers, I heard the tinkling of fountains and I drank in the heady perfumes so full of life and the sun, which make one drunk like champagne.

Standing on the lawn, Hans Christian Andersen fell into reverie: "The sun sank into the sea, which turned pink, stretched across the horizon, reflected with magic lustre in the white marble and decorated walls, filling with splendour the great mirror-clear windows. The air was so warm, so still, so permeated with the scent of flowers that one felt completely spellbound, wafted away from reality."

In 1946 the Cook family sold the house and estate to the Portuguese government, and though the house is still closed, there are efforts to manage the overrun garden once more, through the Friends of Monserrate. But it is a far cry from earlier days when the people working in the garden could have been numbered in hundreds, rather than a handful that might work there today.

## Praia Grande

In January 1981 Raúl Ruiz was in Sintra to shoot his film *The Territory* (1981) around its woods and lakes. Also in attendance was the American independent filmmaker Jon Jost, who had been commissioned to make a documentary on Ruiz, to be called *In Corman's Territory?* (although it was never realized, as the footage was unsatisfactory). One of the actresses in Ruiz's film was Isabelle Weingarten, the girlfriend of Wim Wenders at the time. On the phone to him one night, she explained that they were at a crisis point, almost out of film stock. When one shoots a film it is usual to inform the film manufacturer, particularly when it is black and white, so that they can produce a batch big enough for the whole shoot with the same consistency. But when you are Ruiz you shoot quickly, often at the last minute, and you collect together what you can from a diversity of sources. Wenders was in Zurich, about to go to New York to discuss another project he was trying to set up. Knowing there was some film stock in the fridge of his company's Berlin offices, he detoured to collect and deliver it to Sintra. On arrival he found a "picnic." He had recently suffered at the hands of a production of mishaps in America, filming *Hammett* (1982) for Francis Ford Coppola's company. In Sintra he saw a paradise, "a dream décor." Far from the two hundred technicians in America, he found just a small crew working in the woods, "sheltered from pressure, in a serene manner," with Henri Alekan at the camera. Wenders thought that Alekan had retired. Alekan had filmed Cocteau's *Beauty and the Beast* (1946), as well as films for other directors like Marcel Carné, Joseph Losey and Abel Gance. He was in his early seventies. Wenders was taken by the location and by the way Alekan was working with the notorious light of the region. He started dreaming. And then he came across a deserted hotel on the Praia Grande, one "that had been ravaged by a storm or a hurricane: as a whale beached on the sand." He knew he wanted to film. He asked Alekan if he would be willing to stay. "They only had one week to go on Raúl's film, so I asked if after Raúl was finished, a week later, we could start another film." Likewise, he asked the other technicians and Ruiz's cast. They all agreed, though only half-heartedly, thinking that he would not raise the funds. Wenders flew off to New York and secured enough money to start shooting. Within a few weeks of Ruiz finishing, Wenders was shooting.

That is one version of the story. There are conflicting stories, particularly as the storyline of *The Territory* is about a group of campers who get lost and resort to cannibalism. That Wenders should arrive, ostensibly to save the day, and then cannibalize the cast and crew for his own film has become the myth and the image surrounding events.

Part of the problem seems to be that Ruiz's own production was not going so smoothly. The producer, Roger Corman, had set up the financial backing, but had not provided as much as was promised. (Corman incidentally plays the lawyer in Wenders' film.) Ruiz had wanted to film for Corman's production company, to make the blend between exploitation movie and his own highly aesthetic imagination, an approach that he accomplishes by treating all with equal seriousness. Ruiz, who is a prolific director, even admitting that he has not seen final cuts of some of his films, was undoubtedly distracted by the presence of Wenders, Jost and others at the set, although it appears there was no direct interference. Gilbert Adair, who worked on the script for *The Territory*, describes Ruiz as "a director who tells stories like Sheherazade, as though his life depended upon it." The ground seems to have shifted from under him. Later, talking about the experience, Ruiz said: "we shot in Sintra, a famous place where romantic people go to commit suicide."

Wenders' film *The State of Things* (1982) was largely improvised, as is often his approach. Filming for him is an improvisation because it is about searching, discovering the end only as one proceeds. As with his later film, *Lisbon Story*, this was a film within a film, with the situations around him as the spur. The film he is remaking is Allan Dwan's *Most Dangerous Man Alive* (1961), the Wenders' version being called *The Survivors*. When the film stock runs out, the cast and crew are left to fend for themselves in the damaged hotel at Praia Grande (where they both lived and worked during filming) on the edge of the ocean, while the director, Fritz Munro, sets off for Los Angeles to find the producer and resolve the money crisis. Wenders enjoyed filming on the edge of Europe, as near as he could get to America, to exorcize his all too recent experience there.

After strolling around the woods and parks, along the roads, even losing ourselves out towards the sea, which is somehow regarded as part of Sintra even though it is not, we return to the town. In Wenders' film you could be forgiven for thinking that the sea and the hotel are part of Sintra, given the way they wander around by the station as if just down the road.

Before our return to Lisbon, close to the station we can visit the newly opened Museu de Arte Moderna. The building is a former casino, but now the gambling is on the safe side with international post-war modern art: Pollock, Kline, Guston, Reinhardt, Rivers, Twombly, Beuys, Klein, Tinguely, Sherman, Schnabel, Longo, Koons, and more Koons, Klossowski, Rego... You can peer out of the window, stare up at the Pena Palace, imagine the yellow brick road, and then turn to Warhol's portrait of Judy Garland. As Friedrich Munro (the name also alludes to Marilyn) says to his cast in the hotel before setting off for America and another shooting (by bullet this time): "Stories only exist in stories, whereas life goes by without the need to turn into stories."

# 3. Avenida da Liberdade

The Avenida da Liberdade (Liberty Avenue) is Lisbon's Champs Elysées. Even some of the residents refer to it as such, for it is another way to be part of Europe, to fit in, particularly if it is with fashionable Paris. The Avenida is a long boulevard, about one mile in length, gradually sloping upwards away from the Rossio. It is lined with hotels, restaurants, shops… and offices. This is the street where the biggest contrast between old and new can be seen; many of the Art Deco façaded buildings have been brought down and new blocks erected. Others have been adapted. One example near the southern end, overlooking a square, the Praça dos Restauradores, is the 1930s Art Deco Eden Cinema, as once was, which has been adapted or "disfigured" partly as a Virgin Megastore and partly for its apartments above. The façade has been perforated and an array of plants arranged to offer a resemblance to Eden each morning to the visitors when they yawn and peer through their windows. The preservation order on the cinema's staircase may have been respected, but to no great effect.

Over the road, on the other side of the boulevard is the main *correio* (Post Office), which has been adapted to make better use of space by covering the inner courtyard with a steel and glass framework and paneling, making provision for more counters and more light. Any idea that it would lead to a reduction in the queues was misleading, as that requires a change of attitudes, not facilities. Always to be remembered is that in Lisbon time is on a different plane in real life, and not only in its arts. There might be many tills in the Post Office or a bank, but there is no hurry to serve you or to speed up the process. Clerks wander away and return, while the queues grow longer. No need to lose your temper, or show annoyance, the Portuguese are not impressed. If you prefer your fast-moving other world, there is no reason why you cannot go back there.

The avenue itself is wide, up to 300 feet or so in places. The central parts are flower gardens, ponds and fountains, with bars and restaurants interspersed. It is a place to stroll, to sit and ponder among the palm trees. But it is not the 1880s; today's traffic pours along the center, the pollution from the cars is hardly invigorating and the sight of soulless office façades

is even less stimulating. It does not really match Thomas Mann's description set at the end of the nineteenth century: "One of the most magnificent streets I have ever seen, a triple street indeed, with a path for carriages and riding horses in the center and well-paved avenues on either side, splendidly adorned with flower beds, statues, and fountains. It was on this magnificent *corso* that my palatial quarters were situated."

Parallels with the Champs Elysées are in order at the top, where the Etoile and its busy traffic are matched by a rotary, a perfect circle, with five main arteries locking into this wheel hub, called the Praça Marquês de Pombal (or *Rotunda,* to give it a usable name). Its central reservation is not filled by an arch but a statue, this time of the Marquês, the man who rebuilt the town after the Great Earthquake. He looks back down the avenue, towards the Tagus, and as a result of its slope he gains a magnificent view. Indeed, one could even think that he was looking over the shoulder of his king on his horse two miles away, in the Praça do Comércio, looking down on him, whether as the servant or the master is for others to decide.

## Illusions

Set back behind the Avenida near the top end is the room Tabucchi imagined for the cultural page editor of the daily *Lisboa* in his novel *Declares Pereira.* "I'm only the obscure editor of the culture page of a second-rate evening paper, I write up the anniversaries of famous authors and translate nineteenth-century French stories." His is not the main office of the newspaper, but a satellite office, a room for one, a room upstairs in Rua Rodrigo da Fonseca. "You will find me at number sixty-six Rua Rodrigo da Fonseca, near Rua Alexandre Herculano and just a step along from the kosher butcher." A visit provides one with a clever twist, for the street exists, but not the number. It runs 56, 58, 60, 62 and then a hop, step and jump to 70, 72... No 66. Here is another number game as before in the cemetery and in Rua de Saudade. Nor can one see the buildings on that side of the street harboring the description he gives of his office: "that dismal little room in Rua Rodrigo da Fonseca, with the wheeze of its asthmatic fan and the eternal smell of frying spread abroad by the caretaker, a harridan who cast everyone suspicious looks and did nothing but fry fry fry." The other side of the road, perhaps.

But perhaps a more pleasant place is close at hand, a place where the editor regularly withdraws for a sweet lemonade and omelette. "Do you know the Café Orquídea? asked Pereira, it's in Rua Alexandre Herculano, just past the kosher butcher." At least this place exists as an address, even if now "disfigured," as Bernard Comment remarks, in the 1970s to make a "mediocre snack bar."

This novel is again set in the 1930s, this time 1938, again to highlight the oppression and censorship of Salazar's Portugal. The old journalist who is coasting along quietly in the "independent, nonpolitical" Lisbon daily, is suddenly challenged when he employs a young assistant, a political activist, who makes him take effective action, all the while knowing that the secret police will find their way into his life. He is helped in this change, this regaining of his self-respect, after visiting a friend in Coimbra, when he meets a woman on the train who reads Thomas Mann and who insists that he does something: "surely there's nothing one can't do if one cares enough."

There are always the literary references. Pessoa is not far away. One example occurs when Pereira asks Marta, his assistant's partner, what she does: "I write business letters for an import-export firm, replied Marta, I only work in the mornings, so in the afternoons I have time to read, go for walks…" nudging us towards a comparison with Pessoa.

Tabucchi also wishes us to know that he is not the only Italian to have Portuguese sympathies. Luigi Pirandello was in Lisbon some years before. "In Lisbon the great dramatist first staged his *Sogno (ma forse no)* (Dream, But Perhaps Not)." A fitting title. And the Italian connection is maintained, for the film version of the novel was made in 1996 by another, Roberto Faenza, called *Afirma Pereira* (Pereira Declares), with Marcello Mastroianni in the title role.

A few roads away in the Rua Barata Salgueiro is the home of Portuguese cinema, the Cinemateca Portuguesa, set in a charming former private house with a front garden, and an atrium of wood carvings of oak leaves and acorns to impress as one climbs to the offices and library. This is an ambiance that is more to be expected from a film location than film offices. Besides the films cited in the course of this book there are many others that have Lisbon settings and connections. One of the older directors, Paulo Rocha, who made *Verdes Anos* (Green Years, 1963), a film that helped launch the Portuguese New Wave with its story of a man coming to the capital to seek work as a cobbler, has recently made another set in the city, *A Raíz do Coração* (The Root of the Heart, 2000). The next generation, which includes Pedro Costa who has made a sequel to *Ossos* (Bones), also features Teresa Villaverde with *Os Mutantes* (The Mutants, 1998) on Lisbon's teenage shelters, another gruelling experience of the deprived. And in *Longe da Vista* (Far from View, 1998) João Mário Grilo creates a world of multiple loneliness for its various characters. There are also those from elsewhere who come to

Lisbon with their narratives, like Brazil's Walter Salles, with *Terra Estrangeira* (Foreign Land, 1995), about a young Brazilian who returns to his mother's homeland.

## Morna and Cesaria Evora

Between this haven of film delights and the Rossio, in streets lying just behind the Avenida are a few of Lisbon's varied mix of musical genres. Along the Rua da Glória, in what was once a brothel-cum-music hall, is the Ritz, one of the centers of music from Cabo Verde (Cape Verde), the former Portuguese colony off the African coast. The main reason the music is known today is due to the growing fame of Cesaria Evora, who sings what is called *morna*. Not that she sings it in this club, or in any other club in Lisbon, for her world today is composed of larger theaters, something she accepts though does not necessarily relish. To fortify this lack of intimacy her stage is usually graced with a table and chair so that she can take interludes for a drink, probably still whisky, as if in a bar, while the band swings along with an instrumental. Nor has she lost her barefoot diva tag, refusing to wear shoes, even though at one point not so long ago political pressure forced her to submit, only to kick them off once she had commenced singing.

Since the ending of colonial rule in Cape Verde in 1982, many of its musicians, like those from other ex-colonies like Guinea-Bissau, Angola and Mozambique, have moved to Lisbon, creating an interest in their music. Some say that the interest in *morna* is a reaction against the sadness of traditional *fado*. But *morna* is a music that seems to have derived from *fado*, a meeting of *fado* and African beats at some point under colonial rule, producing a music that is like *fado* with a shuffle. It is a soulful lament, the nostalgia being for the country left behind, for today more Cape Verdeans are abroad than in residence in the islands, (25,000 are thought to live in Lisbon alone), but it is a melancholia mixed with a large splash of hope. To date Cesaria Evora's best-known song, indeed her theme song, is *Sodade*, the creole word for *saudade*.

Various singers and musicians from Africa have arrived in the last forty years on the international stage. Perhaps Miriam Makeba is the most celebrated female singer, emerging from South Africa in the 1960s.

Cesaria Evora's day came in the 1990s. The break occurred not in Lisbon, but Paris, where her friend José da Silva had gone to find work, by day on the railways and by night as a record producer. He made two records of Cesaria's songs and played them to the head of the French label, Mélodie. François Post was smitten. Visiting Cape Verde to confirm his enthusiasm, it was not long before a third album was recorded and she was booked into the famous New Morning jazz club in Paris. From that day she has not looked back, her albums selling across the world. For thirty years she had been singing in the Piano Bar in Mindelo on the island of Sao Vicente, paid in loose change or, more commonly, with drinks. As with the musicians from the Buena Vista Social Club in Cuba, the word retirement is not one that readily springs to her lips.

Lisbon is noticeably a cosmopolitan city, whichever way you look at it. It is in the air. You can breathe it, hear it, see it. It has plenty of good sides, but also the inverse. Half the people employed in the building work of the Expo area and the general rejuvenation are from Africa, as many illegal immigrants were handed residence permits at the high point of construction, when completion dates were knocking at the door. As the work slows, the infusion of cultures continues. Not only of those from the colonies, but from the Portuguese themselves who returned from other parts of Europe as well as the former colonies, whether from exile or from military service in Portugal's own Vietnam in Angola. What will happen to this burgeoning population as fewer jobs are available? Many writers have been confronting these issues for some years now.

António Lobo Antunes published *South of Nowhere* in 1979. It takes the form of a first-person narration that begins in a Lisbon bar and follows the events of a one-night stand between an ex-army doctor and a woman whose voice never appears in the narrative. It is probably a story he recounts regularly on his trips around the bars, during his attempts to seduce women. He tells how Lisbon appears from afar:

*What is certain is that as Lisbon receded from me, my country, do you see? became more and more unreal, my country, my house, my daughter with the clear eyes in her crib became as unreal as these trees, these façades, these dead streets, because Lisbon, understand, is an amusement park, a traveling circus set up beside a river, an invention of tiles that repeat each other, approach and recede, their indecisive colors paling in rectangles on the side-walks. No, seriously, we live in a land that does not exist, it is absolutely useless to look for it on maps because it does not exist, it is only an eye, a name, not our country. Lisbon begins to take shape, believe me, only from a distance, to acquire depth and vitality.*

## Jazz and Carlos Paredes

In the corner of the Praça da Alegria nestles the Hot Clube, a name presumably relating to Hot Jazz, rather than the temperature within, with or without the music, as the cellar space is small. It is reminiscent of the famous Troubadour coffee house in London, where Bob Dylan played on his pre-fame visit and which Tori Amos used as a practice patch before launching herself big time, or Bunjis, that other famous London cellar where scores of famous folk artists have played. Or Ronnie Scott's first Gerrard Street jazz club. These are all cellars where an audience of 100 constitutes full, and to cram in 150 is against all laws known to man, especially that of sanity. The Hot Clube follows in that tradition, to its credit. Hot Jazz. Louis Armstrong played here in the 1950s, when Lisbon was the port of call for those making the transatlantic trip in stages before one-stop flights became the norm.

Charlie Haden, the American bassist, played here too. This is where he met the legendary Portuguese guitarist, Carlos Paredes, which led to them recording together some years later. Charlie Haden became popular with the Portuguese after his stance at a concert on November 20, 1971 in Lisbon, on tour with the Ornette Coleman Quartet, participating in the first International Jazz Festival of Cascais. Haden dedicated his *Song for Che* to "the black people's liberation movements of Mozambique, Angola and Guinea," to the Portuguese that they might be freed from their Fascist dictatorship and that the colonies in Africa might also be freed of colonial control. "It was an act of courage, a prophetic one, that has never been forgotten," as one observer noted. The next day Haden was arrested by the PIDE, the secret police, at the airport and was only released after four hours when the US cultural attaché interceded. The resultant publicity and a further concert, which was canceled and then reinstated, was given media blackout, but the damage was done. A few years later, Haden extracted that dedication from a recording that Ornette had made of the concerts, as he did of all concerts, and built it into the recording *For a Free Portugal* that he made with Paul Motian on drums. The track appeared on his album *Closeness*.

In 1978 Haden was playing at the Avente Festival in Lisbon, and having heard of Paredes, he asked if he could play with him. It was arranged. They met at the Hot Clube, with an audience of 150, more than the place could take. Paredes was accompanied by another guitarist. As Haden wrote: "They were playing as one musician, each anticipating and knowing where the other was going. (...) His approach to music (voicings, melodies, chords, rhythms) was so original that it reminded me of another musician with whom I love to play music: Ornette Coleman." Haden knew that after playing with him that night, one day they would play together again, and hopefully record. This came true twelve years later with an album of improvised music, *Dialogues*, which includes the infamous *Song for Che*. They also played together in the 1990 Lisbon Jazz Festival, this time in the larger Coliseum venue, repeating the concert two days later in Porto.

When you are at the top of your profession, even if your music is regarded as a genre of its own making, like Carlos Paredes', there are always ways to make inroads into the adventures of other forms, as with Charlie Haden. Paredes has also found his music spread further to other edges of contemporary classical playing, the Kronos Quartet commissioning some of his compositions to be arranged for them to play, performing them on their 1998 tour of Europe, which included London and the Lisbon Expo. As Osvaldo Golijov wrote when arranging for the Kronos: "I still ask myself whether it is possible at all to transpose to another medium both the magic of Paredes' playing and that of his unique instrument, with its strange tuning and octave and unison doublings that only the sweet innocence of a whole people or the perversity of a Stravinsky could create. The virtuosism of Paredes is charged with meaning: there is a street wisdom in his playing, a strange, crooked lyricism, and, above all, impeccable taste." The Kronos carve further and further into the musics of the world, taking all manner of turns. Two of the Paredes compositions appear on the Kronos' *Caravan*, as does another composition, *Gloomy Sunday*, a song of Hungarian origins that David Harrington heard and noticed for the first time on tour in Lisbon, sung by Billie Holiday, and which resonated with his mood following the tragic death of his son.

Although Paredes comes from a family of guitarists, he was discouraged from playing guitar and was directed towards the violin and piano. But he picked up one of his father's discarded guitars, one that was cracked, and made himself into the most famous of Portuguese *guitarra* players.

## Parque Mayer

Spilling out of the Hot Clube, within yards one can fall into the arms of the Parque Mayer, though it has seen better days. Some of the theaters, including the old cinema, are closed, but the area still staggers on with some shows and its surrounding restaurants, all of which are aimed at *Lisboetas* rather than foreigners. The shows are popular musical variety entertainments, known as *revistas* (reviews, revues), something of a political burlesque performance with girls, songs and satirical comment. They started in 1859, and seem to be adapted from the idea of the Parisian revue. In the 1920s and 1930s this was a thriving complex, but gradually over the years it has seen parts hived off, left to rot, even failed as porn cinema. In the 1950s and 1960s it is said to have been the only place where the Salazar regime was openly criticized. It has lost its credentials today, with TV supplying its former function.

In *Lucky in Love*, David Mourão-Ferreira ventures there rather than take on the more traditional, and culturally acceptable, *fado*:

> And I greatly admired your duplicity when you suggested to our paedia-tricians that, instead of the inevitable dinner in a fado restaurant, we should, instead, take the "battleship" that Saturday to a musical in the Parque Mayer. Of course our lumbering Canadian enjoyed the show even less than he would have enjoyed the fados. But still, it was a change for you; or rather, for us. And, of course it was a good way for us to see that irreverent farce about Lisbon politics that so many people had been telling us about. But we never did get round to discussing whether it was good, bad or simply the same as all the rest.

For the author the area is also something of a signpost, a dividing line. Talking of another friend's reluctance to travel, or even to step outside Lisbon, he writes: "for over forty years, he has limited himself to living exclusively between the Parque Mayer and the Cais do Sodré. 'Any further north,' he would say, 'any further north, bollocks, don't even think it, that's still Visigoth territory. But to the south, blimey, beware, that's Saracen territory.'" It is what Londoners might say when remarking about not venturing "north of Watford," or "south of the river," for those who live in north London.

## Casa do Alentejo

On the other side of the Avenida, down towards the Rossio, is a street that runs parallel, the Rua das Portas de Santo Antão. It houses one of the magnificent sights of Lisbon, though you wouldn't know from the outside. The entrance is anything but enticing, and once inside you climb a wide staircase before being brought up short by an inner Moorish courtyard "with a small fountain, a glass door and some marble columns lit by red lights, like the lights they use in sacristies." (Tabucchi) And everywhere are ferns and small palms in pots, and walls covered with tiles. There are rooms off in all directions, and there is another staircase that leads to the gallery and two dining rooms, a billiard room, armchaired hallways and a faded ballroom with gilt-mirrors and a chandelier that have seen better days. It is a world of lost grandeur, for faded memories. This is Casa do Alentejo, a private members' club, a kind of Alentejo Social Club which was started some years ago by wealthy Alentejeans who would come in from the countryside to entertain their guests in the capital. Although today it is still intended for those from the region, outsiders and foreigners are allowed to eat in the restaurant.

In an effort to resolve an issue with his dead wife, who committed suicide years before, Tabucchi's character in *Requiem* arranges to meet her in this house: "I arranged to meet someone here at nine o'clock, I said, it was a stupid thing to do, since I'm not a member and I've never been here before, and the person who's coming here belongs only in my memory. The manager of the Casa do Alentejo rested the cue on the table and smiled a melancholy smile. There's nothing wrong with that, he said, you'll feel perfectly at home here, this club is nothing but a memory, now." And while he waits, they play billiards, drink a 1952 bottle of port and talk. In the novel the scene ends with the arrival of

Isabel, but in the film version the ballroom is too good to pass over, and the couple dance, in time to an instrumental *fado*-styled number, laden with *saudade*. They dance and turn, turn and turn, his memory spinning closer and closer in his arms until his friend, Tadeus (or Pierre in the film) is dancing in his place, and he is the lone observer from a sidechair. When the music ends, his wife and friend stand side by side and wave as they fade back to the other world, and the effects of the port and passing time require him to depart and conclude his day's hallucinations, the meeting with Pessoa.

Outside in the street, a left turn takes you back down past the Coliseum to a haven of seafood restaurants. Here you'll find something special: *ginjinha*. *Ginjinha* might be described as a cherry liqueur, a cherry brandy, but if you treat it as such, you'll be in for a shock. The kick is far punchier, almost lethal. Eat the cherry too if you really want a buzz; they have been soaked in alcohol for so many years that it is like ingesting your own personal grenade. Although there are a number of these little bars in this area, and a few others dotted around the city, at the end of the street is the long-established *A Ginjinha* at the Largo de São Domingos. Like the others, it opens early and is almost the last attraction to close at night, its clientele of lowlife and lost souls sent off to look for another way to blast themselves into another sphere. In Eduardo de Gregorio's *Aspern*, the main character Jean stops for a drink at this very bar, needing to fortify himself in order to accomplish his duplicitous deed.

Turning right instead of left from the Casa do Alentejo leads to the Elevador da Lavra. You might have to wait for this funicular as, like a tour bus, it does not seem to depart until a few passengers are aboard, and on arrival at the top you wonder what has been gained. Along the Rua Júlio Andrade is a house that looks like a good substitute for a South American house. In fact it served just that purpose in *The House of the Spirits* (1993), the film version of Isabel Allende's novel with a host of stars including Meryl Streep, Antonio Banderas, Jeremy Irons and more. The view over the city is low key, for this Campo de Santana is the smallest of hills. But where else does it go? Our steps echo in the near deserted streets. Hospitals and various medical institutes. Hospitals and the morgue. A dead end.

**The Metro**

Showers from the word go. It rained. Heavy showers. My notebook was sodden. We went underground, there to discover one of the best art galleries of all: the Metro. It runs straight-arrow along the length of the Avenida and spreads elsewhere at both ends. And it's free. Though you'll have to be careful with your camera because a few of the security guards at strategic points seem to think they have a duty to prevent people from photographing the art or even lingering to look at it. I speak specifically of the Olaias station on the new Oriente line, because these creatures of power feel it is the best display on offer, and hence somehow that they need to protect it from prying eyes.

Lisbon has only started to enlarge its Metro system in the last ten years. Initially it was constructed in the 1950s with a single line, the Caravela (Caravel) line, which was decorated with fairly straightforward *azulejo* patternings. The next phase, the Gaivota (Seagull) and Girassol (Sunflower) lines came later. More recently, not only was the new Oriente (Orient) line added to connect the rest of the system and the city center out to the Expo area and possibilities of new horizons, but a refurbishing of the earlier lines, a sprucing up at least, took place. The Oriente line is the one that has received the most lavish praise and which offers a spectacle to the user of the transport system.

What started out as one aspect of the Lisbon underground system, the use of *azulejos*, has today become the feature of the system. Let us go back to the beginning, take the line back to square one. When the system was first undertaken, the architect Francisco Keil do Amaral and the artist Maria Keil, his wife, despite the financial limitations of the era, were able to accomplish remarkable work. Tiles were not in favor at the time and it was to Keil's credit that she created a different design for each station based on fairly simple patterns. Ten of the initial eleven station designs were hers, the other being decorated by Rogeiro Ribeiro. Her work spanned twenty-five years, starting in 1957, for she later designed the tiles for eight other stations. It would be fair to say that almost single-handedly, by designing these large public works, she brought back into vogue the Portuguese decorative art form that had long been out of fashion. Though many might feel these stations seem plain alongside the latest, all have an understated power, as visits to the stations at

Intendente, Restauradores or Anjos show. In fact, Keil was asked not to incorporate figures; her designs were intended as geometric patterns to provide rhythms to the stations and their architecture.

Later when another line was being developed, other artists contributed and there started an expansion of approaches. There has always been the sense that it was meant to make the underground environment amenable to the user, but that financial restrictions made it difficult to be too elaborate, and also probably that the idea of extravagance was more low-key then than now. Only citizens travel on the Metro, the rich rarely, perhaps not at all in the 1950s. Which is a shame, because not only is the environment fine, but the trains themselves (as indeed the overland trains) are in good health and usually far from abused or vandalized.

At the time, the idea that the artists "decorate" the public spaces was the official terminology, as the design work was still recognized as a decorative art.

I will elaborate on a number of the stations and their designs. If I seem to choose too many, then it is because I think they merit it. In reality, all are worth individual notes, the system is so impressive. In the Laranjeiras station Rolando Sá Nogueira interpreted quite literally the name of the station: orange trees. Using the orange, he applied with a silk-screen technique oranges in groups, isolated, cut in two, distributing them in varying sizes across a white tile background. The effect is almost Pop Art, vibrant and pleasant, playing joyously "as if with the fruits of Paradise," as José Cardoso Pires added.

In the Alto dos Moinhos station Júlio Pomar paid homage to four of Portugal's great writers: Fernando Pessoa, Almada Negreiros, Brocage and Camões. Each has his own area. The calligraphic lines with their sparsity and spontaneity make them art rather than decorations. With hindsight, there are signs creeping in that Pomar's style might become a challenge to others, namely, graffiti artists. Perhaps that is one of his intentions. Although there is only a slight sign of spray-can activity, it might not be long before further public art has to be accounted for.

At the Colégio Militar-Luz station Manuel Cargaleiro has worked with the *azulejo* tradition, creating a pattern inspired by diamond-point and single-picture tiles, and also large panels, with motifs similar to those of his paintings. Here he uses blues and white with some yellow to make forms with letters and other shapes that offer intriguing perspective faces.

Maria Helena Vieira da Silva was asked to work on the Cidade Universitária station. She offered a gouache, *Le Métro*, which she had made in 1942 as the basis of the project. This was enlarged eight-fold to a size of thirteen feet by twenty and transferred to tiles. The image shows artists and intellectuals, along with a couple, a dog, a cat and objects "symbolizing a multitude found in the underground shelter from the violence of war." Fragments from the original are redistributed, and quotes are used from Socrates and Cesário Verde, like: "If only I would never die! And eternally seek and find the perfection of things!"

In the 1990s the need for refurbishment and the reworking of the atriums was as much a priority as the construction of a new line. A whole new approach was needed. The idea of decoration was replaced by the idea of art. The artist was to become more integrated into the design, to produce what could be better regarded as installation art, for not only were walls or objects to be created, but the whole building, the very station itself was to be assessed by the artist. Not that all the artists wanted to go that far, but some took on the challenge of blending their work with the work of the architects, even if we tend to name only the artists who contributed. In the brief for the project attention was also given to deterring vandalism and violence. The sheer scope of what many have accomplished probably impressed potential vandals to desist damaging or offering further painterly additions, an accord with pleasure finding common ground.

The Entre Campos station was the first to benefit from renovation, with Bartolemeu Cid dos Santos providing an engraved stone that paid homage to Portuguese literature. Parque station was refurbished by Françoise Schein and Federica Matta who produced a dark-colored work that is extremely engrossing in its textual detail, based on the Discoveries and the Rights of Man. An hour can easily be passed working one's way around the two platforms.

At the Marquês de Pombal (formerly called Rotunda) station, João Cutileiro, one of the three artists involved, has produced an image of the Marquês that stands between the arches separating the two platforms,

"as counterpoint to the statue above, in the sun and in the shade. A hero in two spaces and two versions: monumental and resounding on the open place; subterranean here, a faceless diplomat." (Cardoso Pires)

The Campo Grande station offers the impressive work of Eduardo Néry, who re-interpreted the eighteenth-century tile motifs of welcoming figures or *figuras de convite*, figures that he has deconstructed and duplicated in fragments, dispersing in a staggered, jarring effect, using a number of tones of blue and creating an amusing work.

By now the boldness of the venture was becoming apparent, and the real display was to follow with the new Oriente line. Of course, one can go about one's daily business and in time visit a number of these stations, or one can travel, as if going to an exhibition and proceed from one station to the next, wandering up and down, and around them. In several instances it is not just a matter of making a painting in tiles on the platform, as many extend through the total concept of the station, from the entrance through the walkways to the platforms. Some work better than others. Many are quite inspired.

The Alameda is the first station where the new line connects to the Caravela line. The original platforms, designed by Maria Keil, have been retained, with four artists working on the new section; one is Alberto Carneiro, whose sculptures represent trees, while a marble floor patterning of different colors is by Juahana Bloomstedt.

One of the most stunning effects is at the Chelas station, where the architect, Ana Nascimento, and the artist, Jorge Martins, have collaborated to provide large and colorful wall coverings that are three-dimensional to match the large red tiled columns along the platform. The whole is set off with a series of twinkle lights along the edges of the platforms that progress through a permutation of changing colors.

Perhaps the most impressive, however, is at Bela Vista, where it is worth the effort to walk the whole station, up the stairways, through the atrium and foyer, along the walkways to the entrances. Querubim Lapa has integrated geometric patternings that work the whole location as an entity, and because the place is so open, viewing from all angles enables one to see the degree of success achieved. This is a station that is not in use to any great degree as yet, evidenced by the absence of staff. The ticket booth was empty, the controller's glass room on the platform too, the monitor videos playing to themselves, and yet there is no damage, no graffiti, and litter bins that are either emptied and cleaned regularly or perhaps scarcely used, for they were scrupulously clean.

One has to note that each of these new stations has its high points to attract and seduce. Olivais, as its name suggests, draws for its theme on olives, with a series of fourteen different scenes by Nuno de Siqueira and Cecília de Sousa. The station that is regarded as the *crème de la crème*, showy in other words, is Olaias, because it is so vast, starting at the cathedral-high platform space with gigantic columns. It thus provides enormous walls to be covered, those by the escalators up from the platforms offering an experience of handprints by Graça Pereira Coutinho that triggers a sense of fun. At the top your mouth is expected to drop open, for flying above are multi-colored glass lit objects, (modern-day "chandeliers," officially termed), as well as a transparent lift in the same style, and a suspended ceiling up the next escalators to the exit likewise lavishly and startlingly covered. The architect for the site was Tomás Taveira, who has worked on some of the buildings in the complex above the station, as well as being the architect of the first shopping mall at the Amoreiras, with all its eye-catching glory. Taveira is the star artist, too, of the four working here, for it is his acrylic-painted works that attract attention above our heads.

The Oriente station itself is a fitting end; in fact, it comprises such an array of work by various artists that it is a gallery in itself. To fit in with the Oceans theme of Expo 98, the exhibition drew on artists from across the continents, even if all do not reside in their places of origin. Most are ceramic tile works, although Magdalena Abakanowicz from Poland presents a large brass sculptural fish. The panels are created by Joaquim Rodrigo (Portugal), Hundertwasser (Austria), Yayou Kussuma (Japan), Raza (India), Errö (Iceland), António Ségui (Argentina), Zao Wou-Ki (China), Abdoulaye Konaté (Mali), Sean Scully (Ireland) and Arthur Boyd (Australia). As with any exhibition, and indeed at all the stations, the artist who created each work has a plaque or sign to indicate their contribution.

Despite all the grandeur, there are moments of delicacy that captivate, such as in the walkways at the Rossio station where Helena Almeida's frieze of a woman walking, as if a series of frames of a film, catches the right balance and lingers longer in the memory than some of the more spectacular images. Or there is the monumental experience that is the new Baixa-Chiado station with its cavernous tunnelings, escalator rides and underground walkways, with space to show its size and only a hint of additional work where the artist Angelo de Sousa has added a gold painting motif near one exit. The project belongs to the architect Alvaro Siza Vieira, who was also responsible for the Portuguese Pavilion and its suspended canopy at the Park of Nations, as well as the Chiado rebuilding above this station. Where once the underground was always somewhere dark and depressing, a deterrent, today's Metro here, and in other cities, brings something exhilarating. Perhaps modern technology, which enables enormous holes to be gouged in the ground, has placed the future before us, and we see the idea of living underground as something credible just as in so many science fiction movies.

One night returning on the Metro in the company of football fans streaming away from a match, at one of the junctions with another line we met fans from another match on their way home. Experience in London teaches one to step aside, or at least be wary. But that is our sadness. Although I'm sure Lisbon fans are far from exemplary, there was little banter between the rather large groups, just a series of cheers. At the cavernous Baixa, which was asking for an echoing din to be created, everyone walked and passed each other with little more than friendliness. Only next day when I checked the papers could I be sure who had won or lost.

Lisbon football is primarily two teams, Benfica and Sporting Lisbon, though many of the stars of Portuguese football and its national team play abroad, often in Spain. Since the heyday of the 1960s when Eusébio was a national hero and known by his surname alone, football has been enjoyed passionately but not always triumphantly. Even if three daily papers (*A Bola*, *Record* and *O Jogo*), the most popular of all the dailies, are dedicated to football, there is a *saudade* for its former glory. Until now, for 2000 saw a resurgence on the international field at the European Championships, and the ascension of one other player into the ranks of surname only status: Figo.

# 4. Jardim Botânico

## Miradouro de São Pedro de Alcântara

Another hill to be climbed, either gradually, though no less tiringly, through the Bairro Alto, or more drastically and in true fellwalking spirit up the slope taken by the funicular of the Elevador da Glória, or alternatively, and more romantically, on the funicular itself,—unless you are the protagonist in José Gil's *Cimetière des Plaisirs* (1990), who hears it is only for the exclusive use of "councillors"—brings one just short of the Miradouro de São Pedro de Alcântara. From this vantage-point one commands a view across the center of the city to the Castelo de São Jorge on the opposite hilltop. A view that makes this *miradouro* a prime spot for visitors, whether the locals who linger seated on the benches, the children who play, or the tourists passing by at varying speeds. The record stops seem to be made by Japanese tour buses from which they pour, cameras in hand, to stand back against the parapet while another takes the photo with the castle as backdrop. And then back on the bus to whistlestop another spot.

For Pessoa, standing on this *miradouro* before "the panorama of the city," his thoughts were of Amiel, the Swiss writer, whose journal bears resemblances to *The Book of Disquietude*. "Amiel said that a landscape is a state of the soul, but the phrase is a flawed gem of a feeble dreamer. The moment the landscape becomes a landscape, it ceases to be a state of the soul. To objectify is to create, and no one would say that a finished poem is a state of thinking about writing one. Seeing is perhaps a form of dreaming, but if we call it seeing instead of dreaming, then we can distinguish between the two."

In Eça de Queirós' *Cousin Bazilio*, Luiza's affair with her cousin finds itself being consummated in a less salubrious area of the city, "over by Arroios in the Santa Barbara quarter, which she vaguely remembered as a heap of shabby old buildings," away from prying eyes in the more affluent areas of town, a stone's throw from here. One time on her way to an assignation, she meets a friend of the family who insists on accompanying her, and try as she may to shake him off, he sticks close to her petticoats.

They enter the *miradouro:* "Subdued to inertia by the pompous voice of the Councillor, Luiza let herself be escorted down the steps to the garden, though very much against her will. 'I still have time.' She thought, 'I can take a cab.'" And they proceed to peruse the "beautiful panorama" at length, as she becomes distraught at being unable to send him on his way. "They made a tour of the garden where white and yellow butterflies were playing; water splashed in the fountains giving rhythm to the beauty of the garden; birds settled on the marble busts that rose between masses of dahlias. The garden delighted Luiza but she hated the high, iron-barred railings." He tells her they are there to prevent suicides. And one wonders whether a different type of suicide isn't staged in this area today. Of all the major *miradouros* this one is in the worst state, the least encouraging, for it has become an area where drug addicts and others seem to hang around, leaving their debris behind. And over the wall, on the garden patio below is not only the rubbish, but the half-burned wreck of a garden house. Enough to forego this viewpoint in the future and move to another.

Just up the way on the Rua Dom Pedro V is the most bizarre of bars that Lisbon has to offer, the Pavilhão Chines (Chinese Pavilion). It is a place that Tabucchi recommends one visit "after midnight," which comes as no surprise if you've read attentively this far, when the atmosphere is at its height. Its extraordinariness is to be found on its walls, which are lined with mirrored vitrines filled with wondrous and ludicrous tableaux of artifacts from around the world, a jumble of curiosities, *objets d'art* and mementos. It is a kitsch display or a veritable Cabinet of Curiosities that we might associate with the American collagist Joseph Cornell.

### Praça do Príncipe Real

Saramago's Ricardo Reis has come up the Rua Dom Pedro V too, and has arrived at "the Praça do Rio de Janeiro, once known as the Praça do Príncipe Real and which one day may go back to that name, should anyone live to see it." That moment was set in 1936. Today it has returned to its former name, as Saramago knew it would. "When the weather becomes hot, one longs for the shade of these silver maples, elms, the Roman pine which looks like a refreshing pergola." But he reminds us: "Not that this poet and doctor is so well versed in botany, but someone must make up for the ignorance and lapses of memory of a man who for the last sixteen years has grown accustomed to the vastly different and more baroque flora and fauna of the tropics." He has, of course, spent that time in Brazil.

Instead, we leave it to Pessoa himself to describe (in 1925) the location on his tour of the city: "This garden contains some fine specimens of trees, the most remarkable one being a spreading cedar, the branches of which resting on iron-work, cover ground enough to hold some hundreds of persons. Under this fine cedar-tree another public library is installed," one of six he informs us that the Town Council at that time had "distributed among the Lisbon gardens." We must remember that Pessoa informs us at every available point of the book about the city's outlets, the libraries and even the daily newspapers. He lives by books and naturally feels that reading is a main root into the town.

Cardoso Pires describes the old there who "remain gathered around the card game which is in some way the reading that lulls them in before the big sleep. At their age they know full well it is no longer the course for life which will give them trumps. That said, wise and resigned, they are content with those that will give them the game in *manille* or *brisque* and which will permit them, as they say, to tot up points." As if to underline Cardoso Pires' remarks, the men play their cards alongside the children's area, beside the slides and sand pits.

The film director, João Botelho, whom some liken to the Japanese director Yasujiro Ozu, lives nearby, and uses the garden to walk with his children. One of his films *Três Palmeiras* (Three Palm Trees, 1994) has various scenes shot in this garden. In 1994, Botelho was commissioned, along with two others, to make a film to celebrate Lisbon, for its European Capital of Culture year. He chose the eight hours from six in the morning to two in the afternoon, dividing the period into eight stories, some of which interconnect. Opening with a death and ending with a birth, the film moves from color to final scenes shot in black and white (like the colors of Lisbon), silent. Using a variety of styles, it enabled him "to express my love for the area I live in, Bairro Alto. The Three Palm Trees are those I see from my window." He wanted to show Lisbon as a village, and using the garden at the Príncipe Real was one way of doing so. There are nods towards Jean-Luc Godard, and towards a musical comedy that has overtones of Bertolt Brecht and Kurt Weill.

There seems to be some comparison in structure with the American director Robert Altman's *Short Cuts*, an echo that Gaudlitz also has with *Taxi Lisboa*, relating back to Fellini's *Roma*. It is a way to approach the city, where so many stories can be told that one has to be selective. And a way to portray the city that Wenders faced, using the history of cinema as a parallel. An earlier film by Botelho, *Conversa Acabada* (The Conversation Is Over, 1981) works with the friendship of Pessoa and Mário de Sá-Carneiro, including scenes from *Lucio's Confession*.

Before we go further, we need some sustenance; after all, the Pavilhão Chines is a night bar. Walking by day requires another spot. We found it in what we would call a corner store. It is indeed perched on a corner, and it does indeed sell food, but it also has a bar and sells *uma bica*. It is almost a converted front room with a few purchases to sustain an income for the owner and his wife, who remains seated in the back room in her armchair. Two little tables with three chairs are crammed into the corner for us to sit, unless one or other of the regulars is in occupation, and though there might well be a seat vacant, one feels an intruder in their daily ritual. Sometimes our visits preceded one old woman, other times she was already installed. But each time was not without her appearance and the entrance of some workers, there to stand at the bar, or spill out of the door if more than three while drinking. We drink *uma bica*, take away some bread, cheese, a banana or other fruit and a bottle of water. Our hands more than full, we pay the small amount asked.

### Jardim Botânico

"Each garden in Lisbon has its phantoms and its secrets," wrote the novelist Urbano Tavares Rodrigues. "The Botanical garden, with its old exotic trunks and its precious species, (is) hidden in the heart of the big city with its oppressive traffic." The Jardim Botânico (Botanical Garden) is one of the ignored, indeed neglected, gardens of Lisbon. Few refer to it, or even point to it. One has to hunt to find the entrance. There is one entrance from below, with an official gate, but perhaps this is rarely opened. The surrounding buildings are ruins, dilapidated beyond repair, hardly a salubrious invitation to step into a garden of foreign wonders. After wandering around the perimeter again, we found ourselves at the top end, strolling beside the university building, the Academia das Ciências, just off the Rua da Escola Politécnica, with its spindly high palm trees as guards, towards a more discreet entrance. As we were to discover, that find numbered us among the few who had gained admittance. Though the authorities would like not to acknowledge it is neglected, it appears little tended, and fallen palm leaves lie rotting across the paths. But that is its charm. It is there to make you feel that you are one of the privileged to have discovered this garden filled with exotic plants lying on the hillside. Trees with roots that wind everywhere. A greenhouse that seems devoid of exhibits, as if schoolchildren had been invited and left with the day's results, dirtied and soiled tables left as evidence. For every sense of negativity there is the sense of affirmation, of wandering at will, discovering emptied giant pods scattered around, rummaging in far-off mindscapes. Has anyone noticed this place before? And then, at our next visit, a street sign points in its direction, and there seems to be an attempt to interest people with a rough plan of the place, photocopied, and a ticket seller who enthuses and tries to direct attention to the special plants as well as to an indoor exhibition of twenty-five vitrines packed with seeds, pods, roots, fruits, stalks and leaves, a collection of tropical plants, recent and past... reminders of the Discoveries, former colonies and the wonders that nature has provided. The ticket seller smiles. We assure him there is no need to sell to us, we are already convinced, we've been before.

In Thomas Mann's *Confessions of Felix Krull, Confidence Man,* the professor on the train to Lisbon insists that:

> *our botanical garden on the western heights ought to be your first goal. There is nothing like it in all Europe, thanks to a climate in which a tropical flora flourishes side by side with that of the temperate zone. The gardens are crowded with araucaria, bamboo, papyrus, yucca, and every kind of palm tree. And there you will see with your own eyes plants that really do not belong to the present-day vegetation of our planet, but to an earlier one—I mean the tree ferns. Go without delay and look at the tree ferns of the Carboniferous period. That's more than short-winded cultural history. That is geological time.*

And so he does visit the garden, though there is a distraction in the form of a woman, or, as he puts it: "This is a fitting place to remark that nature, however rare and interesting her guise, gets scant attention from us when we are engrossed with humanity." Yet he concedes to observe:

*Conifers of gigantic size claimed our amazed attention, half a hundred metres tall, at a guess. The domain abounded in fan palms and feather palms. In places it had the tangled aspect of a primeval forest. Exotic rushes, bamboos, and papyruses, lined the edges of the ornamental waters on which floated bright-hued bride and mandarin swans. We admired the palm lily with its dark-green tuft of leaves from which springs a great sheaf of white, bell-like blossoms. And everywhere were the geologically ancient fern trees, growing close together in wild and improbable little groves, with their massive trunks and slender stems spreading into crowns of fronds, gigantic leaves, which, as Hurtado explained to us, carry their spore capsules. There were very few places on earth, aside from this one, he observed, where there were still tree ferns, But, he added, primitive man had from time immemorial ascribed magical powers to ferns in general, which have no flowers and really have no seeds, especially in the concoction of love portions.*

This garden, which is virtually invisible from the streets that surround it, is just ten acres in size. It was laid out between 1873 and 1878, and is judged to hold around 20,000 exotic species, many labeled (although, as always, the ones you really want to know to satisfy your curiosity seem to bear no tag, nor are noted on the sheet handed at the gate). But there is plenty that is labeled and one can discover the varieties of palm trees—thirty-five here all brought from the former colonies—as well as a number of Ficus trees, including the *Ficus Macrophylla*, some so old that a vast tangle of aerial roots make them an eye-catching display, banana trees and large Sequoias (Big Trees) including the *Sequoia sempervirens*. There are Chorisias, including the floss-silk tree, and an enormous *Dracaena draco* (Dragon Tree) that one can squat beneath and feel reduced in size, though beware of the blood, for it runs red. As we wander, perhaps we will meet José Gil or his protagonist looking for a suitable tree to sit beneath to meditate and dream at leisure, not be disturbed and drawn into a conversation as in *Cimetière des Plaisirs*. This time he should avoid the Himalayas and choose the bench close to the *Ficus sycomorus*, the one near the water.

All is maintained by just four gardeners, as we were to discover, which enables the garden to always have that untended look. Even damage done by the cyclone that hit the city in 1941, overturning some of the statuary and ornamentation, has never been righted, and now seems part of an ancient ruin. The streets on all sides might be resounding with cars, but here there is silence. The trains under feet, carving through the tunnels out of Rossio, are not thought about, only the birds enjoying life in the dense and lush foliage, or in one sectioned off garden frogs croaking merrily until you approach. Only patience and stillness will encourage them to resume, and what appears as only a bright green slime-covered pond is suddenly seen to have pairs of eyes protruding through its surface.

The garden appears to thrive because of a microclimate on these slopes that enables the temperature to change noticeably from the terrace section to various parts of the slope. And its levels of heat do not end there. It is one of those gardens with secluded parts such that if you come across a couple you expect them to be in a compromising position. What I now see labeled and claimed as a toilet on the plan was in fact a former toilet, long past its decently functional stage, lurking in a corner of the garden, that served us well as a shelter one time when it suddenly decided to rain hard, briefly. As if to allow us to sample its Equatorial ambiance.

This environment is a space in which to think, to escape to those other worlds from where the trees originate, to let the vegetal air and nature's sounds whisk one into the imagination of luscious leaves and fallen seeds. I was not surprised to discover that the musician Manuel Mota had made one of his environmental tapes in the garden, part of his collection of rediscovery made around the city.

In *Aspern* (1981), the film that Paris-based Argentinean filmmaker Eduardo de Gregorio shot in Portugal, the garden of the house became the pivotal point for the young critic Jean's attempt to fraudulently obtain the treasured papers from the grand old dame, trying to lure and seduce the young niece into the garden to accomplish it. The film is a fictional world, a film about fiction, one that is appropriate for Lisbon. Adapted from Henry James' *The Aspern Papers*, Lisbon became more relevant to de Gregorio than Venice because it seemed thirty years behind everywhere else, "like Buenos Aires in my childhood, or Rome in 1950." Jean (Jean Sorel) comes to Lisbon to seek the manuscript believed to be in the hands of the last mistress of Aspern, Juliana (Alida Valli), an old lady now, looked after by her young niece, Tita (Bulle Ogier). The writer, who had died young, never existed in reality. Though there is no mention anywhere, by setting it in Lisbon there are enough overtones of Pessoa to draw parallels.

An element of the *fantastique* floats through the film, a house of mirrors distortion, the view through a heat haze, but this is only to be expected from de Gregorio, who was the scriptwriter of *Celine and Julie Go Boating* (1974) for French director Jacques Rivette, in which that house is another world of disorientation, courtesy of the foreign mind-expanding confections they swallow. Here the disorientation comes in the shape of the actress Alida Valli, who is supposed to be a hundred, but who looks younger, and healthier, providing a fundamental disorientation.

It is the garden that Jean uses as his trap. He offers to have it restored, by hired gardeners, as a way to rent rooms in the villa, and then to have the flowers cut and sent to fill the host's rooms. Using the garden's perfume and evening peace to act as the drug to lure Tita among the plants, he takes her into his confidence in his pursuit to grab the papers: Aspern's correspondence, and perhaps an unpublished manuscript. The house and garden were actually shot outside Lisbon, further north, where a greater sense of an uninhabited space could come across. Not that Lisbon is abandoned; other location shots occur around the *miradouro* at Santa Luzia, the Ginjinha bar near the Rossio, a restaurant and more.

The garden is intended for scientific research. I'm sure they mean botanical research, but I think of another who did research with vegetal substances (particularly mescaline), Henri Michaux, the Belgian writer and artist. He wrote to the French poet, Jules Supervielle when he discovered that Lisbon was so agreeable, and decided to stay the 1934–35 winter: "I am no longer obliged to live in revolt and on my nerves, and always suffering, to brood on myself. No? And for the first time too, I write because I want to write."

Pessoa seems to reflect the *Lisboetas'* lack of interest in the garden, an indifference that still appears pronounced. In his book, intended as a tourist guide, he says it all as far as he's concerned: "This building (the university museum) has adjoining it a garden which is one of the most picturesque in Lisbon, and even in Europe; so, at least, many foreigners have said. It contains specimens of the flora of all regions of the world. The garden is on a slope, and this is one of its great points, for the incline has been put to good use to get every possible effect out of the varied vegetation that everywhere rises up, giving the aggregate an Edenic splendour. The garden contains several ponds, cascades, brooks, bridges, labyrinths, a fine hot-house, etc." Hardly an enthusiastic endorsement. He could not get out quickly enough. "The tourist, should he so wish it, can go right through the garden and come out at the lower door, in Praça da Alegria, going on from there to the Avenida da Liberdade…" Or the Hot Clube!

# 5. Gulbenkian

Not to write about Gulbenkian would be to ignore a major portion of today's art and culture in Lisbon and Portugal. Attention must be paid, whether to the man himself or to the results of his actions, for the net spreads further than a couple of museums with their art collections. The Gulbenkian legacy spreads across the world with a foundation that gives grants for the young to travel, finances all manner of cultural activities, and extends into education and health. It is an involvement across the whole board such that every person in Portugal is in some way a beneficiary of this one man's life.

Calouste Gulbenkian was born in 1869 into a wealthy Armenian family, enabling him to come to Britain and study engineering at King's College in London, where he settled, taking British nationality in 1902. His wealth acquired real dimensions when he was awarded a five percent invest in the Iraq oil industry (for his part in its formation). He lived for a time in Paris, but spent the last years of his life in Portugal, his decision to settle made when he was taken ill en route for America and had to be hospitalized in Lisbon. He was so pleased with his treatment that he determined to take up residence.

With his wealth Gulbenkian collected art and antiquities. He was always interested in acquiring the best of something, passing up on treasures that had been damaged or showed signs of too much restoration. His extreme selectivity enabled him to make precise collections. They were given an added bonus when he acquired major works from Leningrad's Hermitage in 1928–1930 at a time when the Soviet Union was desperate for foreign currency.

Gulbenkian's intention had been to leave all his wealth to the country of his nationality, but the British authorities did not look kindly upon him, terming him a "technical enemy" for remaining honorary economic advisor to the Iranian embassy in Paris during the Second World War. As a consequence he looked around him in the country in which he was staying, Portugal, and decided to bequeath all to his hosts, setting up a structure that not only provided homes for his not inconsiderable art collections, but also provided foundations to fund work of "a charitable, artistic, educational and scientific nature." He died in 1955, aged 86.

In his name today there is not only the park with his two museums, but also the system of funding grants and scholarships for Portuguese artists to travel and study abroad. Add to this the financing of Portuguese libraries abroad and at home, in villages as in towns, as well as the funding necessary for schools, medical facilities, research laboratories, hospitals and centers for the disabled, and you have a network that has made him a cultural patron in the widest sense, a name that has become part of the daily fabric of Portugal itself.

In his collecting Gulbenkian had passions for specific antiquities, including Turkish and Persian carpets, Armenian and Arabic manuscripts, and Greek and Roman coins. His interests veered through ancient Egyptian art and Chinese porcelain to illuminated manuscripts and French book bindings, taking in Japanese lacquer boxes and the exotic art of René Lalique (with whom the collector had a contract, his 169 pieces of jewelry making his Lalique collection second to none). He also collected Western painting, with outstanding works by Rubens, Rembrandt, van Dyck, Frans Hals, Fragonard, Gainsborough, Turner, Manet, Monet, Degas and Renoir among many others.

In 1969 the Museu Calouste Gulbenkian (Gulbenkian Museum) was opened in Lisbon to house the collections, set in a garden that includes sculptural works as well as an open air auditorium. Unlike many museums where the overwhelming quantity creates cultural indigestion, this museum is uncluttered, enabling visitors to focus on the quality of the art.

Across the garden is the Centro de Arte Moderna (Modern Art Center) with a collection of Portuguese art from the twentieth century that shows succinctly where it has been during that period, with acknowledgments to the Paris days noted by the inclusion of Fernand Léger, André Masson and Francis Picabia as well as Sonia and Robert Delaunay, or Berlin with a George Grosz.

Those who went through Paris in the early days of that century make up a list of all Portugal's major artists: Amadeo de Souza-Cardoso and Eduardo Viana, Sarah Afonso and José de Almada-Negreiros, Carlos Botelho, Mário Eloy and Maria Helena Vieira da Silva. Most returned afterwards. With the war raging, the Delaunays took refuge in Vila do Conde in northern Portugal for a couple of years from 1915 to 1917, attracting Amadeo de Souza-Cardoso, whom they had met before in Paris, along with José de Almada Negreiros and Eduardo Viana. All these artists felt isolated in Lisbon, after the whirl of Paris.

Berlin was another destination. Bernardo Marques visited in 1929, the influence shown in his work of busy city life, with its cafés and theaters. As the years passed his work became more depopulated, moving away from the city bustle into the fields. Until his suicide in 1962 he only exhibited in group shows. Marques had seen George Grosz as a role model, as had Mário Eloy, who also ventured to Berlin in 1927, after initially trying Paris and finding it too amiable. On return to Lisbon he felt excluded and increasingly isolated. The cityscapes he painted are poetic, revealing a drama going on within him, their scenes with naked women having more to do with aesthetics than erotics, whatever his intentions.

Although the intervening years saw the emergence of other artists, those were lean times. The Salazar regime's restrictions on outside influences created a dearth of art, and while many left for cities besides Paris, like London and Munich, the quality was lacking in strength until late in the century. Since 1974 political normality has meant that art influences from abroad have been reflected in all the home-based work. All periods are shown in the museum, including many already mentioned in relation to the Metro art, along with others like Lourdes de Castro, Júlio Pomar, Paula Rego and younger artists like Julião Sarmento, recently the subject of a solo show at the museum.

## Paula Rego

It seems clear that Portuguese art has two major artists within its recent history, both of them female, namely Maria Helena Vieira da Silva and Paula Rego. Both chose to live and work outside their country as a result of Salazar's dictatorship in their formative years.

Paula Rego has lived and worked in London for many years. She came to study at the Slade school in the 1950s, met and married the artist Victor Willing, and then for a number of years moved back and forth between London and Ericeira, just outside Lisbon. Her work is firmly rooted in her childhood and aspects of Portuguese culture.

She regularly acknowledges and comments on her sources, noting that, for example, her use and liking for films dates from her father's influence. He made films for his own and his friends' amusement, creating a small cinema in the basement of her grandparent's flat where he showed his as well as other films. She has memories, too, of going to the cinema to see Walt Disney with her grandmother and the nurse, Luzia, seeing *Fantasia, Snow White* and *Pinocchio*, which have had an enormous influence on her, and *The Wizard of Oz*, another key influence. Only Luis Buñuel's films can match Disney's, she says, a liking she acquired in her adulthood, of course.

As is evident from much of her work, domination is a major factor. Victor Willing wrote: "Domination takes many forms. We see, for example, the child dominated by the parent or teacher; the individual by the State; the psyche by the dream or ideal; the personality by passion; conscience by guilt." Paintings like *Salazar Vomiting the Homeland* (1960) or *The Policeman's Daughter* (1987), with the girl cleaning the knee-length boot, have obvious sexual overtones and indicate her political position. That her work was unnerving to others in Portugal was witnessed at the opening of her first solo exhibition, which was held in Lisbon in January 1966 at the Galeria de Arte Moderna in the Sociedade Nacional de Belas Artes. Many appeared shocked at her freedom of expression, which revealed that though they thought they had confronted the status quo, perhaps they still tacitly accepted it. One man turned to her at the opening and pronounced: "You must be a slut to paint these pictures," to which she replied, quite politely: "No. Sluts paint churches." The poet Alberto de Lacerda, writing on a Portuguese group show, noted: "The suffering and penalties of those who stayed are immeasurable. In the arts the most criminal fascism that Portuguese fascism caused was self-censorship."

Humor and a playfulness not unconnected with childhood concerns are continually at work in Rego's paintings. Indeed, her studio is often described as an enchanted toy cupboard, or "like a playroom" as she puts it, with "a dressing up box." Her studio takes on the aspect of a little theater as she constructs the tableaux for her paintings, for the need to have a story element dates to her childhood, in what the critic Ruth Rosengarten terms the "will-to-narrative." A childhood that still has working practices, like kneeling on the floor on all fours to draw.

As she works, Paula listens to music: opera in the morning, *fado* and samba in the afternoon. Predominantly the same works: the *fado* of the incomparable Amália Rodrigues, and the opera of Verdi. Although she knew the operas from her father's recounting of the narratives and playing selections on his gramophone, it was not until she was thirteen that he took her to the São Carlos Opera House in Lisbon. Bizet's *Carmen* was her first experience, and *La Traviata* was another adored. *Rigoletto* was her favorite, and also her father's, "which he saw thirty-two times."

The idea is to have a working routine. "The place is the Portugal I like, an idea of my childhood, not a memory." Though the element of time passed is in the work, a memory of childhood hopes, promises, fears and nightmares, it is not direct childhood memory. The intention is to make an environment "like a source of feeling. If you have a source of feeling, then you can have thoughts, ideas... then thoughts and ideas can come."

An issue that has also affected her centers on the ordinary Portuguese working woman. Having been brought up in a wealthy family home, she was used to an environment where wealthy women were idle, while the servants did the work. This has had a profound effect on her, resulting in her portrayal of women as servants, stocky and solid, hairy and powerful figures. "Most women in my pictures are Portuguese. I use Portuguese models, simply because I identify with them very very closely, and I do have a profound admiration for these particular women. They are so brave. I mean they endure such a hard life."

In recent years, on one of her visits to Lisbon, Rego created *azulejos* for one of the manufacturers there. In 1990, when she was invited to be the first artist-in-residence at London's National Gallery, one of the works she produced was for the brasserie in the Sainsbury Wing. Based on *Crivelli's Garden* in their collection, she used the idea of *azulejos* as the basis of the mural. The preparatory drawings and the first panel were actually painted just outside Lisbon in Estoril during the summer. "The mural's title may be Crivelli's Garden but of course it's really my garden, a Portuguese garden. In my bedroom at Ericeira there were tiles from floor to ceiling, arabesques in cobalt blue—the same color I've used for the tiles I've painted on the walls at the lower level of the mural."

## Maria Helena Vieira da Silva

Maria Helena Vieira da Silva and her husband, the Hungarian painter Arpad Szenes, are both represented in the Gulbenkian collection, though they also have their work extensively exhibited in their own museum not far away in an old silk factory in the Amoreiras district. Facing the Jardim das Amoreiras, the Fundação Arpad Szenes-Vieira da Silva was set up in 1994, devoted to their work and supplemented by special exhibitions by others with close affinities. Vieira da Silva was born in 1908, on June 13, St. Anthony's day, like Pessoa, and left Lisbon to study in Paris in 1928. She rarely returned because of the political climate. When she was forced to in 1939 for the duration of the war, her stay was only brief, as she preferred to pass through and travel to Rio de Janeiro instead. In 1970 when the Gulbenkian showed her first retrospective, which had already toured other European capitals, she refused to attend or accept an award in protest at the dictatorship and the earlier destruction of one of her commissioned paintings by the government because it appeared inappropriate to them. Although she had taken French nationality in 1956, her work was always marked by Portugal. By going away, it seems that she discovered more about the Portuguese within her. She died in 1992.

While Vieira de Silva's work is abstract, a spatial research with the geometric form of the square as the recurrent motif, images of the city are part of the whole, more clearly perceived at times than others, dependent on the perspective shifts. It is often said that her work relates to memories of her childhood, *azulejos*, and the special light of Lisbon that is always at play, helping to bring out her own sense of coloration. Indeed, she acknowledged herself that she had always been sensitive to the light, that Lisbon light is unique, "especially when one crosses the Tagus and sees the city from the middle of the river. There one questions all the mysteries of the city." And yet Virgílio de Lemos writes that she told him, as an aside, that "it was her soul that made the light of her paintings. Like a weaver. Nothing to do with the light of azulejos or the light of my childhood in Lisbon." A deflection probably to encourage less obvious observations .

"Perspective is one of my passions," she said at another time. "Not scientific perspective, but that which I rediscover, make out of rhythm, out of music… with the aid of which it is possible to suggest a huge space on a tiny piece of canvas." Time is perhaps the Portuguese factor that is hiding in her blues. Vieira da Silva's work is about waiting, "waiting for something to happen," in order to "give space to space," eminently captured by Sophia de Mello Breyner in her poem, *Maria Helena Vieira Da Silva or The Ineluctable Itinerary*:

> The labyrinth is minuteness. Wall by wall
> Stone against stone book upon book
> Street after street stairs after stairs
> The labyrinth forms and unforms itself
> The labyrinth is a palace and within it
> The halls multiply and the chambers
> Of Babel, raucous and red, gleam
> The labyrinth is the past: its gardens flower
> And from the back of memory ascend the stairs
> The labyrinth is a cross-roads and a cavern and a grotto
> Library net inventory bee-hive;
> The labyrinth is an itinerary
> Like the scent from an ineluctable star—
> But he who traverses it meets
> No solar bull nor sun nor moon
> But only the recurrant glass of the void
> And a shimmer of azulejos, cool magnet
> Where mirrors devour images
> Exhausted by the labyrinths we walk
> In the minuteness of the search in the intentness of the search
> In the changeable light: from square to painting
> We come upon detours nets and cast
> Towers of light corridors of fear –
> But one day we shall emerge and the equipoised
> Cities will show their white
> Their whitewash their dawn their wonder.

## Amoreiras

"It resembles an immense sphinx, above the city, ready to devour us all." That is how Vieira da Silva saw the vast Amoreiras complex, which is just up the road from the museum, an area of Lisbon where she kept a house even if she rarely stayed there. Amoreiras means mulberry trees, and it was in this area that they were grown to provide food for the silkworms of the local silk factories.

The shopping center of Amoreiras, with its attendant luxury apartments and offices, was the first of the big complexes to be constructed in the 1980s. Although today there are others, this one is still looked upon affectionately. It is variously described as an Egyptian cut-out model that children stick together, or an assemblage of Licorice Allsorts with smoked glass for licorice, or a fantasy birthday cake, and indeed it has traces of all those. The complex was an awakening for the architecture of Lisbon, the architect Tomás Taveira's style using an eclecticism of popular imagery and a playfulness that challenged notions of austerity and created a frivolity of decoration and sense of color. It is reputedly inspired by a cluster of chess pieces. Its grandeur was said to be staged as a counterpoint to the Castelo de São Jorge, though one is in ruins, the other not yet. Others think the three office blocks with their decorous crowns were unnecessary mirrors in a city with an abundance of light. Another touch was to include many entrance doors, though none are large, with a complex layout within so that one loses oneself and just continues spending in its two hundred and forty stores, fifty or so eating places and ten cinemas. These days it has lost some of its inner attractiveness, appearing faded and frayed in places, but the exterior has placed it firmly on the map, as was intended, and it is for this endearing quality that the public still seems to venture there.

# PART FIVE

# *THE WEST*

*"I wanted to record it as it was, before it got all cleaned up and looked
as though it had never had any history."*
Luísa Ferreira

## 1. Janelas Verdes

**Museu Nacional de Arte Antiga**
The Museu Nacional de Arte Antiga (National Museum of Ancient
Art), with its steps up from the Jardim 9 de Abril, is the National
Gallery, the main collection showing the history of early Portuguese art.
It is often referred to as "green shutters," after the street along which one
side of it runs, the Rua das Janelas Verdes. It is partly housed in the
former palace of the Counts of Alvor and the haunted chapel of the
razed Convent of Santo Alberto. The collection covers Portuguese art
from the eleventh century to the nineteenth and decorative arts from
magnificent ecclesiastical silverwork to eighteenth-century furnishings,
all illustrating the nation's involvements with Flanders, Africa, India,
China and Japan. It also has a section on European art that includes a
few splendid works, including the extraordinary Bosch painting, *The
Temptation of St. Anthony.* It is this painting that draws the most
attention. Not only do the visitors, the tourists, move towards it like a
magnet, but Tabucchi in *Requiem* takes it as a major point in his book,
his hallucination, and later the film.

But as in much of Lisbon culture, a casual attitude reigns in the museum, and you are not always fortunate enough to see what you came to see, though it seems the Bosch is always available. As I have found, confirmed by others, rooms are inexplicably sectioned out of bounds. One expects that this means refurbishments or work in progress. Not necessarily. Often it means that the museum just hasn't the staff that day, so sections are closed without warning or apology. Last time we pursued our inquiries, determined to get to the bottom of the closures, and found that lunchtime is the worst period to visit, as it is regular practice to close off rooms with the reduced staff available. The tendency is not to close the Portuguese Art on the top floor, or the rooms leading to the Bosch. After that straws appear to be drawn.

Pride of place among the Portuguese Primitives goes to *The Adoration of St. Vincent*, which was painted in the late 1460s as the *retábulo* (retable) for the chapel in the Sé Catedral and later moved to the São Vicente de Fora. Attributed to the Portuguese master, Nuno Gonçalves, this is his only painting still in existence. It is believed that he learned his craft from the Flemish artist Jan van Eyck, who visited Lisbon in 1428, invited by Dom João I to paint his daughter, the Infante Isabel. It was almost lost, only being found at the end of nineteenth century, dismantled, covered in grime, its order not specified. Composed of six large panels, it contains sixty characters, many of them recognizable portraits of contemporary dignitaries, including Prince Henry the Navigator (included posthumously it would appear), alongside knights, monks, rabbis and fishermen, and even a beggar, while Dom Afonso V and Dona Isabel kneel to receive a blessing from the patron saint of the city, the attention to detail of the portraiture being one of its noteworthy features. Also included in this polyptych is the artist himself, on the far left corner of the central left panel.

There are some good paintings by, among others, Albrecht Dürer, Joachim Patinir, Lucas Cranach and Hans Holbein, and a self-portrait of touching sensitivity by Andrea del Sarto. Velázquez is represented, of course, attributed to Diego de Velázquez de Silva (or Diego da Silva Velázquez, as the Portuguese prefer to call him). The Portuguese have a special affection for him because many regard him as more Portuguese than Spanish. His mother, Jerónima Velázquez, was of Spanish origin and his father, Juan Rodríguez de Silva, Portuguese, and yet he was known as Diego Rodríguez de Silva y Velázquez, which became Diego Velázquez, and, of course, just Velázquez is enough for us today. Though he was born in Seville in 1599, the family had only settled there earlier in the sixteenth century from Portugal. Which is why many think that he is really Portuguese and to strengthen their claim point to his great work, *Las Meninas*, explaining that not only is it a Portuguese word, but that the very coolness of the painting is more Portuguese than Spanish. Or as Sitwell notes: "Where in Velazquez are the morbid fantasy and the love of death; the cold austerities of Ribera and Zurbarán, or Goya's nightmares? The cool tones in Las Meninas are of Portugal: and so, they add, are the sanity and restraint that paint things as they are and know when to curb their hand."

Many of the gold and silver extravagances in the decorative arts collection date from the eighteenth century, ordered by Dom José I to replace treasures lost in the earthquake. One that escaped destruction because it belonged to the Monastery of Belém, which was left standing on the edge of the city's devastation, was the *Custodia dos Jerónimos* (Monstrance of Belém), dating from 1506. It was wrought by Gil Vicente, the medieval playwright and goldsmith, using the first gold Vasco da Gama brought back from the Indies, as a gift from the King of Qilva.

With St. Vincent in the museum, it should only be fitting that St. Anthony should also be in residence. Richard Zimler in *The Last Kabbalist of Lisbon* leads us to the painting's existence. In the process of his investigation Berekiah Zarco goes to visit the Count of Almira at the Estaus Palace, and while waiting looks at a painting: "We are invited to sit, but on the wall to the right of the entrance hangs a disturbing triptych which grabs our attention. It depicts a bearded, prostrated saint begging in a ruined city peopled by rat-headed priests and all manner of sphinxes." The Count enters and notices them admiring the painting: "'Frightful what saints have to put up with,' he says. 'Not worth it, I should think. It's by a Lowlander named Bosch. King Manuel received it as a gift. But he hates it. And hangs it here for me when I'm in Lisbon.' He smacks his lips. 'We always enjoy the King's leftovers.'"

## The Temptation of St. Anthony

*The Temptation of St. Anthony* by Hieronymus Bosch was painted around 1500. Although St. Anthony appears in other paintings by Bosch, this is his main work on the saint. He drew for the subject matter on the *Lives of the Fathers* and the *Golden Legend,* books that related the lives of the saints, though the episodes were embellished by his fantastic imagination as evidenced in all his work. St. Anthony is seen four times. In the left panel he is being borne by others, including Bosch himself, after being beaten by a horde of demons and left unconscious, and again in the sky held aloft by other demons. In the right panel, also drawn from the stories, is the attempt at seduction by the Devil-Queen, her hand showing a false modesty as she covers her pudenda, intent on luring him to her city in the background. The central panel has the saint kneeling, his head turned towards the viewer and offering a blessing, while around him demons arrive from all directions and a village burns in the background. It is a reference perhaps to St. Anthony's Fire, the disease of ergotism, in which, as the art critic Walter Gibson notes: "one phase of the disease is characterized by hallucinations in which the sufferer believes that he is attacked by wild beasts or demons." The triptych is filled with demons in various monstrous forms, flying, swimming, walking and crawling, shifting forms as much as deformities, like a lizard-tailed monster aboard a rat, or a horse-skulled demon astride a plucked goose with a sheep's head. Here is a multiplicity of hideousness that has its own beauty, for the array of vibrant colors seduce and tempt us into admiration, all the more so since its restoration in recent years, which makes it one of the best preserved of all Bosch's works. Though St. Anthony is shown to be tempted, he averts his eyes in all cases, his strength of faith all conquering. Lust apparently has been designated as the main vice at play. And yet today perhaps we view it differently, not as an apocalyptic vision of our world only, not as a horror, a lesson or warning, but a sign of imaginative strength, and a work of beauty. As with most of his work, Bosch's detail is so rich that one's eye can play for as long as one desires.

Tabucchi takes us into the museum on his trip in *Requiem.* He is there to see the Bosch, but the heat leads him straight to the bar, where he engages the Barman in conversation, finally partaking of the

Barman's special concoction, the Janelas Verdes' Dream, which, as the name suggests, is not real. Nor perhaps is the story of the previous day's visitor and its reportage in the newspaper: "O Publico's colour supplement gave it a big photo spread." Or did Tabucchi do as Saramago and spend his time in the newspaper library?

"Guess what, I asked. Guess who was here yesterday, he said. I don't know, I said, I haven't a clue. The President of the Republic! exclaimed the Barman at the Museum of Ancient Art proudly, the President of the Republic was here in person, he came with a foreign guest who's on an official visit to Portugal, the prime minister of some Asian country, and they came to visit the museum." And then he launches into details of how the president recognized him from his days in exile in Paris, with Daniel at the famous Harry's Bar in the Rue Daunou, a well-known American bar in Paris (though there's also a Harry's Bar in Lisbon today).

Realizing that the museum is about to close, he asks the Barman if he can arrange to spend a bit of time with the Bosch painting, if a warder could hold on for a little longer. "I need at least an hour, could you ask the guard who's in charge of that room if I could stay on for an hour? I can try, said the Barman at the Museum of Ancient Art with a conspiratorial look, the staff don't leave until an hour after closing time anyway, because of the cleaners, you might be able to stay on for a while. Then he lowered his voice, as if what he was asking were a secret: Which painting is it? The Temptation of St Anthony, I said. Haven't you ever seen it? he asked. Dozens of times, I said. Then why do you want to see it again, if you've already seen it? he asked. It's just a whim, I said, let's just call it a whim."

The visit arranged, Tabucchi's hero goes up to the room. It is not empty. A Copyist is at work painting a detail. Which is not absurd of course, for when we look at paintings illustrated in art books we see them in that form, particularly Bosch. Or when we buy our postcards in the museum foyer, the choice is as likely to include "details" as the complete image. So Tabucchi's hero never really looks at the painting, sidetracked. Indeed, he looks at the back of the painting, at the outer wings. "I would like to have seen the painting on my own without other eyes looking at it, without the slightly discomforting presence of a stranger. It was perhaps because of that feeling of unease that instead of standing in front of the painting, I went round to the other side to study the back of the left-hand panel, the scene that shows Christ being arrested in the Garden." Perhaps Tabucchi feels betrayed and is having a glancing joke, for that very panel shows Judas' betrayal of Christ.

They engage in conversation. He looks at the painting on the easel "and saw that he was reproducing a detail from the right-hand panel that depicts a fat man and an old woman travelling through the sky mounted on a fish. The canvas was over six feet across and three feet high, and the effect of blowing up the Bosch figures to that size was most odd: the monstrous size seemed to emphasize the monstrousness of the scene. But what are you doing? I asked in a shocked voice, what are you doing? I'm copying a detail, he said, can't you see? I'm simply making a copy of a detail." Then the Copyist explains how he has been coming there for ten years, painting details for ten years of this one painting, all because he had been looking for inspiration early on and started to paint a copy of a detail. Then he turns back the clock to that first work, a detail of a fish: "One Sunday I set to painting a detail from the Bosch, it was a joke really, it could have been anything, but because I like fish I chose the ray in the central panel, just above the gryllos, see? Gryllos? I asked., what does that mean? That's what the torso-less creatures Bosch painted are called, said the Copyist, it's an old name that was rediscovered by modern critics like Baltrusaitis, but in fact it's a name that dates from Antiquity, it was Antiphulus who coined the word, because he used to paint creatures like that, creatures without a torso, just a head and arms."

Detail is everything with Tabucchi, whether the painting, the recipe for the cocktail, and particularly anything connected with food, fish in particular. A preoccupation with the stomach throughout the book is relevant, partly as a tribute to the Portuguese interest in food, and to Tabucchi's too, as an Italian. So it is no surprise that the fish are singled out in the painting.

The Copyist then describes how an American approached him intent on making a purchase, his refusal, the insistence. " I'm very sorry, he said, but this painting is going to my ranch in Texas, (…) and I have a ranch in Texas the size of Lisbon. I have a house without a single painting in it and I'm mad about Bosch, I want that painting for my house."

Since then the Copyist has filled commissions to supply details of the whole triptych, back and front, all six feet across.

Picking up on the painting again:

*I know this painting like the back of my hand, he said, for example, you see what I'm painting now? well, all the critics have always said that this fish is a sea bass, but it isn't at all, it's a tench. A tench, I said, that's a fresh-water fish, isn't it? It is indeed, he said, it lives in swamps and ditches, it loves mud, it's the greatest fish I've eaten in my life, where I come from they cook a rice dish made with tench which is just swimming in grease, it's a bit like eels and rice only even greasier, it takes a whole day to digest. The Copyist paused briefly. Anyway, he said, these two characters are off to meet the devil mounted on this greasiest of fish, do you see, they've obviously got some devilish rendezvous, they're certainly up to no good.*

And while Walter Gibson alludes to one aspect of St. Anthony's Fire, the Copyist adds more to the flames. "There's something else too, said the Copyist, in the old days this painting was thought to have magical powers, sick people would file past it hoping that some miraculous intervention would put an end to their suffering. The Copyist saw the surprise on my face and asked: Didn't you know that? No, I said, I didn't actually. Well, he said, the painting was on show at the hospital run by the order of St Anthony in Lisbon, it was a hospital that cared for people with skin diseases, mostly venereal in origin, and a ghastly affliction, a sort of epidemic erysipelas, which they used to call St Anthony's Fire, in fact people in the country still call it that, it's a really terrible disease because it appears cyclically and the area it affects becomes covered in horrible blisters, which are really painful, but it has a more scientific name now, it's a virus, it's called herpes zoster." Shingles, we call it.

Tanner's film of *Requiem* gives us the gallery scene, not the prelude in the bar. If one is lucky and the keeper is not around one can step on the dais and look at the details, otherwise it's a question of good eyesight.

## Rua das Janelas Verdes

As if Tabucchi doesn't hallucinate enough, the Dutch writer Cees Nooteboom has a similar problem in *The Following Story* (written before *Requiem*). His main character, Herman Mussert, goes to bed in Amsterdam, but wakens in a hotel room in Lisbon, where twenty years before he had slept with another man's wife. "So I had not turned into someone else, I was merely in a room I could not possibly be in, not if I had any understanding of the rules of logic. And I knew that room, because I had slept there twenty years ago with another man's wife."

The hotel appears to be the York House in the road alongside the museum, suitably transformed in the story into the Essex House. "Essex House—silly name for a Portuguese hotel—in the Rua das Janelas Verdes, close to the Tagus." Of course he can place it, but he cannot believe it. "Armed with all Newton's laws I stood there, glued to the red tiles in the bathroom of room 6 of the Essex House in Lisbon, and I thought of Maria Zeinstra, biology teacher at the school where her husband, Arend Herfst, also taught. And where I too taught, of course."

He knows that if he tries to leave he will be stopped and questioned. He passes reception. There is no problem, he is recognized and acknowledged. Nothing is wrong. He steps out. "August, the imperial month. The pale blue remnants of the wisteria, the shaded patio, the stone steps descending, the same doorman stewed in twenty years of slowly passing time. I recognize him, he acts as if he recognizes me. I must turn left, to the small pastelaria where she used to gorge herself on little brioches the colour of egg-yolk, the honey varnishing her eager lips. The pastelaria is still there, the world is everlasting."

But whereas Tabucchi is working with hallucination as his pivot, Nooteboom's pivot is time, as he makes clear a little later as he turns to see a clock remembered, with its inscription: "Whosoever attempts to interfere with time, wheresover that may be, whosoever seeks to stretch it, retard it, channel it, stem its flow, divert it, should know that my law is absolute, that my magisterial hands indicate the ephemeral, non-existent now, as they always do. They stand aloof from corrupting division, from the mercenary now of the scholar, mine is the only true now, the durable now encompassing sixty counted seconds."

The York House in Rua das Janelas Verdes is one of the city's famed hotels, partly because of the quirkiness of its origins, dating from 1880 when two Yorkshire women took the ex-Carmelite convent and turned it into an inn, and partly for its ambience, the garden and its restaurant. It is also the hotel for two writers who have passed through, giving it that particular touch relating to Englishness and espionage. The writers: Graham Greene and John le Carré.

Graham Greene's MI6 posting to headquarters at St. Albans in 1943 brought him into the embrace of Portugal, first as understudy to Charles de Salis who was responsible for Portugal and its dependencies, and later when de Salis went to Lisbon, and Greene took over the Portuguese desk. The purpose was to counter enemy intelligence activities, taking information coming in from field officers in Lisbon and Portugal or from Enigma decodes. Later the counter-espionage operation moved to Ryder Street in London. *Our Man in Havana* (1958) owes much to material that Greene picked up during the 1943–44 period. Wormold was inspired by Paul Fidrmuc, alias "Ostro," an agent in Lisbon, as well as Juan Pujol García, known as "Garbo," also in Lisbon. Greene's main work was to compose a Purple Primer on all enemy agents with known connections, sorting the fake from the real, and identifying the commercial firms used as covers. It was a "labyrinth of spies and intrigue," as his biographer Norman Sherry observes. For as we have seen, the place was a hive of agents, with British and American spies alongside their German counterparts, the Portuguese authorities, as well as the Portuguese security police, the PIDE who were German-trained and similarly inclined. Greene resigned his position in June 1944, just prior to the Allied invasion of Europe; the reason, ostensibly, was that it was dull, "it was like working in an office." Others are less satisfied with that reason, or variants on the theme, some wondering whether he had an intuitive feeling that his colleague Kim Philby was a Russian agent, and that he would not want to be put in a position to betray him.

Greene's own visits to Lisbon are not on record, as the final volume of his biography has yet to appear.

It seems only fitting with Graham Greene's involvement and the reputation of Lisbon during the war that John le Carré should be attracted to Lisbon and to this hotel, set in an area not far from the embassies and the homes of those who work in that world, for his spy story, *The Russia House* (1989). The central character, Barley Blair (played by Sean Connery in the film version), is a London publisher with Russian interests, who hides away in Lisbon when he feels like a break. Having inherited a stray few thousand from a remote aunt, he has "bought himself a scruffy pied-à-terre in Lisbon, where he was accustomed to take periodic rests from the burden of his many-sided soul. It could have been Cornwall, it could have been Provence or Timbuktu. But Lisbon by an accident had got him, down on the waterfront, next to a bit of rough parkland, and too near the fish market for a lot of people's sensitivities." The suggestion is that it is located not far from the hotel, in an area called the Santos, closer to the Ribeira fishmarket, although the film version prefers the Alfama.

While cut off from London life there, Blair is contacted by MI5, who have picked up on a message sent to him from a Russian he had met at a bookfair. They need him to go to Russia and act for them, to collect the manuscript waiting for him—if they can find him in Lisbon. They locate him in the bar at the York House, naturally (though the film opts for a more traditional *tasca*, among local people). "The hotel—it prefers to call itself a humble *pensão*—was an old convent, a place the English loved."

Once tracked down, Blair is taken to the Embassy, ostensibly on minor formalities, although in reality he is delivered into the arms of MI5 in another location, a house rented for the purpose, as in all good spy stories. "They had rented the town house of a former member of the Service, a British banker with a second house in Cintra. Old Palfrey had clinched the deal for them. They wanted no official premises, nothing that could afterwards be held against them. Yet the sense of age and place had its own particular eloquence. A wrought-iron coaching lamp lit the vaulted entrance. The granite flagstones had been hacked to stop the horses slipping." The film has chosen a house in the Chiado, probably in the Largo da Biblioteca, so that the view through the window as MI5 officers question Connery's Blair looks over the Baixa, the castle, the river…

Afterwards, as mentioned earlier, they stretch their legs at the crack of dawn on the Portas do Sol, which is still a way away, though near the flat they have sited for Connery (whereas the book happens in the opposite direction, in the Largo dos Santos):

*The shade tree is in a public garden near the waterfront. I have stood under it and sat under it and watched the dawn rise over the harbour while the dew made teardrops on my grey raincoat. I have listened, without understanding, to an old mystic with a saintly face who likes to receive his disciples there, in that self-same spot by daylight. They are of all ages, and call him the Professor. The bench is built round its trunk and divided by iron arm-rests into seats. Barley sat at the centre with Ned and Walter either side of him. They had talked first in a sleepy sailors' tavern, then on a hilltop, Barley said, but Ned for some reason refuses to remember the hilltop. Now they had come back into the valley for their final place. Brock sat wakefully in the hired car keeping a view of them across the grass. From the warehouses on the other side of the road came a whine of cranes, a pumping of lorries and the yells of fishermen. It was five in the morning but the harbour is awake from three. The first clouds of dawn were shaping and breaking like the First Day.*

At the end of the book, returning from Russia, after not carrying through what was intended for him, Blair moves quietly to Lisbon and prepares his home for Katya (Michelle Pfeiffer in the film version), the Russian woman and her children whom he has saved, who will join him. They arrive by boat, along the front before the Alfama.

Not far away too, in the Casino at Estoril, the seaside limb of Lisbon and the playground for the wealthy, Ian Fleming found inspiration in the 1940s for his novel, *Casino Royale*, in the shape of a Yugoslav spy he watched at the gambling tables.

## Doca de Santo Amaro

Alain Tanner has trawled along these docks with his cast and crew—or perhaps the word is traveled (from "traveling shot" in film terminology)—as his character Paul (Bruno Ganz) in *In the White City* paces along the docks. Eventually we reach the steel bridge, the Ponte 25 de Abril, that bridge which fascinates so many filmmakers, but particularly Tanner and Wenders. That bridge with the traffic droning above their heads, that noise that both are intent to heighten, unlike many others. It is the relevant aural backdrop to this area, a sound, we have noted, that has enticed Rafael Toral to record it as part of his soundcapes and one that many locals have learned to live with.

Wenders might only be passing through Lisbon briefly on his world tour in *Until the End of the World*, but his lead female, Claire Tourneur (Solveig Dommartin), has time to walk and ruminate beneath the bridge.

For Wenders this magnet is also a location where various transport systems can be encompassed in one shot. Since he filmed there in 1994 for *Lisbon Story*, there has been a further addition at the bridge. Always conceived to take rail traffic on the level beneath the road, the finance has now been found to incorporate it. Wenders would have been ecstatic to witness, as we did, an image of the bridge with its road traffic on the main tier, along with a train rolling beneath on the lower level, and coming in to land at the airport a large jet in the blue above the bridge, with, naturally, a sizeable ship passing beneath the central span, and up close along the newly streamlined sparseness of a quay one man jogging and another strolling... and a child on a bike, though she deflected before completing the image. Later, two men sitting on the edge presented a composition of peacefulness as the haze started to settle, the image bearing no hint of the incessant drone.

The docks are extensive, and the area of transformation is extensive, but perhaps the worst part, or best, depending on your viewpoint and interest, is just before the bridge, across the expanse mentioned above, called Doca de Santo Amaro. This has become the new playground for nightlife, a riverside strip with bars, restaurants and clubs that have been encouraged to move from the Bairro Alto to populate the area, or, as seems more likely, which have sprung up as new ventures. The old

warehouses that have been transformed look little more than modern warehouses, each with their own themes. Rather than the slight uneasiness one gains from the Bairro Alto, here is modern nightlife, with its chic and expensive ways, with vast spaces to park cars whether for the nightlife or for the daytime marina activity, and its leisure craft.

Past the eastern end of the strip is the old Gare Marítima de Alcântara (Alcântara Maritime Station), which was built in the 1940s as a modernist terminal for the liners, or as it turned out, a "Palace of Tears" for families to wave goodbye to their sons and husbands as they boarded the boats to take them as soldiers to the killing fields of the colonial wars. The government wanted the building to be impressive and to decorate it with Portuguese Realism, still to be seen in large mural works by Almada Negreiros that stretch high into the vast waiting hall, comprising eight paintings, two triptychs and two single compositions, depicting life along the docks and at sea. Not that it is always accessible by day, although perhaps it is more so at night, because the area is lively, the Salsa Latina bar with its Latin dancing being attached to the building.

### Alcântara Mar

Set back from the dock in the side streets is one of the first nightspots to set up in the area, the Alcântara Mar. Today it is working hard to combat the latest trend to go in the opposite direction, eastwards along the docks to the Lux, which is certainly set to become the heart of the next focal area.

Tabucchi sets his meeting with Pessoa here, to be consummated over a meal, although the film version doesn't follow his step. Earlier in the Praça do Comércio he had asked the Seller of Stories where he should take his guest to eat and the suggestion was the Alcântara Mar, though not by name. Indeed they do go there and talk about literature and food, and Europe which "was something remote, far off, it was a dream." Not what it has come to today, looking around the nightspot. "But I never left Lisbon, he said, I never left Portugal, oh, I liked Europe, but only as an idea." Pessoa sent others abroad, noting the disenchantment that his friend Mário de Sá-Carneiro experienced after venturing to Paris. As for him, Pessoa, what he liked most was going to the Rossio station, where the Paris trains arrived at that time, and "reading about the journey on other people's faces."

In *Backwards out of the Big World*, Paul Hyland seeks out the venue, although he does not recognize the place from the outside at first, expecting a nightspot, not a converted warehouse. "Inside, the club is larger than its walls. I step into a darkness where my eye roams towards infinity when it's not caught and enthralled by gilt and glitz that shimmers and gleams in shocking close-up or disarticulated middle distance." And he proceeds to describe the people and the place. But it's just fashion. Not long after we visit, it has had a makeover, as all fashion-conscious people and venues must do, and has sought a *new look* to counter the Lux. And as if taking his cue from the eclectic world where "anyone can turn up, in period costume, drag, high fashion or DMs in this warehouse of dreams," Hyland finds the way forward to pursue the characters he could choose to meet, whether Ricardo Reis, or Pessoa, or other "Portuguese celebrities".

If this all sounds tiring, or too much like excitement, head back towards the center, but not by the docks or the main road. Find a parallel course along the Rua Sacramento, where the houses have more in common with the Bica and the Alfama than lip-gloss in all its shades. You can soon forget modernity if you wish, but you can never forget the drone close at hand, day or night, that continues in your ears for quite some distance.

# 4. Belém

## Torre de Belém

Earlier we went east, up river to the Expo 98 site, with its own startling new bridge, the Ponte Vasca da Gama. Now we come further west to the original suburb of Lisbon, to Belém, with its suspension bridge in close proximity, the Ponte 25 de Abril. Belém is signified by its tower, the Torre de Belém (Belém Tower). It is the image that graces many leaflets or brochures about the city. One imagines a large tower. In reality it is not very high, dwarfed by trees and other things that give it a truer perspective.

The tower squats in the Tagus, forming its own peninsula. When it was built in the early sixteenth century, it was positioned further into the river, almost in the middle it is purported, off the *praia* (beach) of Restelo (the district's earlier name). This was the famous point from which the

caravels rode at anchor, loading their supplies before departure for the Discoveries. Since that time, however, the earthquake has shifted the course of the river slightly, carved into the far bank and silted on the north side, reducing the tower's isolation and today making it almost a land-tied monument reached by an unimpressive wooden causeway.

It was planned as a fort to protect the entrance to Lisbon, a strange fort, for the elaboration of its Manueline style seems to place it at odds with its purpose. Pessoa described it as "a magnificent stone jewel," and a friend as "an enchanted cake." Although the intention was for it to act as a lookout for any unwelcome corsairs, and there are cannon platforms and sentinels in evidence, it was also a point from which harbor dues were collected once a tax was imposed on imported goods. Or indeed as Henry Fielding later showed, it was from here that the inspector, "the magistrate of health," came to check the ships arriving, to ensure that no illness would be brought ashore.

The Belém Tower is a five-story construction with projecting bastion. Today it shines a bright white, having been cleaned, although it has always had a strong whiteness about it, as Pessoa remarked: "It is lace, and fine lace at that, in its delicate stone-work which glimmers white afar." The man who designed this erection, Francisco de Arruda, had worked on Portuguese fortifications in Morocco, hence the Moorish trimmings. It is also the most complete example of Manueline architecture, for unlike others it was made afresh and not restored from an earlier building, and neither was it damaged by the earthquake. The sentry posts have melon-shaped domes, "like the many cupolas of the Koutoubia mosque at Marrakesh," Sitwell noted, which Arruda would have visited. There are carved balconies and balustrades and ornamentation of rope molding, and the crenellations bear the Cross shields of the Order of Christ, belonging to the Knights Templar. Blakeston described it as:

> *pinnacles with spiralled pompoms like pierrots' hats, in belvederes (real belvederes surmounted by stone coronets capped with heads of chess queens), with pawn-like columns, with stone astrolabes and (happiest of the personal discoveries of personal response which give the lie to the snob idea that one should not visit the sight to which "everyone" goes) a gargoyle playing a violin.*

Hollywood in its enthusiasm to use the landmark, returned it to its former use as a lookout, in the Ray Milland film, *Lisbon*, with the customs officers stationed there. Another use that many might want to see forgotten was in the Spanish director, Jess Franco's infamous film *Succubus* (1967). Although filming took place all over Lisbon, taking in various major landmarks and viewpoints, the main location was the tower, with its interior settings. The film was shown under various names, like *Necronomicon*, and *Delirium*, not unlike its director, who has spun out a string of pseudonyms that must be comparable in quantity to Pessoa's heteronyms. His original name was Jesús Franco, which he changed to Jess, his name today as a director. To avoid red tape and excessive taxes when shooting in various European countries, Franco earlier evolved a series of names for use in different countries. Being a prodigious creator and shooting films back to back, he thus made up to a dozen low-budget films some years under names like Clifford Brown (after the jazz trumpeter, a hero of his), Jess Frank, James P. Johnson, Franco Manera, Frank Hollman, Roland Marceignac, James Gardner, Dan Simon, Dave Tough, Charles Christian, A.M.Frank, David Khune Jr., Jeff Manner, James Lee Johnson and Pablo Villa. Something in excess of 150 bizarre films are credited to this man who improvises films as if a jazz musician. The Belém Tower probably does not have Franco and his soft porn sleaze films high on its priority remembrance list, but then aspects of its history, especially its damp storerooms below the water level, which were used as dungeons for political prisoners, doubtless have their own unhealthy tarnishings.

## Mosteiro dos Jerónimos

In earlier times, almost on the banks of the Tagus was the Mosteiro dos Jerónimos (Jeronimos Monastery), the other fine example of Manueline architecture and the other main tourist attraction. People come for various reasons. Here rest the sarcophagi of Luís Vaz de Camões opposite that of Vasco da Gama, both brought here in the 1890s "when Portugal was desperate for glory" (Hyland). The chances of Camões' ashes being comprised of any of his body are slight, however, as they were first rescued from the plague pit where he was buried and moved to a church and then to this pantheon.

Pessoa (in four of his guises), with his bleak marble and stainless steel pillar, stands poised in the cloister, a cloister that is finally getting a cleaning to bring its whiteness up to the gleaming standard of the neighboring environment.

Belém means Bethlehem and derives its name from this church and monastery of the Hieronymite friars, dedicated to St. Mary of Bethlehem. Its first modest building on the site in 1460 was a hermitage, founded by Henry the Navigator, where the monks cared for the temporal and spiritual needs of the seafarers. But within forty years, the monastery was under construction, after Vasca da Gama returned from India, for Dom Manuel I had vowed to build it as an act of thanksgiving to the Virgin Mary should his captain return safely. In the event, his fleet of four boats not only discovered the sea route to India, but returned (at least two of them) to their starting point almost two years later to the day in July 1499, bearing a cargo of pepper that was itself enough to finance the voyage sixty times over. Subsequently the king imposed a five percent tax, called the "pepper penny," on the ensuing flow of spices and precious stones. But it is not Vasco da Gama who graces the portal over the entrance, but Henry the Navigator, the spiritual father of all Portuguese seafarers.

What is regarded as Manueline style, the name derived from the king during whose time it flourished, stems from late European Gothic and comprises a mixture of other influences from Spanish Plateresque (finely detailed motifs in low relief, a silversmith style) to the Moorish revival called *mudéjar*. There are also maritime motifs of ropes, cables and the flora and fauna of the seas, as well as the king's seal, the ubiquitous armillary spheres with bands to represent the equator and tropics. From the outside, the monastery's most conspicuous example of Manueline style is the south portal, which you can't fail to see as you walk towards it, its reliefs illustrating episodes from the life of St. Jerome.

The interior of the church has a grand sense of space, mainly because the nave and aisles are of the same height, while the richly decorated columns, like palm trunks, climb the 75 feet and fan out as leaves to make the rib-vaulting of the roof. The two cloisters, one atop the other, have different creators, and the upper story is noticeably more sober than the lower with its fantasy embellishments of animal and human faces that

peer through plant ornamentation tied with ropes and anchors. Hyland describes it: "the precise elaboration of multiple arches has the flexibility of rope and the swell of ocean, the sense of an enclosed submarine world, of coral-laced caverns where saint-spires shelter beneath scallops."

Although Thomas Mann's character Felix is preoccupied with other matters—"to wit, how I could make love comprehensible to the forthright Zouzou"—he too is captivated by the cloisters: "The incredible, magic delicacy of the cloister of Belém, belonging to no time and like a child's enchanted dream, with slender towers and delicate columns in the niche-vaults, the lightly patinated white sandstone cut into such fairytale magnificence that it seemed as though the stone could be worked with the slightest of fretsaws to produce these gems of lacy openwork." Not everybody has been captivated by the Manueline style. Aubrey Bell commented with regard to the monastery that "one longs to strip off some of its laced traceries and surfeit of unnecessary details, so noble and splendid is its main structure."

The history of the building did not always favor wealth. Hard times followed and the monks later found it hard to sustain their existence. One means by which they gathered funds was to sell *pásteis de nata*. Part of the building was used to house army units in the nineteenth century, and when the monasteries were dissolved in 1834, it became an orphanage for 700 boys until the 1940s.

Built on the white limestone that was quarried to construct it, the monastery resisted the 1755 earthquake, only minor damage being sustained. Its whiteness helps to confirm the name "white city" on Lisbon, for here too the buildings as well as the ground shine whitely.

There is a story surrounding the monastery, according to which in 1515 an unusual battle was to be staged on the forecourt. Dom Manuel and others wanted to know which was the mightiest animal on earth, the elephant or the rhinoceros. A specimen of each was shipped to Lisbon, the first time either animal had set foot in Europe. The story goes that the elephant fled when faced by the other snorting pachyderm. Pope Gregory XII was to be presented with the winner, but it drowned in the process of being shipped on to Rome.

Passing reference to Gil Vicente has been made as a goldsmith, but he is primarily the great playwright of Portugal, considered the main dramatist in Europe prior to Shakespeare. Not that it is conclusive that the two professions are tied to the same man, as the use of homonyms was not unusual at that time. But if both are not the same man, then little is known about Gil Vicente the playwright except his plays, which received their productions here at court in Belém from 1502 to 1536. It seems that plays and sketches poured from his pen at a prodigious rate: farces and comedies as well as contemplative tragic works.

## Monumento dos Descobrimentos and Centro Cultural de Belém

Belém has a variety of other museums and palaces for the tourist to walk around. Two are quite distinct. The first, the Monumento dos Descobrimentos (Monument of the Discoveries), which was finally erected after a twenty-year wait in 1960 as a five-hundredth anniversary salute to Henry the Navigator, smacks of being a Fascist emblem. Its jutting prow of a stylized caraval has the prince to the fore and others lined up behind, some identifiable as various navigators and associated dignitaries, but many anonymous. The second, which is no more inspiring, is the Centro Cultural de Belém (Cultural Center of Belem). Although built in the 1990s as a sign of political and economic awakening, it looks and feels so depressing as to readily fit its nickname "The Bunker." A center that houses not only cultural events such as concerts and exhibitions, but also many business and political conferences, it is a "tomb" for culture, I was told, as far as many are concerned. Now that the Expo site and the surrounding community are up and running, and growing, it is as if a different form of earthquake has occurred. A new shift has taken place within the city, making the new site a far more interesting and invigorating proposition as a center than this quaint suburb. The Park of Nations even has its own *miradouro* in the Vasca da Gama Tower, which juts towards the Tagus with a more acceptable look than Belém's Monument of the Discoveries.

## Pastéis de Belém

All this amounts to nothing if you cannot take time out to step into the most famous of the *pastelarias*, which is the real reason for coming to Belém in the first place. For the monuments of the district are just side attractions to the serious business of the delights of a *pastéis de nata*, here called *pastéis de Belém*. They are served in the Casa dos Pastéis de Belém, which has been making these custard tarts since 1837. They need to be served at a specific temperature, their caramel coating of the right crispness and dusted with powdered sugar and cinnamon. In order to counterbalance the sweetness one drinks the bitterness of the espresso, *uma bica*.

It is here that many *Lisboetas* and visitors alike come to sit in the warren of rooms that make up the café, with its tiled walls of seventeenth-century life, or to lean on the glass counter, looking at the selection of other *bolos* (little cakes) that could be eaten. Despite temptations, it is the *pastéis de Belém*, the original custard tarts that derived from this shop, which have become a national favorite and our main focus. Reputedly only three bakers are party to the recipe that makes these tarts different from other attempts to bake them, and this tradition has been handed down ever since the original recipe was acquired from the monks of the nearby monastery in the 1830s, when they sold them in their desperation to acquire some income. Even though one can take some tarts away in a cardboard tube (the card helping to preserve the heat), there is simply no reason why you have to spoil the pastries, having come all the way out here, by not eating them at the right temperature while you can.

## Ponte 25 de Abril

What better way to go than with a *pastéis de Belém* and *uma bica* in one's stomach? Outside, back down by the river, looking along to the Ponte 25 de Abril and beyond, is something we've omitted to mention until now, the large statue, the Cristo Rei (Christ the King), erected high on the south bank, peering across at the city. Tabucchi, when contemplating the possible suicide points around the city, viewed the Christ statue as a favored contender. A way to leave the city, as to leave the world, as to leave the book—which is why Tabucchi makes it his final invitation in *The Flying Creatures of Fra Angelico*: "Undeniably this Christ is an invitation writ in stone, a sculptor's hymn in praise of the leap, a suggestion, a symbol, perhaps an allegory. This Christ offers us the very image of the *plongeur*, his arms outspread on a springboard from which he is ready to hurl himself. He is not an impostor he is a companion, and that brings a certain comfort. Beneath flows the Tagus. Slow, calm, powerful. Ready to welcome the body of the volunteer and carry him down to the Atlantic…"

Cees Nooteboom concurs in *The Following Story*: "I looked at the absurd statue of Christ high on the south bank, arms outstetched, ready to jump." This invitation for mankind to jump is another Salazarist statement, a copy of the Christ figure on Mount Corcovado in Rio de Janeiro, though not so large, albeit monumental enough.

*Taxi Lisboa* offers us Machedo, the old taxi-driver in his Oldsmobile, making his entrance over the Ponte 25 de Abril, ready to start his day's work, the camera whirling above, around him and the Christ figure, the allusion to Rio resounding in the music of the soundtrack. Spino in Lopes' *The Edge of the Horizon* is going in the opposite direction, crossing the bridge out of Lisbon, heading for the church at Cabo Espichel in search of some information from a monk, played by director Paulo Rocha, in an acting role this time.

Julien Green, speaks for many when he says he will leave the city with some sadness: "Why must going away be so melancholic? You've been happy there, but *there* always represents something that one must leave. When one arrives in Portugal by air and likewise when one leaves, it is the softness of its light that seems to percolate into every colour of the ground. And the softness, the gentleness of the inhabitants is in keeping with the appearance of the country and the amenity of its climate."

For João de Melo, from the Azores but living today in Lisbon, the city is another island, a metaphor for his quest for a happiness that he makes from the simplest things. "To navigate unclearly between the lie and reality, between vision and invisibility, without having either the clarity or the consciousness of anything; to say that the city only exists through the imagination and the written, as simple invention, desire and expression of literature."

"For Europe, we're a country that's almost invisible," Saramago remarked. He is perplexed, for despite its contribution to the history of civilization, the discoveries, its culture, its literature, Portugal still remains invisible. And yet how can it be when it has one of the major languages in the world? "The world can't ignore a language—the world can't pretend that a language doesn't exist when it's spoken by 150 million people, when it's the fifth or sixth language in the world. If the world considers that a contribution on this scale and of this importance can be disregarded and ignored then we'll continue to be invisible. But it won't be because we're small it will be because the world is blind."

Noticeable throughout this book, as underlying strata, is repeated reference to the disappearance and non-existence of the city. No other city seems to run this line of thought so repetitively. Wenders provides it too in *Lisbon Story*, when Friedrich, the director, talks about filming in Lisbon, the city which he loves, and which he wants to film with a hand cranked camera, as if cinema was just beginning: "And most of the time I really saw it, in front of my eyes. But pointing a camera is like pointing a gun, and each time I pointed it, it felt like life was drained out of things. And I cranked and I cranked. And with each turn of the old handle the city was receding, fading further and further, like the Cheshire Cat. Nada."

Behind Wenders' thinking is Pessoa, whose texts are variously referenced throughout his film. For it is Pessoa who moves behind his names, who leads us into this inference, this concept of non-existence. In connection with one of his heteronyms, he wrote: "If they were to tell me that it is absurd to speak thus of someone who never existed, I should reply that I have no proof that Lisbon ever existed, or I who am writing, or any other thing wherever it might be."

# Resources

## Books

Alphant, Marianne, *Vers le chant*. Editions Léo Scheer: Paris, 2000.

Andersen, Hans Christian, *A Visit to Portugal 1866*. Peter Owen: London, 1972. Trans. Grace Thornton.

Auster, Paul, *Wall Writing*. The Figures: Berkeley, 1976.

Auster, Paul, *The New York Trilogy*. Faber & Faber: London, 1987.

Bair, Deidre, *Simone de Beauvoir*. Cape: London, 1990.

Barreno, Maria Isabel, Horta, Maria Teresa & Costa, Maria Velho da, *New Portuguese Letters*. Readers International: London, 1994. Trans. Helen Lane.

Beauvoir, Simone de, *The Mandarins*. Collins: London, 1957. Trans. Leonard Friedman.

Beauvoir, Simone de, *Force of Circumstance*. Penguin: Harmondsworth, 1968. Trans. Richard Howard.

Bell, Aubrey, *In Portugal*. John Lane: London, 1912.

Bell, Aubrey, *Portuguese Literature*. Oxford University Press: Oxford, 1922.

Bernhard, Thomas, *Extinction*. Penguin: London, 1996. Trans. David McLintock.

Blakeston, Oswell, *Portuguese Panorama*. Burke: London, 1955.

Blanc, Guillaume le, *Lisbonne au coeur*. Editions du Laquet: Martel, 2000.

Boujut, Michel, *Wim Wenders*. Edilig: Paris, 1982.

Bowe, Patrick, *Gardens of Portugal*. Tauris Parke: London, 1989.

Bradley, Fiona et al, *Paula Rego*. Tate Gallery Publishing: London, 1997.

Brett, Guy, *Kinetic Art*. Studio Vista: London, 1968.

Bridges, Ann & Lowndes, Susan, *The Selective Traveller in Portugal*. Chatto & Windus: London, 1958.

Brion, Patrick, *Casablanca*. Editions Yellow Now: Crisnée, 1990.

Camões, Luís Vaz de, *Epic & Lyric*. Carcanet: Manchester, 1990.

Camões, Luís Vaz de, *The Lusiads*. Oxford University Press: Oxford, 1997. Trans. Landeg White.

Cardoso Pires, José, *Ballad of Dogs' Beach*. Dent: London, 1986. Trans. Mary Fitton.

Cardoso Pires, José, *Lisbonne, livre de bord*. Gallimard: Paris, 1998.

Carita, Helder & Cardoso, Homen, *Portuguese Gardens*. Antique Collectors' Club: Woodbridge, 1990.

Clair, Jean, *Henri Cartier-Bresson—Europeans*. Thames & Hudson: London, 1998.

Delaunois, Alain, *Conversations à Brooklyn et ailleurs avec Paul Auster*. Cirque Divers: Liège, 1997.

Dos Passos, John, *The Portugal Story*. Hale: London, 1969.

Eça de Queirós, José Maria, *The Mandarin and Other Stories*. Bodley Head: London, 1966. Trans. Richard Franko Goldman.

Eça de Queirós, José Maria, *Cousin Bazilio*. Carcanet: Manchester, 1992. Trans. Roy Campbell.

Eça de Queirós, José Maria, *The Relic*. Dedalus: Sawtry, 1994. Trans. Margaret Jull Costa.

Eça de Queirós, José Maria, *To the Capital*. Carcanet: Manchester, 1995. Trans. John Vetch.

Evans, David, *Portugal*. Cadogan Guides: London, 1998.

Faye, Jean-Pierre (ed), *Portugal: The Revolution in the Labyrinth*. Spokesman Books: Nottingham, 1976.

Ferreira, Paulo, *Correspondance de quatre artistes portugais*. Presses Universitaires de France: Paris, 1972.

Ferreira, Vergílio, *Ton Visage*. Gallimard: Paris, 1993.

Fielding, Henry, *The Journal of a Voyage to Lisbon*. Dent: London, 1932.

Francis, Claude & Gontier, Fernande, *Les écrits de Simone de Beauvoir*. Gallimard: Paris, 1979.

Frébourg, Olivier, *Souviens-toi de Lisbonne*. La Table Ronde: Paris, 1998.

Gallop, Rodney, *Portugal, a Book of Folk-ways*. Cambridge University Press: Cambridge, 1961.

Gibson, Walter, *Hieronymous Bosch*. Thames & Hudson: London, 1973.

Gil, José, *Cimetière des Plaisirs*. Editions de la Différence, 1990.

Gonçalves, Rui Mário, *100 Pintores Portugueses do Século XX*. Publicações Alfa: Lisbon, 1986.

Green, Julien, *Villes*. Editions de la Différence: Paris, 1985.

Guyotat, Pierre, *Progénitures*. Gallimard: Paris, 2000.

Hamm, Manfred & Radasewsky, Werner, *Lisbon*. Nicolai: Berlin, 1989.

Hancock, Matthew, *Lisbon*. Rough Guide: London, 1998.

Henriques, Paulo, Martins, Fernando Cabral, et al, *Modern Art in Portugal 1910–1940: The Artist Contemporaries of Fernando Pessoa*. Edition Stemmle: Zurich, 1998.

Hopkinson, Amanda (ed), *Reflections by ten Portuguese Photographers*. Frontline/Portugal 600: London, 1996.

Hyland, Paul, *Backwards out of the Big World*. Flamingo: London, 1997.

Kaplan, Marion, *The Portuguese*. Penguin: London, 1998.

Kaufman, Helena & Klobucka, Anna (ed), *After the Revolution: Twenty Years of Portuguese Literature, 1974–1994*. Associated University Presses: New Jersey, 1997.

Keenoy, Ray, Treece, David & Hyland, Paul, *The Babel Guide to the Fiction of Portugal, Brazil & Africa in English Translation*. Boulevard: London, 1995.

Kendrick, Thomas, *The Lisbon Earthquake*. Methuen: London, 1956.

Kotowicz, Zbigniew, *Fernando Pessoa: Voices of a Nomadic Soul*. Menard: London, 1996.

Lancastre, Maria José de, *Fernando Pessoa*. Hazan:Paris, 1997.

Larbaud, Valéry, *Jaune bleu blanc*. Gallimard: Paris, 1991.

Le Carré, John, *The Russia House*. Hodder & Stoughton: London, 1989.

Léglise-Costa, Pierre, *Des Nouvelles du Portugal 1974–1999*. Métailié: Paris, 2000.

Lisboa, Eugénio with Taylor, L.C. (eds), *A Centenary Pessoa*. Carcanet: Manchester, 1995.

Llansol, Maria Gabriela, *Un Faucon Au Poing*. Gallimard: Paris, 1993.

Lobo Antunes, António, *South of Nowhere*. Chatto & Windus: London, 1983. Trans. Elizabeth Lowe.

Macaulay, Rose, *They Went to Portugal*. Cape: London, 1946.

Macaulay, Rose, *They Went to Portugal Too*. Carcanet: Manchester, 1990.

Macedo, Helder & de Melo e Castro, E.M. (eds), *Contemporary Portuguese Poetry*. Carcanet: Manchester, 1978.

Mann, Thomas, *Confessions of Felix Krull, Confidence Man*. Secker & Warburg: London, 1955. Trans. Denver Lindley.

Mason, Haydn, *Voltaire*. Paul Elek: London, 1981.

Massie, Allan, *Byron's Travels*. Sidgwick & Jackson: London, 1988.

McEwan, John. *Paula Rego*. Phaidon: London, 1997.

Mello Breyner, Sophia de, *Log Book: Selected Poems*. Carcanet: Manchester, 1997. Trans. Richard Zenith.

Monaco, James, *The New Wave*. Oxford University Press: Oxford, 1976.

Monegal, Emir Rodríguez, *Borges*. Dutton: New York, 1978.

Moreau, Annick, *Lisbonne n'est pas*. Le Temps qui'il fait: Cognac, 1996.

Mortaigne, Véronique, *La Voix du Cap-Vert*. Actes Sud: Le Méjan, 1997.

Monteiro, George (ed), *The Man Who Never Was*. Gávea-Brown: Providence, 1982.

Mourão-Ferreira, David. *Lucky in Love*. Carcanet: Manchester, 1999. Trans. Christine Robinson.

Nin, Anaïs, *The Journals of Anaïs Nin 1939–1944*. Peter Owen: London, 1970.

Noël, Bernard, *Poèmes 1*. Flammarion: Paris, 1983.

Noël, Bernard, *Le Reste du voyage*. P.O.L.: Paris, 1997.

Nooteboom, Cees, *The Following Story*. Harvill: London, 1994. Trans. Ina Rilke.

Oliveira, Manoel de, *Lisbonne culturelle*. Dis Voir: Paris, 1995.

Peary, Danny, *Cult Movies*. Vermilion, London, 1981.

Pérez-Reverte, Arturo, *The Dumas Club*. Harvill: London, 1996. Trans. Sonia Soto.

Pessoa, Fernando, *Poesias Inéditas (1930–1935)*. Edições Atica: Lisbon, 1960.

Pessoa, Fernando, *Selected Poems*. Penguin: Harmondsworth, 1982. Trans. Jonathan Griffin.

Pessoa, Fernando, *Always Astonished*. City Lights: San Francisco, 1988. Trans. Edwin Honig.

Pessoa, Fernando, *Lettres à la fiancée*. Rivages: Paris, 1989.

Pessoa, Fernando, *The Book of Disquiet*. Quartet: London, 1991. Trans. Iain Watson.

Pessoa, Fernando, *The Book of Disquietude*. Carcanet: Manchester, 1991. Trans. Richard Zenith.

Pessoa, Fernando, *Lisbon: What the Tourist Should See*. Livros Horizonte: Lisbon, 1992.

Pessoa, Fernando, *Message*. Menard /King's College London: London, 1992. Trans. Jonathan Griffin.

Pessoa, Fernando, *Lisbonne*. Anatolia Editions: Paris, 1998.

Petit, Catherine, *Les Voyages de Wim Wenders*. Editions Yellow Now: Crisnée, 1985.

Petrie, Graham, *The Cinema of François Truffaut*. Zwemmer/Barnes: London, 1970.

Remarque, Erich Maria, *The Night in Lisbon*. Hutchinson: London, 1964.

Rimmer, David (ed), *Time Out: Lisbon*. Penguin: London, 1999.

Robertson, Ian, *Portugal, A Traveler's Guide*. Murray: London, 1992.

Rolin, Olivier, *Sept villes*. Rivages: Paris, 1988.

Rose, Phyllis, *Jazz Cleopatra*. Vintage: London, 1991.

Sabo, Rioletta & Falcato, Jorge Nuno, *Portuguese Decorative Tiles*. Abbeville: New York, 1998.

Sá-Carneiro, Mário de, *Lucio's Confession*. Dedalus: Sawtry, 1993. Trans. Margaret Jull Costa.

Sá-Carneiro, Mário de, *The Great Shadow*. Dedalus: Sawtry, 1996. Trans. Margaret Jull Costa.

Saporiti, Teresa, *Lisbon Tiles of the 20th Century*. Edições Afrontamento: Lisbon, 1992.

Saramago, José, *The Year of the Death of Ricardo Reis*. Harvill: London, 1992. Trans. Giovanni Pontiero.

Saramago, José, *Manual of Painting & Calligraphy: A Novel*. Carcanet: Manchester, 1994. Trans. Giovanni Pontiero.

Saramago, José, *The History of the Siege of Lisbon*. Harvill: London, 1996. Trans. Giovanni Pontiero.

Schwerner, Armand, *Sounds of the River Naranjana & The Tablets I-XXIV*. Station Hill: Barrytown, 1983.

Sherry, Norman, *The Life of Graham Greene, Volume Two: 1939–1955*. Cape: London, 1954.

Sitwell, Sacheverell, *Portugal and Madeira*. Batsford: London, 1954.
Solier, René de, *Vieira da Silva*. Le Musée de Poche: Paris, 1956.
Southey, Robert, *Portuguese and French Journals*. Oxford University Press: Oxford, 1960.
Symonds, John, *The Great Beast, the life and Magick of Aleister Crowley*. Mayflower: London, 1973.
Tabucchi, Antonio, *Vanishing Point*. Chatto & Windus: London, 1991. Trans. Tim Parks.
Tabucchi, Antonio, *Requiem*. Harvill: London, 1994. Trans. Margaret Jull Costa.
Tabucchi, Antonio, *Les trois derniers jours de Fernando Pessoa. Un délire*. Seuil: Paris, 1994.
Tabucchi, Antonio, *Declares Pereira*. Harvill: London, 1995. Trans. Patrick Creagh.
Tabucchi, Antonio, *Dreams of Dreams*. City Lights: San Francisco, 2000. Trans. Nancy J. Peters.
Thomas, Donald, *Henry Fielding*. Weidenfeld & Nicolson: London, 1990.
Tohill, Cathal & Tombs, Pete, *Immoral Tales*. Primitive Press: London, 1994.
Ugresic, Dubravka, *The Museum of Unconditional Surrender*. Phoenix House: London, 1998. Trans. Celia Hawkesworth.
Vernon, Paul, *A History of the Portuguese Fado*. Ashgate: Aldershot, 1998.
Vieira, Edite, *The Taste of Portugal*. Grub Street: London, 1995.
Volodine, Antoine, *Lisbonne, dernière marge*. Minuit: Paris, 1990.
Voltaire, *Candide*. Penguin: Harmondsworth, 1947. Trans. John Butt.
Wenders, Wim, *Le Souffle de l'Ange*. Cahiers du Cinéma: Paris, 1988.
Wilkinson, Julia & King, John, *Portugal*. Lonely Planet: London, 1997.
Wohl, Hellmut, *Portuguese Art Since 1910*. Royal Academy of Arts: London, 1978.
Zimler, Richard, *The Last Kabbalist of Lisbon*. Arcadia Books: London, 1998.

**Magazines, newspapers and miscellaneous**
A number of magazines dating back to the early 1970s have been most invaluable, particularly as regards film. They include: *Cahiers du Cinéma* (Paris), *Les Inrockuptibles* (Paris), *Monthly Film Bulletin* (London), and *Sight & Sound* (London).

While newspaper clippings from Lisbon have been received, some with no source details, others of relevance include: *The Independent* (particularly articles by Simon Calder, Michael Church, and Elizabeth Nash), *The Observer*, and, from Paris, *Libération* and *Le Monde*.

Afterimage 10, Myths of Total Cinema. London, Autumn 1981.

Arcane 14/15. Paris, 1996.

Autrement, La Nostalgie du futur. Paris, April 1988. Special issue on Lisbon.

Ennemi, L', Lisbonne d'un bout à l'autre du siècle. Paris, 1996.

Framework 15/16/17. London, Summer 1981. Portuguese Cinema.

Kronos Festival catalogue. Royal Festival Hall: London, 1998.

Magazine Littéraire 291. Paris, September 1991. Special Pessoa issue.

Magazine Littéraire 385. Paris, March 2000. Portuguese writers.

Modern Poetry in Translation 13/14. London, 1972. Portuguese feature.

Número 3, hangar. Lisbon, Autumn 1999.

Número 4, Contaminações. Lisbon, Winter 1999.

Paris Exiles 2. Paris, 1985.

Passport to Portugal. Huntingdon, 1994.

Quinzaine littéraire 194. Paris, Sept 1974.

Quinzaine littéraire 301. Paris, May 1979.

Substance 47. Madison, 1985.

Times Literary Supplement. London, October 1997. Portuguese literature feature.

Ulysse 71, Lisbonne. Paris, March-April 2000.


## Recordings

I have noted artists, titles and dates. International licenses and distribution make these the only details necessary. Amália Rodrigues' records and *fado* collections are too numerous to list and are not uncommon.


Bevínda, *Fatum*, 1994.

Bevínda, *Pessoa Em Pessoas*, 1997.

Evora, Cesaria, *Mar Azul*, 1991.

Evora, Cesaria, *Miss Perfumado*, 1992.

Evora, Cesaria, *Live à l Olympia*, 1996.

Evora, Cesaria, *Cabo Verde*, 1997.

Evora, Cesaria, *Café Atlantico*, 1999.

Evora, Cesaria, *São Vicente,* 2001.

Haden, Charlie, *Closeness*, 1976.

Haden, Charlie & Paredes, Carlos, *Dialogues*, 1994.

Kronos Quartet, *Caravan*, 2000.

Madredeus, *Os Dias da Madredeus*, 1987.

Madredeus, *Existir*, 1990.

Madredeus, *Lisboa*, 1992.

Madredeus, *O Espírito da Paz*, 1994.

Madredeus, *Ainda*, 1995.

Madredeus, *O Parisco*, 1997.
Madredeus, *Antologia*, 2000.
Mota, Manuel M, *Environmental Analysis Report*, 1997.
Osso Exótica VI, *Organ Church Works*, 1998.
Paredes, Carlos, *Guitarra Portuguêsa*, 1987.
Paredes, Carlos, *Movimento Perpétuo*, 1988.
Rodrigues, Amália, *Fado Português*, 1989.
Toral, Rafael, *Sound Mind Sound Body*, 1994.
Toral, Rafael, *Wave Field*, 1995.
Toral, Rafael, *Chasing Sonic Booms*, 1998.
Toral, Rafael, *Aeriola Frequency*, 1998.

**Films**
Films are listed by director, title and date.

August, Bille, *The House of the Spirits*, 1993.
Biette, Jean-Claude, *Trois Ponts sur la rivière*, 1998.
Botelho, João, *Conversa Acabada (The Conversation is Over)*, 1981.
Botelho, João, *Três Palmeiras (Three Palm Trees)*, 1994.
Costa, Pedro, *Ossos*, 1997.
Curtiz, Michael, *Casablanca*, 1942.
De Gregorio, Eduardo, *Aspern*, 1982.
Faenza, Roberto, *Afirma Pereira (Pereira Declares)*, 1996.
Franco, Jess, *Succubus*, 1967.
Fuller, Sam, *Street of No Return*, 1989.
Gaudlitz, Wolf, *Táxi Lisboa*, 1996.
Grilo, João Mário, *Longa da Vista (Far from View)*, 1998.
Hackford, Taylor, *White Nights*, 1985.
Laurent, Christine, *Vertiges*, 1985.
Lopes, Fernando, *O Fio do Horizonte (The Edge of the Horizon)*, 1993.
Milland, Ray, *Lisbon*, 1956.
Monteiro, João César, *Recordações de Casa Amarela (Recollections of the Yellow House)*, 1989.
Monteiro, João César, *A Comédia de Deus (God's Comedy)*, 1995.
Nunes, Pedro, *Cacilheiros*, 1998.
Oliveira, Monoel de, *Lisboa Cultural*, 1982.
Oliveira, Manoel de, *A Caixa (Blind Man's Buff)*, 1994.
Polanski, Roman, *The Ninth Gate*, 1999.
Rocha, Paulo, *Os Verdes Anos (Green Years)*, 1963.
Ruiz, Raúl, *The Territory*, 1981.
Ruiz, Raúl, *Three Crowns of the Sailor*, 1982.
Ruiz, Raúl, *Dark at Noon*, 1992.

Salles, Walter, *Terra Estrangeira (Foreign Land)*, 1995.
Schepisi, Fred, *The Russia House*, 1990.
Tanner, Alain, *Dans la ville blanche (In the White City)*, 1983.
Tanner, Alain, *Requiem*, 1998.
Truffaut, François, *La Peau Douce (Soft Skin )*, 1964.
Verneuil, Henri, *Les Amants du Tage (The Lovers of Lisbon)*, 1955.
Villaverde, Teresa, *Os Mutantes (The Mutants)*, 1998.
Wenders, Wim, *The State of Things*, 1982.
Wenders, Wim, *Until the End of the World*, 1991.
Wenders, Wim, *Lisbon Story*, 1994.

# Index of Literary
# & Historical Names

# Index of Places